THE PUBLIC
ECONOMY

THE PUBLIC ECONOMY

RICHARD E. WAGNER

The Urban Institute

MARKHAM PUBLISHING COMPANY / Chicago

MARKHAM ECONOMICS SERIES
Julius Margolis, Editor

Arrow, *Essays in the Theory of Risk-Bearing*
Bowles and Kendrick, *Notes and Problems in Microeconomic Theory*
Buchanan, *Cost and Choice: An Inquiry in Economic Theory*
Harberger, *Project Evaluation: Collected Papers*
Haveman and Margolis, eds., *Public Expenditures and Policy Analysis*
Klein, *An Essay on the Theory of Economic Prediction*
Tobin, *Essays in Economics, Volume I: Macroeconomics*
Wagner, *The Public Economy*

Views expressed in this book are those of the author, and should not be interpreted as reflecting the views of The Urban Institute or its sponsors.

Copyright © 1973 by Markham Publishing Company
All Rights Reserved
Printed in U.S.A.
Library of Congress Catalog Card Number 72-95719
Standard Book Number 8410-2035-3

*To Barbara, Stephanie,
and Valerie*

Preface

My purpose in writing this book is to present systematically both a set of analytical tools and a point of view that will assist us in understanding and interpreting the public economy. The fiscal life of the state is essentially a two-sided affair, which is reflected in the organization of this book into two main parts. On the one side, the state supplies public services for its citizens. In Part I, we examine the processes within which these budgetary choices are made. On the other side, the state must somehow finance the services it supplies. We examine the alternative instruments for financing public spending in Part II.

This text is selective rather than comprehensive in its coverage. I have attempted neither to describe prevailing institutions fully nor to examine theoretical constructions exhaustively. Rather, I have attempted both to develop a point of view toward fiscal affairs and to explain some analytical principles that in combination provide a foundation for exploring the conduct of the public economy. Because fiscal institutions are continually evolving, an intensive cultivation of a few principles seems more likely to produce the analytical flexibility that is necessary for dealing with changing institutions than would an extensive exposure to institutional facts and theoretical models.

Stimulation and assistance in preparing this volume has come from several sources, and I should like to express my deep appreciation to all participants. Professor Martin David of the University of Wisconsin and Professor Harold Lofgreen of Arizona State University prepared exceedingly helpful commentaries on an earlier manuscript version of this volume. Professor Martin J. Bailey of the University of Rochester and the U.S. Office of Tax Analysis provided helpful suggestions regarding Part II. Jacques Melitz, of Tulane University until 1971 and the French Ministry of Finance since then, was a source of insight into numerous issues raised throughout this volume. Students at Tulane University between 1968 and 1972 were exposed to much of this material in various forms and provided many constructive suggestions for revision. Elaine Liang typed the manuscript with uncommon graciousness and extraordinary effort in order to satisfy my unduly stringent, self-imposed schedule. I am especially thankful because my wife and children lovingly tolerated the hurried meals, the unread stories, and the various other irritations that occurred so often while I was preparing this book.

Richard E. Wagner
Washington, D.C.

Contents

1. An Agenda for Fiscal Analysis

One of the dominant themes of recent history has been the steady growth of the state's role as an economic agent. Table 1-1, which shows the percentage of gross national product collected by taxation, illustrates the growth of the public economy for 26 nations between 1955 and 1968. Only 1 nation among these 26—New Zealand—had a percentage of gross national product collected by taxation lower in 1968 than in 1955. While 9 of these nations had tax revenues exceeding 25 percent of GNP in 1955, 16 had exceeded the 25 percent level by 1968. And while no nation had tax revenues exceeding one-third of GNP in 1955, 9 had surpassed that level by 1968.

Table 1-2 illustrates the growth of the American public economy at 10-year intervals since 1931. With all four measures of income and product—gross national product, net national product, national income, and personal income—the relative share of government expenditures increased steadily over the 40-year period. By 1971, total government expenditures exceeded 32 percent of gross national product and 35 percent of net national product. Additionally, government expenditures had surpassed 40 percent of national income and were nearing 40 percent of personal income.

These measures show clearly that government is one of the largest industries in the American economy. Moreover, the relative size of government has expanded continuously over the past forty years. Linguistically, it is unconventional to speak of government as an *industry*. It is common to speak of the *housing* industry, the *transportation* industry, or the *recreation* industry, but not of the *government* industry. Yet individual governments provide services to their citizens or customers just as do the individual firms that comprise any other industry. We now spend more for the services of government than we spend for the services of any other

TABLE 1-1

Tax Revenues as a Percentage of Gross National Product,
Selected Countries, 1955, 1960, 1968

Nation	Tax Revenues as a Percentage of GNP		
	1955	1960	1968
Australia	21.9	22.9	24.4
Austria	29.3	30.5	35.9
Belgium	22.6	25.2	33.0
Canada	23.7	25.0	31.2
Chile	16.9	24.8	29.9
China (Taiwan)	15.9	14.7	16.7
Colombia	12.3	11.3	14.2
Denmark	24.0	25.31	34.7
Ecuador	15.0	15.2	16.1
Finland	26.6	27.6	33.3
France	32.1	33.8	37.0
Germany	31.9	33.9	34.7
Ireland	21.5	21.6	28.4
Italy	24.3	27.9	30.5
Jamaica	11.9	14.3	17.2
Japan	18.2	18.4	19.0
Korea, Republic of	6.1	10.2	12.2
Netherlands	26.2	30.1	37.8
New Zealand	26.4	27.4	26.0
Norway	29.2	32.4	38.2
Philippines	9.5	9.7	11.1
Portugal	15.9	16.7	19.6
South Africa	14.9	15.4	18.1
Sweden	27.9	30.9	42.2
United Kingdom	28.5	27.1	34.4
United States	24.9	27.3	30.0

Source: *Facts and Figures on Government Finance,* 16th ed. (New York: Tax Foundation, Inc., 1971), p. 32.

industry. During 1971, Americans spent nearly $140 billion for food and drink and approximately the same amount for housing and household operation. During this same year, we spent more than $200 billion for the services of government excluding transfer payments, more than $300 billion including transfer payments. It seems quite reasonable to speak of government as an industry, with the individual units of government comprising the firms of the industry.

For many purposes, it is fruitful to examine the fiscal affairs of the state by treating a government as if it were such a multiproduct, nonprofit organization, whether it is a government or a club. What will be the total that a person voluntarily joins a country club and may leave at will, whereas he necessarily acquires membership in a government by virtue

TABLE 1-2
Total Governmental Expenditures in Relation to National
Income and Product,
Selected Years, 1931–71

Governmental Expenditures as Percentage of	*1931*	*1941*	*1951*	*1961*	*1971*
Gross national product	16.75	23.15	24.06	28.65	32.59
Net national product	18.28	24.78	25.72	31.38	35.85
National income	20.83	27.66	28.43	34.88	40.10
Personal income	18.88	30.02	30.92	35.76	39.81

Source: *Economic Report of the President, 1972* (Washington, D.C.: U.S. Government Printing Office, 1972), Tables B-13, B-14, B-70.

of residence and can escape its jurisdiction only by migrating. Nevertheless, we should not overemphasize the contrast between the voluntary nature of a club and the compulsory nature of a government, for, as we shall see later, the difference is more formal than substantial in many respects.

An analysis of the budgetary affairs of a government would have much underlying similarity to an analysis of the budgetary affairs of a country club. Both a country club and a government provide a variety of services for its members. A member receives swimming and golfing services from his club. He receives protection from his government. While the members of a club are assessed *dues* and the members of a government are assessed *taxes,* this difference in nomenclature should not be allowed to obscure the essential similarity: in both cases, the organization supplies services on the one hand and receives payments on the other.

One task of fiscal analysis is to explain the spending decisions of an organization, whether it is a government or a club. What will be the total amount of expenditure? How much will be spent for the various services that are supplied? How will a club allocate its resources between swimming and golfing; how much will it spend in total? How will a government allocate its resources between police protection and education; how much will it spend in total? The other task of fiscal analysis is to examine the ways in which the budget is financed. In the case of a country club, we might examine the relationship between the size of initiation fees and annual dues, the classes of membership and their respective rate schedules, and the extent to which such activities as golfing are financed by direct charges or by general fund outlays. In the case of a government, we might examine the types of taxes that are used, the extent to which public services are financed through debt issue and user pricing, and the manner in which the cost of public services is apportioned among the citizenry.

Our study of the public economy will involve an examination of the budgetary affairs of a government, but remember that the scope of the public economy may extend beyond that indicated by the public budget. Any effect that can be achieved through some change in budgetary policy can be duplicated—at least conceptually—by some change in the legal framework. Before warfare became highly capital-intensive, wars were sometimes "financed" by requiring certain citizens to provide their bodies, their food, their clothing, and their weapons. Under this legal framework, states could wage war with little direct budgetary outlay. Resources were still channeled into public uses, but by legal sanctions rather than through budgeting. Roughly identical results could have been obtained by having the state purchase the military services through market institutions and pay for those services by levying taxes on its citizenry. Under the former institutional arrangement, there would be little budgetary outlay. Under the latter institutional arrangement, the government would have recorded budgetary outlays equal to the market value of the resources it purchased. Yet this is merely a difference in institutional form, and the substantive workings of the economy are practically unchanged between the two settings.[1]

The ability to substitute legal for fiscal means of exercising collective control over resources makes it impossible to assess precisely the extent of governmental participation in the economy. Instead of providing public education through public budgets, for instance, the state could simply require that parents send their children to approved schools for a stipulated number of years. For instance, it is common for a locality to require that citizens have their dogs licensed and vaccinated. There is no reason why vaccinations could not be provided free of direct charge, with the cost of the service financed by taxation. Thus, indirect provision through legal requirements and direct provision through budgets are substitutes for one another. While our examination of the public economy must necessarily focus on budgetary magnitudes, we should keep in mind that through the exercise of its legal powers, the state exerts a pervasive influence in the economy.

THE ORGANIZATION OF FISCAL CHOICE

Through its fiscal apparatus, the state extracts resources from its members in order to supply them with a wide variety of services. Typically, it edu-

---

[1] Military conscription is a remnant of that institutional form. As another illustration, some of the American colonies built roads by requiring men to donate specified amounts of time to road construction. As a result of this legal sanction, budgetary outlays on road construction were less than they would have been had all resource inputs been purchased in factor markets. Yet the impact of the state on road construction would be roughly identical under the two alternative institutions in spite of the considerable difference in direct budgetary measure.

cates its members, protects them from fire and from other humans, dams rivers, constructs superhighways, insures against unemployment, and subsidizes retirement, as well as providing numerous other services. Tables 1-3, 1-4, and 1-5 illustrate various dimensions of public spending on twelve functions. Table 1-3 shows total spending by function on all levels of government for fiscal 1970. Table 1-3 shows that national, state, and local governments spent a total of $333 billion in fiscal 1970, with the national government spending $185 billion, state governments $56 billion, and local governments $92 billion.

Table 1-4 shows how each level of government distributed its spending among the twelve functions. The national government apportioned 50 percent of its spending to military related activities (national defense, foreign aid, and veteran's payments), and payments from its insurance trust programs—predominantly Social Security payments—were the only other item of relative significance, totaling 22 percent of federal spending. By contrast, state governments devoted one-quarter of their spending to educational activities and one-fifth to transportation (primarily highways) and commerce. State governments also spent more than ten percent of their budgets on welfare, insurance trusts, and miscellaneous activities.

Table 1-5 shows how responsibility for each function is distributed among the three levels of government. National government accounted for 56 percent of government spending, while state and local governments accounted for 17 percent and 28 percent respectively. The federal government made 100 percent of all military expenditures, and it also accounted for the major share of spending for insurance trust programs, for interest payments, and for recreation and natural resources. State governments did not account for a majority of spending for any function, but they did spend more on welfare and on transportation and commerce than national or local government spent. Local governments were responsible for the major portion of total spending on sewerage and sanitation, police and fire protection, education, and housing and urban renewal. The pattern that emerges is one of extensive overlapping among levels of government in their responsibilities for particular functions. The only functions in which all levels of government do not participate are military and sewerage and sanitation.

Why do the various governments provide the services they do, and in those particular amounts? Why did the federal government spend $185 billion in fiscal 1970 instead of, say, $205 billion or $165 billion? Why did state governments spend $56 billion in 1970 rather than $66 billion or $46 billion? And why did local governments spend $92 billion rather than, for instance, $107 billion or $77 billion? Unless we are content to treat the size of the budget as an unexplainable, random circumstance,

TABLE 1-3
Public Spending by Function and by Level of Government,
Fiscal Year 1970 (in millions of dollars)

Function	All Governments	Federal Government	State & Local Governments	State Governments	Local Governments
All functions	$332,985	$184,933	$148,052	$56,163	$91,889
Military related	93,332	93,332			
Education	55,771	3,053	52,718	13,780	38,938
Health and hospitals	13,587	3,919	9,668	4,788	4,880
Welfare	17,517	2,837	14,679	8,203	6,477
Police and fire	6,927	409	6,518	688	5,830
Sewerage and sanitation	3,413		3,413		3,413
Recreation and natural resources	13,357	8,737	4,620	2,158	2,462
Transportation and commerce	28,095	10,097	17,998	11,395	6,603
Housing and urban renewal	3,189	1,051	2,138	23	2,115
Interest	18,411	14,037	4,374	1,499	2,875
Insurance trust	48,521	41,248	7,273	6,010	1,263
Other	30,364	5,713	24,651	7,618	17,032

Source: U.S. Bureau of the Census, *Governmental Finances in 1969-70* (Washington, D.C.: U.S. Government Printing Office, 1971), Tables 5 and 7.

TABLE 1-4
Public Spending by Function, as Percentage of Total Spending,
Fiscal Year 1970

Function	All Governments	Federal Government	State & Local Governments	State Governments	Local Governments
All functions	100.00%	100.00%	100.00%	100.00%	100.00%
Military related	28.03	50.47			
Education	16.75	1.65	35.61	24.54	42.38
Health and hospitals	4.08	2.12	6.53	8.53	5.31
Welfare	5.26	1.53	9.91	14.61	7.05
Police and fire	2.08	0.22	4.40	1.23	6.34
Sewerage and sanitation	1.02		2.31		3.71
Recreation and natural resources	4.01	4.72	3.12	3.84	2.70
Transportation and commerce	8.44	5.46	12.16	20.29	7.19
Housing and urban renewal	0.96	0.57	1.44	0.04	2.30
Interest	5.23	7.59	2.95	2.67	3.13
Insurance trust	14.57	22.30	4.91	10.70	1.37
Other	9.12	3.09	16.61	13.56	18.54

Source: Computed from Table 1-3.

TABLE 1-5

Public Spending by Level of Government, as Percentage of Total Spending, Fiscal Year 1970

Function	All Governments	Federal Government	State & Local Governments	State Governments	Local Governments
All functions	100.00%	55.54%	44.46%	16.87%	27.60%
Military related	100.00	100.00			
Education	100.00	5.48	94.63	24.74	69.89
Health and hospitals	100.00	28.84	71.16	35.24	35.92
Welfare	100.00	16.20	83.80	46.83	36.98
Police and fire	100.00	5.90	94.10	9.95	84.16
Sewerage and sanitation	100.00		100.00		100.00
Recreation and natural resources	100.00	65.41	34.59	16.16	18.43
Transportation and commerce	100.00	35.94	64.06	40.56	23.50
Housing and urban renewal	100.00	32.96	67.05	0.74	66.32
Interest	100.00	76.24	23.76	8.14	15.62
Insurance trust	100.00	85.01	14.99	12.39	2.60
Other	100.00	18.82	81.18	25.09	56.09

Source: Computed from Table 1-3.

it becomes necessary to explain why the budget is one size rather than another. We must explain, for instance, why $185 billion was an equilibrium level of federal spending in 1970.

We must also ask why governments allocate their budgets in the manner they do. Why does the federal government spend 50 percent rather than 60 percent or 40 percent of its budget on military services? Why do state governments devote 20 percent of their spending to transportation and commerce rather than some alternative percentage? And why do local governments spend 42 percent of their budgets on education? Moreover, why was 56 percent of total government spending made by the national government? Again, as we are unwilling to attribute these outcomes to unexplainable, random forces, we must try to explain why the pattern of spending takes on one particular level and composition.

The numerous issues relating to the organization of fiscal choice and the attainment of fiscal equilibrium comprise the subject matter of Part I of this book. Chapter 2 describes three principles that have been advanced for the conduct of fiscal affairs: efficiency, equity, and justice. Chapter 3 presents a theoretical explanation of fiscal equilibrium in an isolated state, while Chapter 4 examines some of the peculiarities that result when fiscal choices are made simultaneously by a multitude of governments. Chapter 5 studies the actual processes of budgetary choice and compares their properties with those of our theoretical models. Some analytical techniques that have been developed to assist public officials in making more efficient decisions about public spending are described in Chapter 6, and the manner in which changes in the cost and reward structure faced by public officials may promote greater efficiency in public spending decisions is examined in Chapter 7.

THE INSTRUMENTS OF PUBLIC FINANCING

The state must somehow pay for the services it supplies to its members. The financing of public spending forms the second major branch of fiscal analysis. Tables 1-6, 1-7, and 1-8 illustrate various dimensions of public revenue for fiscal 1970. From Table 1-6, we see that the three levels of government raised a total of $361 billion in fiscal 1970: $233 billion in taxation, $48 billion in user charges, $53 billion in trust fund revenue, and $27 billion in debt creation.

Table 1-7 shows the importance of each source of revenue at each level of government. The federal government received 41 percent of its revenue from the taxation of personal income, 19 percent from its trust fund revenue, and 15 percent from its taxation of corporation income.

TABLE 1-6
Public Revenue by Source and by Level of Government, Fiscal Year 1970 (in millions of dollars)

Source	All Governments	Federal Government	State & Local Governments	State Governments	Local Governments
Total revenue, own sources	$361,031	$222,761	$138,270	$71,146	$67,215
Taxation	232,877	146,082	86,795	47,962	38,833
Individual income	101,224	90,412	10,812	9,183	1,630
Corporation income	36,567	32,829	3,738	3,738	
Sales & excises	48,619	18,297	30,322	27,254	3,068
Property	34,054		34,054	1,092	32,963
Other	12,412	4,544	7,868	6,695	1,173
User charges	48,217	17,500	30,717	11,293	19,424
Insurance trust	52,716	41,980	10,736	9,437	1,299
Debt issue (net)	27,221	17,199	10,022	2,455	7,568

Note: Because of rounding and sampling variation, detail may not add to totals.

Source: U.S. Bureau of the Census, *Governmental Finances in 1969–70* (Washington, D.C.: U.S. Government Printing Office, 1971), Tables 2, 4, and 14.

TABLE 1-7
Public Revenue by Source, as Percentage of Total Revenue, Fiscal Year 1970

Source	All Governments	Federal Government	State & Local Governments	State Governments	Local Governments
Total revenue, own sources	100.00%	100.00%	100.00%	100.00%	100.00%
Taxation	64.50	65.58	62.77	67.41	57.77
Individual income	28.04	40.59	7.82	12.89	2.43
Corporation income	10.13	14.74	2.70	5.25	
Sales and excises	13.47	8.21	1.93	38.31	4.56
Property	9.43		24.63	1.54	49.04
Other	3.44	2.04	5.69	9.41	1.75
User charges	13.36	7.86	22.22	15.87	28.90
Insurance trust	14.60	18.85	7.76	13.26	1.93
Debt issue (net)	7.54	7.72	7.25	3.45	11.26

Source: Computed from Table 1-6.

TABLE 1-8

Public Revenue by Level of Government, as Percentage of Total Revenue, Fiscal Year 1970

Source	All Governments	Federal Government	State & Local Governments	State Governments	Local Governments
Total revenue own sources	100%	61.70%	38.30%	19.71%	18.62%
Taxation	100	62.73	37.27	20.60	16.68
Individual income	100	89.32	10.68	9.07	1.61
Corporation income	100	89.78	10.22	10.22	
Sales and excises	100	37.63	62.37	56.06	6.31
Property	100		100.00	3.21	96.80
Other	100	36.61	63.39	53.94	9.45
User charges	100	36.29	63.71	23.43	40.28
Insurance trust	100	79.63	20.37	17.90	2.46
Debt issue (net)	100	63.18	36.82	9.02	27.80

Source: Computed from Table 1-6.

State government revenues accrued in a considerably more diffused pattern: sales and excise taxes supplied 38 percent of state revenue, user charges provided 16 percent, and insurance trusts and personal income taxation each provided 13 percent. In contrast to state governments, local governments raised their revenue in a relatively concentrated pattern: 49 percent from property taxation, 29 percent from user charges, and 11 percent from the net issue of debt.

In Table 1-8, the importance of each source of revenue among the three levels of government is shown. The federal government collected the predominant share of the total revenue from corporation income taxation (89.78 percent), personal income taxation (89.32 percent), insurance trusts (79.63 percent), and debt creation (63.18 percent). State governments took the majority share of revenue from only sales and excise taxation (plus the category of miscellaneous taxes), where they collected 56 percent of total revenue raised by that source. Local governments collected the majority of revenue from only one source—97 percent of all revenue raised by property taxation.

The means by which budgets are financed will affect the operation of both the public economy and the market economy. Changes in the degree of progressivity in the personal income tax may alter the equilibrium size and composition of the public budget, as may replacement of the corporate income tax with some form of value-added tax. In addition to disturbing the budgetary equilibrium, a change in the degree of progressivity in the personal income tax may also change the level of saving, the rate of economic growth, and the distribution of income. The size of the budget and the means by which it is financed may also affect the levels of income, employment, and prices. Government decisions as to whether budgetary changes should be effectuated by raising or lowering taxes, by creating or retiring debt, or by expanding or contracting the supply of money can exert a significant impact on the aggregate level of economic activity. In the second half of our study of the fiscal affairs of the state (Part II of this book), we shall examine the impact of alternative methods of paying for public spending on the size and composition of the public budget on the one hand and on the functioning of the private market economy on the other.

Chapter 8 examines user pricing and related instruments for financing public services. User pricing is a system by which the state finances the supply of some service by charging a price to the consumers of the service. The supply of public utilities in many localities is a prominent example of user pricing. While the revenues from such trust funds as the highway and Social Security trusts are collected in the form of taxes, taxation clearly is regarded merely as the form in which the price is collected. Because this is so, trust funding and tax earmarking may be regarded as a form of user pricing. Taxation, the dominant instrument of public financing to-day, will be discussed in Chapters 9 through 12. There are numerous par-ticular tax forms: income, property, sales, excise, use, turnover, value-added, import, estate, inheritance, and gift taxes are but a sample. The numerous particular forms of tax may be aggregated into a few broad clas-sifications. Taxation may be based on the value of flows or on the value of stocks, and on either the product or factor side of the market. Taxation of individual income and corporation profit—treated in Chapters 9 and 10 respectively—are taxes on flow values on the factor side of the market. Chapter 11 considers the taxation consumer expenditure, which is taxation on the product side of the market. Chapter 12 considers the taxation of asset value: the taxation of stocks rather than flows. Finally, Chapter 13 explores the use of debt creation and money creation as instruments of public financing, paying particular attention to the similarities among and differences between these two instruments.

I

The Organization of
Fiscal Choice

2. The Normative Basis of Fiscal Organization

Much effort has been invested in trying to formulate norms for assessing the performance of the public economy. Few people would quarrel with the dictum that the public economy be operated efficiently. Nor would many disagree that the public economy should be operated equitably. A common fear is that the requirements of efficiency and those of equity will conflict and thereby present a dilemma. If efficiency in the allocation of resources conflicts with equity in the distribution of income, it becomes necessary to decide at what rate equity should be sacrificed to attain efficiency, or vice versa.[1] First, efficiency and equity will be described as principles for fiscal organization, after which a third principle, justice, a principle that may nullify conflict between efficiency and equity, will be examined.

EFFICIENCY AS A NORM FOR FISCAL ORGANIZATION

Any political unit must make three interdependent fiscal choices. First, it must choose the total size of its budget which is a choice about the share of the community's resources to be allocated collectively rather than privately. Second, the community must allocate its budget among competing uses: a decision must be made on how the budget will be apportioned among such public services as police protection, fire protection, and recreation. And, finally, the community must apportion the cost of its services among its members. Efficiency as a norm for fiscal organization states that

[1] For a development within this frame of reference, see Koichi Mera, "The Trade-Off Between Aggregate Efficiency and Inter-Regional Equity: A Static Analysis," *Quarterly Journal of Economics,* 81 (November 1967), 658–74.

these budget choices should be efficient. But what is an efficient fiscal choice? How do we distinguish efficient and inefficient budgetary choices?

The concept of a collective good is a major analytical construction of modern fiscal theory.[2] A collective good is generally defined as one for which $X = X_i$, where X is the total quantity of the good and X_i is the amount of X consumed by individual i. A private good, by contrast, is generally defined as one for which

$$X = \sum_{i=1}^{n} X_i$$

A private good, then, is one that is apportioned among individual users in such a way that the sum of the amounts consumed by each person equals the total consumption of the good. By contrast, a collective good is one for which each user is able to consume the total supply of the good.

A lighthouse has long served as a standard illustration of a collective good. It simultaneously protects all ships in its vicinity. Each ship consumes the entire output of the lighthouse, the protective beam. Beer may serve as a contrasting example of a private good. Beer consumed by one person cannot be consumed by another. Rather, the sum of each person's consumption of beer equals the total consumption of beer. With a private good, then, one person's consumption precludes another's. With a collective good, one person's consumption does not reduce the amount available for consumption by others.

Admittedly, the private good and the collective good are merely polar cases, and there is a spectrum of in-between cases.[3] The lighthouse provides more protection for ships that pass relatively close to dangerous areas than for ships that pass relatively far from such areas. The number of patrolmen policing an area may be varied, affording more protection to some neighborhoods than to others. Moreover, assuming that the size of the police force remains constant, increasing the number of policemen in one neighborhood means decreasing the number in other neighborhoods, given the total size of the police force. Nonetheless, it is possible to array the goods and services available in our economy along a spectrum ranging from purely private to purely collective. Thus, military protection would lie close to the collective end of the spectrum, as would the provision of monetary stability, while consumption of beer or housing would lie close to the private end of the spectrum.[4]

---

[2] Paul A. Samuelson, "The Pure Theory of Public Expenditure," *Review of Economics and Statistics,* 36 (November 1954), 387–89.

[3] Julius Margolis, "A Comment on the Pure Theory of Public Expenditure," *Review of Economics and Statistics,* 37 (November 1955), 347–49.

[4] We should perhaps note that whether a service is private or collective depends

Now that we have examined the distinction between a private good and a collective good, let us see how the concept of a collective good is used in describing the characteristics of an efficient fiscal system. Our discussion will not be impaired if we simplify it and assume that the community supplies itself with only a single service. Such an assumption eliminates any question concerning the efficient composition of the budget, which permits us to concern ourselves with only two questions about the budget: its size and the distribution of cost among the citizenry. Let y denote the collectively supplied good and x the privately supplied good. Our assumption that a single public good is supplied reduces our problem to a choice of two goods, one public and one private. The community faces some set of production possibilities, $p = f(x, y)$, which indicates the various combinations of x and y that can be produced by the community. Given this set of production possibilities, there will be some marginal cost of y in terms of x, $(-)f_x/f_y$, where f_x denotes $\delta f/\delta x$ and f_y denotes $\delta f/\delta y$. Each individual citizen, i, will have some utility function, $U^i = g^i(x, y)$, which indicates his preferences for x and y. Each person is willing to substitute x for y at the rate $(-)g_x^i/g_y^i$, where g_x^i denotes $\delta g^i/\delta x$ and g_y^i denotes $\delta g^i/\delta y$. Efficiency in the supply of the collectively supplied service, y, is attained when

$$\sum_{i=1}^{n} (g_y^i/g_x^i) = f_y/f_x.$$

The efficient sized public budget, then, is the one that supplies the indicated amount of y.

When this equality is attained, the rate at which the members of the community are willing to give up x to get y, the term on the left-hand side of the equation, is equal to the rate at which the members of the community are able to get y by giving up x, the term on the right-hand side of the equation. If the value of the left-hand term should exceed the value of the right-hand term, the members of the community would value additional y more highly than they value the x they would have to give up in payment, so efficiency would require a larger budget. And if the value of the left-hand term should be smaller than the value of the right-

---

on either the technology of or prevailing practices toward the definition and enforcement of property rights. The lighthouse beam or the television signal, to choose two common illustrations, have the property of equal consumption either because it is technologically impossible to exclude nonpayers from consuming the service or because such exclusion is simply not permitted under the prevailing system of property rights. It is possible to exclude nonpayers for consuming television signals by using scrambling devices, but such devices are currently illegal. If exclusion rights were granted to suppliers, broadcasting would become a private service.

FIGURE 2-1
Efficiency in Budgetary Choice

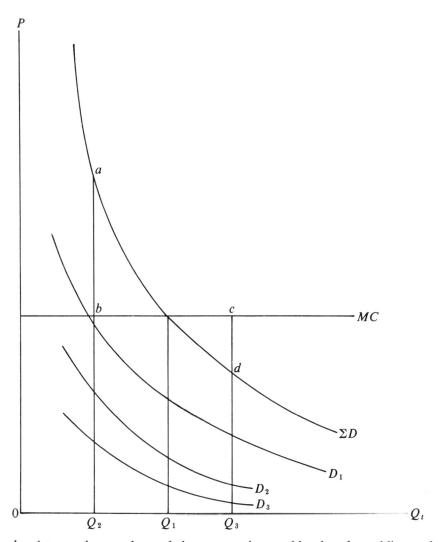

hand term, the members of the community would value the public good
y less highly than they regard the private good *x* that they would have
to sacrifice in payment.

Efficient distribution of marginal cost among the members of the community results when each individual pays a marginal tax price of

$$(-)f_y{}^i/f_x{}^i = (-)g_y{}^i/g_x{}^i.$$

Moreover, under conditions of constant cost,

$$\sum_{i=1}^{n} (f_y{}^i/f_x{}^i) = f_y/f_x = \sum_{i=1}^{n} (g_y{}^i/g_x{}^i).$$

This indicates that total tax collections will equal the total cost of providing the service when each individual is charged a price for public service equal to his marginal valuation of that service. If y is supplied under conditions of increasing cost and tax prices are set equal to marginal valuations, however, a budget surplus will result. And if y is supplied under conditions of decreasing cost and each person is charged a tax price equal to his marginal valuation, a budget deficit will result. Under conditions of nonconstant cost, then, budgetary efficiency requires not only that tax prices differ over individuals, but also that tax prices differ over sequential units of output.

Figure 2-1 illustrates this resulting equilibrium, although some generality is lost in the process. We assume marginal cost (f_y/f_x) to be constant over various rates of output, and the marginal valuation functions $(g_y{}^i/g_x{}^i)$ for three individuals are shown as the demand functions D_1, D_2, and D_3. The efficient budgetary choice is the output rate Q_1, at which point the sum of the individual marginal valuations equals the marginal cost. At any other rate of output, the community's resources will not be allocated in the most efficient manner. At the rate of output Q_2, for instance, the sum of the marginal valuations of the collective good exceeds the marginal cost of the good by the amount ab. Because the value placed on the collective good by the members of the community exceeds the value placed on the other goods that must be sacrificed to get the collective good, Q_2 represents an inefficiently small budget. Similarly, at the rate of output Q_3, the sum of the marginal valuations of the collective good is less than the marginal cost by the amount cd. Thus, Q_3 represents an inefficiently large budget. Only at Q_1 is the budget efficient, for only at that rate of output is the marginal value placed on the collective good by the members of the community equal to the marginal cost.[5]

The properties of fiscal efficiency that were shown above may also

---

[5] An individual's average tax price need not equal his marginal tax price. If marginal prices are not uniform over quantity, an individual's total tax payment is not the product of his marginal tax price and quantity. While the income effects generated by non-uniform marginal tax prices restrict the generality of the analysis by making it capable only of explaining the characteristics of an equilibrium position without being able to locate that position, the essential equilibrium and efficiency properties of the analysis are undisturbed. For a thorough discussion of these relations between marginal and average tax prices, see James M. Buchanan, *The Demand and Supply of Public Goods* (Chicago: Rand McNally, 1968), pp. 37–46.

be examined by the following numerical example, which is basically an algebraic representation of Figure 2–1. Assume that a community of 3,000 residents faces the task of choosing how many sanitation crews to provide per month. Let the monthly cost per crew be \$2,000, and let each of the following marginal valuation functions be possessed by 1,000 citizens:

$$V_1 = 12/x,$$
$$V_2 = 6/x,$$

and

$$V_3 = 3/x.$$

The efficient supply of sanitation crews per month is provided when the sum of individual demand functions equals the marginal cost of providing sanitation services. Solution of $1,000V_1 + 1,000V_2 + 1,000V_3 = 2,000$ gives $21,000/x = 2,000$ or $x = 10.5$ crews per month as the efficient rate of supply.

At a monthly output of 10.5 crews, the marginal valuations of the members of V_1, V_2, and V_3 are \$1.14, \$.57, and \$.29 respectively. Of the \$2,000 cost of the marginal unit of sanitation services, \$1,140 is paid by members of V_1, \$570 by members of V_2, and \$290 by members of V_3. If we assume further that each person pays an average tax price equal to his marginal tax price, we can determine each person's total tax bill. All we neeed do is to multiply the price for the marginal unit by the number of units (10.5). Thus, members of V_1, V_2, and V_3 would pay \$11.97, \$5.985, and \$3.045 respectively as their share of financing the sanitation services.

A more intuitive formulation of the conditions for fiscal efficiency might be helpful. Consider some given, initial rate of supply of sanitation services. At this initial rate of supply, there will be some value that each citizen places upon a slight increase in the level of cleanliness. This is the citizen's marginal valuation for cleanliness, which normally will fall with increases in the level of cleanliness. There also will be some sacrifice of private consumption that will be required to generate a slight increase in the level of cleanliness, for resources must be transferred from production for private uses to production for public cleanliness. This sacrifice of private consumption is the marginal cost of cleanliness to the community. As long as the marginal cost of cleanliness to the community is less than the marginal valuation of cleanliness by the community, the sacrificed private services will be valued less than the greater cleanliness will be, and budgetary efficiency requires an increase in the number of sanitation crews. Budgetary efficiency will be attained only when the supply of cleanliness has been expanded to the point where the marginal valuation of cleanliness equals the marginal cost.

The conditions of fiscal efficiency convey a simple message. When the conditions are satisfied, all of the gains from trade from possible budgetary changes have been fully exploited. It is no longer possible for the members of the community to agree on mutually profitable expansions or contractions in the size of the budget. Conversely, as long as the conditions for budgetary efficiency are unsatisfied, gains from trade from budgetary change will remain unexploited. Under such conditions, budgetary changes are possible so that at least some members of the community benefit without harm to any other member. As long as an activity of the state is a more productive use of resources than the best alternative use of those resources, it is conceptually possible to reach unanimous consent over expansion of the activity. While some may lose from expansion because the marginal cost to them of the additional output would exceed their marginal valuations of that output, in principle, those who gain from expansion could buy the consent of those who lose and still be better off than they were before the expansion. Thus, net social costs are inflicted on the members of the community as long as the conditions for budgetary efficiency are not satisfied, for productive resources would not be allocated to their most profitable uses.

Although these conditions for budgetary efficiency ordinarily have been treated as a prescription of *results* that government should strive to attain, these conditions also may be viewed as *predictions* of the outcomes of budgetary choices. If the number of individuals is sufficiently small to facilitate reaching a group decision and if each individual is free to secede from the group, actual budgetary choices are likely to approximate the conditions for budgetary efficiency. The budgetary choices of all sorts of voluntary, club-like organizations will tend to approximate these conditions. In the same way, budgetary choices of local governments also may tend toward efficiency if individuals are able to migrate among local governments in search of budgetary patterns more to their liking.[6]

This analysis of fiscal efficiency frequently is referred to as the benefit principle for fiscal organization—the precept that persons should be assessed marginal tax prices equal to their marginal valuations of public services. This principle should be distinguished from the principle that particular taxes should be levied on those who receive differential benefits from particular public services. Not only is the latter principle widely respected, but also it is used in such practices as levying special assessments

---

[6] The similarity of local government to voluntary associations is examined in Charles M. Tiebout, "A Pure Theory of Local Expenditures," *Journal of Political Economy,* 64 (October 1956), 416–24.

to finance such public improvements of property as installation of sewers, lighting, and curbing. But this particular application of benefit-based taxation is really a form of user pricing, which we will examine in Chapter 8, and it should not be identified or confused with the benefit principle for fiscal organization.

EQUITY AS A NORM FOR FISCAL ORGANIZATION

A second principle for fiscal organization is that the state's fiscal choices should be equitable. To give empirical content to the principle of equity, criteria must be specified to distinguish equitable choices from those that are inequitable. As it is usually formulated, the principle of equity is separated into horizontal equity and vertical equity. Horizontal equity is the principle that equals should be treated equally; vertical equity is the principle that unequals should be treated unequally.

Horizontal Equity

Horizontal equity is a precise, unambiguous principle, once an index of equality has been chosen. If personal income is selected as the appropriate index, the principle states that all persons with equal incomes should pay equal taxes.

Selection of an index of equality is a major obstacle to use of the equity principle. We must establish a basis on which to judge two people to be equal for purposes of taxation. Some people have contended that consumption is the most appropriate index, but most people support an index based on income. Nevertheless, this consensus with respect to income is largely limited to generalities and vanishes when the discussion focuses on specifics. Even if income is selected as an appropriate index, numerous questions must be answered about the specific application of the principle of horizontal equity. Income must itself be defined and possible exceptions to an income comparison must be delimited.[7]

Income is not limited to monetary receipts. The value of home-grown food consumed by farmers is a common illustration of a nonmonetary form of income. While the consumption of home-grown food enhances the farmer's welfare, the food is not traded on the market, so a measure of income is not registered. The imputed rental value of owner-occupied

[7] For a thorough discussion of these issues concerning empirical implementation, see Richard A. Musgrave, *The Theory of Public Finance* (New York: McGraw-Hill, 1959), pp. 160–83.

housing is another major illustration of a nonmonetary form of income. Of two people who have equal money incomes, the one who lives in his own home will have a higher total income than the person who lives in a rented home will have. There are numerous other nonmonetary forms of income, although many of them are comparatively insignificant. Because not all income is monetary, an application of the equity principle based only on monetary income will inappropriately classify as equal some who should be considered unequal.

Moreover, in many instances, the use to which income is put is considered to be a legitimate basis for modifying the application of horizontal equity. It is widely felt that two families with equal incomes but with unequal medical expenses should not be treated equally for purposes of taxation. The basis for this difference in tax treatment is that such items as medical expenses and occupational expenses are considered expenses of living rather than a source of potential consumption. It is also widely felt that two families with equal incomes but with unequal numbers of dependents should not be treated equally for purposes of taxation, in this instance reflecting the belief that the tax base ought to measure equal levels of well-being for different taxpaying units.

One of the strongest limitations on the principle of horizontal equity—one that perhaps renders it useless for all except its use as a safeguard against flagrant tax discrimination—is its restriction to the taxing side of the budget. Horizontal equity requires that all families with $5,000 income should pay the same amount of tax. But what if some receive greater benefits from public expenditures than do others? While some may make substantial use of a public park, others may avoid the park entirely because they are allergic to insect bites. All are taxed equally, but not all families are treated equally by the government's fiscal operations. As another example, some families live in subsidized housing while others do not. Those that live in the subsidized housing are treated more favorably by the government's combined taxing and spending activities than are those that do not. Since fiscal affairs are two sided—one side taxing and the other spending—a principle of equity that is limited to one side of the budget can have only limited applicability.

Vertical Equity

Vertical equity[8]—a corollary of horizontal equity—states that unequals should be treated unequally. Even when there is complete agreement in regard to the appropriate index of equality, vertical equity, in sharp con-

---

[8] The principle of vertical equity is sometimes cited as the principle of ability-to-pay taxation. See Musgrave, *Theory of Public Finance*, pp. 90–115 and 160–61.

trast to horizontal equity, is imprecise and ambiguous in its application. Assume for purposes of discussion that income is considered the appropriate index of equality. While horizontal equity requires that all families with incomes of $10,000 be treated equally, vertical equity requires that families with incomes of $10,000 be treated differently than families with incomes of $5,000.

But what, precisely, does unequal treatment of unequals require in this instance? A proportional income tax at a 10 percent rate collects $1,000 from the more wealthy families and $500 from the less wealthy families. Unequal amounts of tax are collected from families with unequal amounts of income. Thus a proportional rate of tax might be considered consistent with the requirements of vertical equity.

Certain regressive rates of tax, however, might also be considered consistent with vertical equity. As long as the average rate of tax falls less rapidly than the rate at which income rises, total tax payments will rise with income. If the average rate of tax is, for instance, 10 percent on incomes of $5,000 and 6 percent on incomes of $10,000, the more wealthy family still pays a larger tax bill than does the less wealthy family—$600 as against $500.

Moreover, progressive rates of tax might also be considered consistent with vertical equity. The more wealthy family could be taxed at an average rate of 50 percent and the less wealthy family at a rate of 20 percent. Or the more wealthy family could be taxed at 45 percent and the less wealthy family at 30 percent. Yet the principle of vertical equity does not itself assist in selecting one tax schedule from among the infinite number of acceptable alternatives. Thus, even if there were complete agreement concerning the appropriate index of equality, an unambiguously equitable tax schedule could not be selected under vertical equity as it could be under horizontal equity.

Presumably, vertical equity would be violated if the rank orderings of persons by their pretax incomes were reversed in terms of their posttax incomes. The rate distribution of 50–20 percent that we used above left the more wealthy person still wealthier after tax, although the differential between them was reduced from $5,000 to $1,000. However, if the rate distribution were 56–8 percent, posttax income of the less wealthy person would exceed that of the initially more wealthy person by $200, thereby reversing the rank orderings and violating vertical equity.

Vertical equity would thus appear consistent with complete equalization of posttax incomes on the one hand and consistent with no disturbance in the relative income differentials among persons on the other hand, as well as with an infinite number of rate schedules in between. The irreducible ambiguity inherent in the principle of vertical equity and the lack of such ambiguity in the principle of horizontal equity suggests that horizontal equity is the more significant and useful principle.[9]

JUSTICE AS A NORM FOR FISCAL ORGANIZATION

Efficiency as a norm for fiscal organization is based on an explicit acceptance of the appropriateness of consumer's sovereignty. Efficiency simply denotes a state of affairs that results when individuals have fully exploited the gains from trade open to them. By contrast, vertical equity is based on an explicit denial of the appropriateness of consumer's sovereignty. Instead, judgements about vertical equity usually are based on the observer's personal preferences about the desired degree of inequality in the distribution of income. Whatever agency is held responsible for the attainment of vertical equity is supposed to transfer income among individuals through tax and expenditure changes until an appropriate distribution of income results. Individual preferences obviously can play no role in such an analytical framework. Thus, the principles of efficiency and vertical equity exist in a state of strong conflict. One principle accepts individual values, the other denies them. No mutual ground exists between efficiency and equity, at least as long as those principles are examined within their usual frames of reference. Because efficiency and equity conflict with one another, we must think in terms of trade-offs between allocative efficiency and distributive equity: a decision must be made as to how much inequity (inefficiency) should be accepted in order to get additional efficiency (equity).[10]

As long as efficiency and equity are viewed within their traditional frame of reference, fiscal economists must remain schizoid: they are as impartial spectators when they discuss the efficiency of fiscal institutions, but they become partisans for particular groups when they discuss fiscal equity. Analytical schizophrenia can be avoided, however, and in the process, *efficiency* and *equity* may be reduced to a single principle, *justice*.[11] The orthodox formulation of fiscal efficiency implicitly assumes that individuals are completely self-seeking: They are concerned about only their own well-being and they try to maximize some appropriately defined utility

[9] The same strictures about the neglect of the spending side of the budget hold for vertical equity as were cited above for horizontal equity.

[10] See, for instance, Mera, "Trade-Off Between Efficiency and Equity."

[11] It is noteworthy that Wicksell spoke of his seminal work as expounding an approach to just taxation, not to efficient or equitable taxation. See Knut Wicksell, "A New Principle of Just Taxation," in Richard A. Musgrave and Alan T. Peacock, eds., *Classics in the Theory of Public Finance* (London: Macmillan & Co., 1958), pp. 72–118.

function. Typically, people are both self-seeking and self-giving. In fact, this capacity for self-giving is the characteristic that makes genuine community possible. If people are concerned about and interested in the well-being of others as well as of themselves, utility functions are interdependent: a person's utility function typically will contain among its arguments the well-being of his fellows. Thus, there will be circumstances under which a person will voluntary choose to restrict his own consumption in order to increase the consumption of his fellows. Hence, some fiscal transfers from more wealthy to less wealthy persons may be necessary to achieve fiscal efficiency.

Interdependence of utility functions may be either general or specific, with the fiscal implications dependent on the form of the interdependence. General interdependence may be characterized by utility functions of the form: $U^A = f^A(C^A, C^B)$, and $U^B = f^B(C^B)$, where the superscripts A and B refer to the more wealthy and the less wealthy person or set of persons respectively, and where C denotes the person's rate of consumption.[12] Specific interdependence, by contrast, may be represented by utility functions of the form: $U^A = f^A(C^A, X_j^B)$, and $U^B = f^B(C^B)$, where X_j^B is but one good among the set of goods consumed by person B.[13]

Because the general level of B's consumption enters A's utility function under general interdependence, transfers should take the form of transfers of general purchasing power. Efficiency requires some equalization of income in this instance. In contrast, with specific interdependence, only B's consumption of particular items enters A's utility function. In this case, transfers should take the form of transfers of those particular commodities. If X_j^B refers to B's consumption of education, for instance, B should receive a transfer in the form of subsidized education, not a transfer in the form of generalized purchasing power. With specific interdependence, efficiency requires some equalization in the consumption of particular commodities rather than some equalization of income.

In addition to interdependent utility functions, there is one additional basis of saying that fiscal efficiency may require some equalization of income. Orthodox fiscal theory implicitly assumes that fiscal choices for each budgetary period are made *de novo.* If the length of the budgetary period is one year, we assume that each year we must choose the size and composition of the budget on the one hand and the distribution of the tax burden

---

[12] General interdependence and its implications are examined in Harold M. Hochman and James D. Rodgers, "Pareto Optimal Redistribution," *American Economic Review,* 59 (September 1969), 542–57.

[13] For a discussion of specific interdependence and its implications, see James Tobin, "On Limiting the Domain of Inequality," *Journal of Law and Economics,* 13 (October 1970), 263–77.

on the other. Typically, individual income rises until the middle years of life and falls off on retirement. Because this is so, individuals who are faced with the task of choosing tax structures annually will tend to favor a rate of progressivity greater during their earlier and later years (when their income will be relatively low) than the rate during their middle years (when their income will be relatively high).

Fiscal choice on Uranus would work quite differently than it works on Earth. Fiscal institutions on Uranus would be chosen once every eighty-four earth-years, so the average earthling would be confronted by only one tax institution during his lifetime. Under these circumstances, he might prefer progressive taxation to proportional taxation because progressive taxation would enable him to reduce his tax payments in years of low income and increase them in years of high income, thus achieving a smoother time path of consumption. Once we recognize that a tax institution may remain unchanged for a long period of time, progressive taxation need not be viewed wholly as a zero sum transfer of income among individuals at one point in time. Instead, it may be viewed at least partially as a transfer of income from an individual at one point in time to himself at some other point in time. Within this alternative perspective, progressive income taxation takes on some of the characteristics of a form of income insurance.[14]

When we introduce considerations of income insurance and individual capacities for self-giving, the traditional distinction between efficiency and equity vanishes, and fiscal economists may escape their schizoid frame of reference. When utility functions are expanded to permit interdependence among individuals and fiscal institutions are viewed as semipermanent, the distinction between efficiency and equity is nullified. Justice is the only principle for fiscal organization: an efficient fiscal organization is also equitable. In the following discussion, however, we shall speak of fiscal efficiency rather than of fiscal justice simply because it represents more familiar terminology. Yet we do not consider trade-offs between efficiency and equity because an efficient fiscal organization is also equitable. To claim that a conflict exists between equity and efficiency is merely to admit that one's conflict of efficiency is insufficiently broad.

[14] This point is explored thoroughly in James M. Buchanan, *Public Finance in Democratic Process* (Chapel Hill: University of North Carolina Press, 1967), pp. 225–40 and 293–97. Also see James M. Buchanan and Gordon Tullock, *The Calculus of Consent* (Ann Arbor: University of Michigan Press, 1962), pp. 189–99.

3. Budgetary Choice in a Democratic State

Now that we have examined some principles for fiscal organization, let us see how various political and fiscal institutions relate to the attainment of efficiency, equity, and justice. If we can explain why government budgets take on one size and composition rather than another, we should be able to explain such matters as how a change in the progressivity of the personal income tax will affect the equilibrium size and composition of the government budget. Within a Paretian-Wicksellian frame of reference, we can ask whether the size of the budget tends toward optimality or whether it tends systematically to be too large or too small. Similarly, we can examine whether the composition of the budget is optimal or whether spending is excessive for some functions and deficient for others. Spending might be biased toward military services or toward nonmilitary services, on the one hand, or toward short-term expenditures or toward long-term expenditures on the other. Spending also might be biased toward expenditures that benefit particular segments of the population. The issues are a sample of the topics that a theory of fiscal choice aims to elucidate.

THE POLIS AND THE FISC

While considerable effort has been invested in refining the theory of public goods, a conspicuous characteristic of the private good-public good construction is its inability to assist in separating publicly undertaken activities from those that are privately undertaken. While the state undertakes many activities that are predominantly public as defined by Samuelson,[1] it also undertakes many activities that are predominantly private. Similarly, pri-

---

[1] Paul A. Samuelson, "The Pure Theory of Public Expenditure," *Review of Economics and Statistics,* 36 (November 1954), 387–89.

vate markets provide numerous goods that are predominantly public. The state directly supplies about 50,000 housing units annually and underwrites another 250,000 units, yet housing is primarily a private good. Governments provide a variety of park facilities, but private individuals also provide a variegated supply. Movie theaters are supplied through market institutions and libraries are provided publicly almost universally, yet there is little essential difference between the two. While a library book can be read by only one person at a time and a theater seat can hold only one person at a time, a library book may be passed from reader to reader and a theater seat may be passed from viewer to viewer.

The standard distinction between private goods and public goods is designed to answer the question: "what activities should be undertaken by government?" not the question: "what activities will be undertaken by government?" Within this standard frame of reference, goods that are predominantly public should be supplied publicly and goods that are predominantly private should be supplied privately. While such a frame of reference can be useful in supplying normative advice, it cannot contribute to our understanding of the actual conduct of our fiscal affairs. Because many activities undertaken by governments must be classified as private and many activities undertaken by private entrepreneurs must be classified as public, it seems more appropriate in conducting a positive analysis to classify goods as public or private according to their source of supply rather than to their technological characteristics. For this reason, we shall label those activities that are undertaken collectively as public goods and those activities that are undertaken privately as private goods.[2]

By using such a classification, of course, it is no longer possible to assign all goods uniquely to one class or the other. It is no longer a matter of assigning, say, recreation, food, education, or police to either the public good or the private good category. Education is supplied by both government and private firms. Most police services also are provided by government, but many businesses and individual citizens hire private police services in addition to those supplied by the government. Similarly, recreation is supplied by both government and private firms: campgrounds, for instance, are supplied by the national government, by state and local governments, and by private firms. While, food is almost entirely distributed through private markets, the production of food is heavily dependent on collectively financed irrigation projects and agricultural research.

The typical industry is composed of numerous producers, some private and some public. The outdoor recreation industry is a good example.

---

[2] A classification based on the source of supply is followed in James M. Buchanan, *Public Finance in Democratic Process* (Chapel Hill: University of North Carolina Press, 1967), p. 11.

The national government provides numerous facilities within its national parks, forests, and seashores, many of them operated by private concessionaires. The various state and local governments supply a wide variety of recreational facilities, ranging from small-scale community parks and playgrounds to large-scale state parks that often are similar to some of the national parks and seashore preserves. Such recreational facilities as fishing, water skiing, and camping also are supplied by private enterprise, and with wide variation in the provision of modern accoutrements. A description of the outdoor recreation industry, as a description of most any industry, would show a substantial intermingling of collective and private agencies.[3]

A person's demand for fresh-water fishing does not depend on whether the opportunity to fish is supplied collectively or privately. If there are opportunities for profit from satisfying demands for fresh-water fishing, entrepreneurs will compete among themselves to satisfy that demand. This entrepreneurial exploitation of profit opportunities manifests itself both privately and collectively. A private entrepreneur may supply the opportunity to fish by creating a reservoir, stocking it with fish, and charging a price for the right to fish. His profits will accrue in the form of money. Private entrepreneurs compete among themselves to provide goods and services desired by the populace, and the more successful they are the more they will profit. A political entrepreneur may also supply the opportunity to fish. Political entrepreneurs, as private entrepreneurs, compete among themselves to provide goods and services desired by the citizenry, and the more successful they are, the more they will profit. Customarily, however, political entrepreneurs reap their profit in the form of future electoral support rather than directly in the form of money.[4]

We shall use the private goods-public goods terminology in this book, for it seems firmly affixed to the vocabulary of modern fiscal analysis, but because we place more emphasis on positive analysis than on normative prescription, our distinction usually will be based on the source of supply rather than on the technical characteristics of the good. Usually, public

---

[3] For a development of this theme, see Vincent Ostrom and Elinor Ostrom, "A Behavioral Approach to the Study of Intergovernmental Relations," *The Annals,* 359 (May 1965), 137–46

A nonrandom sample of states found that Maryland has 28 public campgrounds with space for 1,948 tents and 40 private campgrounds with space for 2,102 tents. Similarly, Virginia has 68 public campgrounds with space for 4,529 tents and 120 private campgrounds with space for 9,354 tents. See *1972 Campground and Trailer Park Guide* (Chicago: Rand McNally, 1972).

[4] For a discussion of political entrepreneurship in relation to private entrepreneurship, see Albert Breton and Raymond Breton, "An Economic Theory of Social Movements," *American Economic Review,* Proceedings, 59 (May 1969), 198–205; and Richard E. Wagner, "Pressure Groups and Political Entrepreneurs," *Public Choice,* 1 (1966), 161–70.

goods will refer to those services that are supplied collectively, while private goods will refer to those services that are supplied privately.

THE INSTITUTIONAL FRAMEWORK
FOR FISCAL JUSTICE

The mere derivation of the conditions for budgetary efficiency in no way ensures that those conditions will be satisfied through ordinary processes of budgetary choice.[5] Only if government is viewed as some sort of costlessly working, perfectly performing automaton is the task of economic analysis ended on mere specification of the conditions for efficiency. The automaton can be instructed to see that the postulated conditions are satisfied and it will do so. Nevertheless, once we recognize that politicians compete for voter support just as firms compete for consumer support, we can no longer look on government as a perfectly performing automaton. Rather, it becomes necessary to extend the purview of economic analysis to include the specification of the institutional constraints that are required for political competition to produce budgetary efficiency.[6]

In the late nineteenth century, Knut Wicksell recognized that the fiscal theorist's primary task was to specify the institutional framework necessary if efficient budgets are to emerge from the political process.[7] Wicksell suggested that efficient budgets necessarily will emerge only under a rule of unanimity, which he later relaxed to a requirement of approximate-unanimity. Wicksell also specified a set of procedural rules to follow in implementing the rule of unanimity. A proposal for public expenditure would always be combined with some proposal for covering the cost, and the tax-expenditure package would be voted on as a unit. Because the sum of the individual marginal costs would exceed the sum of the individual marginal valuations for an inefficient tax-expenditure proposal, at least one person would be required to pay a tax price that would exceed his marginal valuation for the service. Because this person would reject the

[5] The discussion in this section draws heavily on Richard E. Wagner, *The Fiscal Organization of American Federalism* (Chicago: Markham, 1971), pp. 6–16.
[6] For a seminal work stressing the similarities between market competition and political competition, see Anthony Downs, *An Economic Theory of Democracy,* (New York: Harper, 1957). The institutional focus in market analysis is shown clearly in Nathan Rosenberg, "Some Institutional Aspects of *The Wealth of Nations,*" *Journal of Political Economy,* 68 (December 1960), 557–70.
[7] Wicksell's work on budgetary choice is translated into English as "A New Principle of Just Taxation," in Richard A. Musgrave and Alan T. Peacock, eds., *Classics in the Theory of Public Finance* (London: Macmillan & Co., 1958), pp. 72–118. Wicksell's contribution on the need for institutional theorizing is discussed in J. G. Head, "The Welfare Foundations of Public Finance Theory," *Rivista di diritto finanziario e scienza della finanize,* 23 (May 1965), pp. 410–12.

proposal, the inefficient proposal would fail under a rule of unanimity. With an efficient budgetary proposal, by contrast, no person need pay a tax price greater than his marginal valuation, so the proposal is capable of receiving unanimous consent. An efficient budget, then, is the largest tax-expenditure proposal that receives unanimous support.

Although budgetary efficiency increases as the voting rule becomes more inclusive, the costs of taking budgetary action also increase as the voting rule becomes more inclusive. It is more difficult to secure the consent of three-quarters of the members of some group than of a simple majority. It is even more difficult to secure the consent of nine-tenths of the group. The more inclusive the voting rule, the more indispensable becomes any one person's consent. This growing indispensability strengthens the motivation to become a strategic holdout—a "free rider"—in an effort to capture a greater share of the gains from trade. Wicksell recognized the free-rider dilemma associated with unanimity and suggested approximate unanimity—somewhere between 75 and 90 percent consent—as a means of reducing the cost of reaching agreement.[8]

Delay in failing to take an efficient action is costly. The longer the delay, the greater the potential returns that remain unreaped. To illustrate, consider some activity that would yield an annual return of $1 million for three years once provisions to implement the activity were enacted. Suppose that unanimous approval were required for passage. By introducing greater bargaining over tax-sharing schemes, this requirement would delay the project one year, while immediate passage could be gained with majority voting. At a 10 percent rate of interest, the delay would reduce the present value of the project by $.23 million, from $2.49 million to $2.26 million. Although unanimity eliminates inefficient budgetary choices, the amount of inefficiency produced by majority rule might be less than $.23 million. Under such circumstances, majority rule is more efficient than is unanimity, for the amount of inefficiency produced by majority rule is less than the cost of eliminating the inefficiency.

The choice of a voting rule for making budgetary choices may thus be constructed as a problem of cost minimization,[9] as illustrated by Figure 3-1. As the voting rule becomes more inclusive, the expected cost of bud

---

[8] As a complement of approximate unanimity in voting on a proposed expenditure, a previously approved expenditure would be eliminated from the budget if a motion for elimination of the expenditure received somewhere between 10 and 25 percent support, for such a vote would indicate that the program no longer commanded approximately unanimous support.

[9] This theme is examined fully in James M. Buchanan and Gordon Tullock, *The Calculus of Consent* (Ann Arbor: University of Michigan Press, 1962), pp. 63–64.

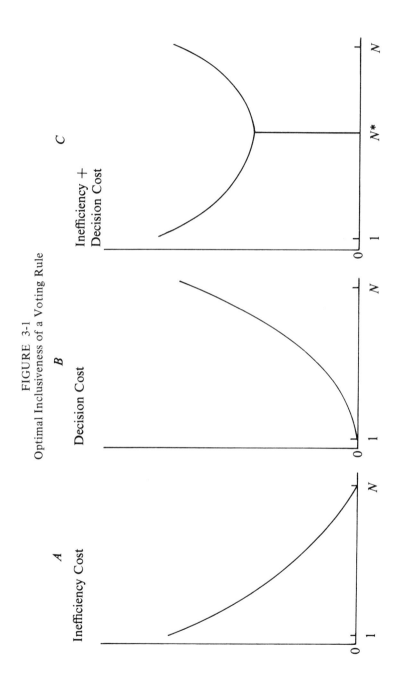

FIGURE 3-1
Optimal Inclusiveness of a Voting Rule

A
Inefficiency Cost

B
Decision Cost

C
Inefficiency +
Decision Cost

getary inefficiency falls. If any single person can enact budgetary choices
that are binding on the entire community, the inefficiency cost will be substantial. Under unanimity, by contrast, the inefficiency cost must be zero.
This relation between expected inefficiency cost and the voting rule is illustrated by panel A. As the voting rule becomes more inclusive, the expected
cost of securing the required degree of consent rises. If any single person
is able to make decisions for the group there will be no cost of group
agreement as such. As the voting rule approaches unanimity, the motivation to become a strategic holdout in order to secure a more favorable
distribution of the gains from trade will strengthen rapidly. The expected
decision cost would thus increase rapidly as the voting rule approaches
unanimity, as illustrated by panel B. The efficient voting rule is the one
for which the fall in direct inefficiency is offset by the rise in the cost of
securing consent among the participants, or where the combined costs are
minimized. This is illustrated by panel C, where the efficient voting rule
is N^*/N.

Perhaps the most significant feature of the cost minimization formulation of an efficient voting rule is that no special significance is attached
to majority rule, for majority rule will be efficient only by accident. Contrary to customary usage, majority rule should not be considered synony-
mous with democracy.[10] Unanimity, not majority consent, is the appropriate benchmark that is analogous to perfect competition as a benchmark
for market organization. Yet many commentators have rejected unanimity
as the appropriate benchmark by voicing the belief that unanimity is dicta-
torial in that it permits a one-man veto.[11] If all but one member of a community want to take some action, the recalcitrant member can prevent the
group from taking that action. While unanimity is equivalent to a one-man
veto, it is not equivalent to one-man rule. The recalcitrant person can prevent the group from taking action, but he cannot initiate action to be undertaken by the group. The distinction between the ability to take action
and the ability to prevent action from being taken is a crucial one.

But what is wrong with the one-man veto or veto by some qualified
minority? Instances in which we allow the one-man veto and consider if
fully apropriate are numerous. We generally declare that we do not want
to allow majority coalitions to dictate to the members of the minority on
the latter's form of religious observances, on the types of food they must
eat, or on whether they can continue to live. In these instances, and in
many others, the one-man veto is considered fully appropriate.

[10] One definition of democracy in *Webster's New International Dictionary* is:
"government by the people; *esp:* rule of the majority."
[11] See, for instance, William J. Baumol, *Welfare Economics and the Theory
of the State* 2nd. ed. (London: G. Bell & Sons, 1965), pp. 43–44.

It is tempting to suggest that one list could specify for which activities one-man veto is appropriate and another list could specify for which activities majority rule is appropriate. Once this has been done, majority rule could be applied generally. But such a separation of activities is not self-policing. Controversy will always arise over the applicability of the rules, and suggestions will always be made for revising the rules and their applicability. The discussion below will show that majority rule itself may tend to produce an expansion in the range of activities subject to majority rule. The list of activities that a collectivity will designate as appropriate for majority decision may itself be larger if political decisions are made by majority vote than it would be if they are made by unanimous consent.

We are faced by a dilemma in choosing an appropriate voting rule for making budgetary decisions. If majority coalitions are wholly unconstrained, majority voting will tend to produce socially wasteful budgetary choices. More inclusive voting rules will reduce the amount of direct social waste, but the social saving from use of such rules may be less than the additional cost of reaching decisions under more inclusive voting rules. In some cases it may be possible to develop a set of fiscal rules that will constrain the budgetary power of majority coalitions. If we are successful, our dilemma might be averted or reduced in force. Properly chosen supplementary fiscal rules would exclude from consideration some of the inefficient budgetary outcomes that would result under majority rule without incurring the additional decision costs of more inclusive voting rules.[12]

To illustrate the use of fiscal rules, consider the problems involved in an attempt to implement Wicksell's proposal for budgetary choice. If marginal benefit taxation is actually attempted, personal tax payments will depend directly on expressed preferences. Understandably, there will be strong incentives to understate preferences in order to reduce tax liability. This difficulty can be avoided by establishing tax institutions that levy tax charges independent of personal evaluations. Suppose the government collects its revenues by means of a personal income tax. Personal tax payments then will depend on income rather than on personal evaluations of public services. Thus no longer is there an incentive to understate personal evaluations. But suppose further that individual citizens have unitary income and price elasticities of demand for the public services as well as similar preference patterns. Under these circumstances, a rule of proportional income taxation will produce results similar to those that would be produced under marginal benefit taxation, yet the free-rider dilemma will

---

[12] On the substitutability of fiscal rules and political rules, see Buchanan, *Public Finance in Democratic Process*, pp. 287–91; and James M. Buchanan, *The Demand and Supply of Public Goods* (Chicago: Rand McNally, 1968), pp. 163–66.

be avoided.[13] An increase in income will increase the demand for public services, but it also will increase the price paid for public services, thereby reducing the quantity demanded. With unitary elasticities, a 10 percent rise in income will generate a 10 percent increase in demand, but it also will generate a 10 percent rise in price, thereby producing a 10 percent reduction in quantity demanded. Under these circumstances, a fiscal rule of proportional income taxation is a perfect substitute for a political rule of unanimous consent, for all citizens will choose the same amount of public service. In the remainder of this chapter and throughout this entire book, this substitutability between fiscal institutions and political institutions shall serve as a major focal point of our analysis.

FISCAL CHOICE WITH MAJORITY RULE

In this section, the present state of the fiscal theory of majority rule will be described. For the most part, we shall think in terms of a three-person community. Such a small-scale model enables us to examine the salient properties of majority rule and, at the same time, abstract from the purely computational complexities associated with larger numbers of people. Furthermore, we shall assume that the state faces only one budgetary issue, the rate of supply of x. To add descriptive concreteness, we can designate x as sanitation services. (Budgetary choice with multiple issues will be discussed in the next section.)

We assume that each member of the community has a demand curve for the collectively supplied service. The demand curves for our three-person community are shown in Figure 3-2 as D_1, D_2, and D_3. For now, we assume that each individual faces the same price per unit for sanitation services, P_0, which implies that the per unit cost of sanitation services is $3P_0$. On the basis of this information, the preferred rates of supply are x_1, x_2, and x_3 for persons 1, 2, and 3 respectively.

By the very nature of collective choice, however, a single rate of supply must be chosen for the entire community. Duncan Black has shown that in this type of choice situation, the preference of the median voter, x_2, will be chosen by the collectivity.[14] At any motion besides x_2, a majority will support some alternative motion. Only at x_2 can no majority be found. Consider the motion x_1', for instance. Because both persons 2 and 3 would prefer motions to the right of x_1', this motion is not an equilibrium motion.

[13] James M. Buchanan, "Fiscal Institutions and Efficiency in Collective Outlay," *American Economic Review,* Proceedings, 54 (May 1964), 227–35.

[14] Duncan Black, *Theory of Committees and Elections* (Cambridge: University of Cambridge Press, 1958).

FIGURE 3-2
Budgetary Choice Under Majority Voting

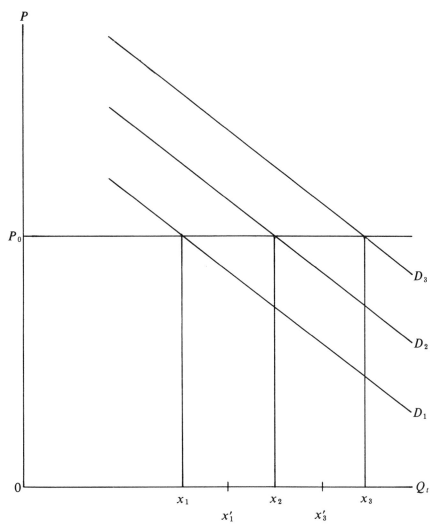

A similar situation exists with respect to motion x_3'. For any motion except x_2, there will be at least one alternative motion that two of the three voters prefer. Only x_2 is an equilibrium motion, for only on that motion will no majority coalition support budgetary change. At x_2 only one person, 1, wants less sanitation, and only one person, 3, wants more sanitation. Majority rule, in effect, delegates budgetary choice to the person whose preferences are median for the group.

TABLE 3-1
Preference Orderings:
Three Voters and Three Motions

v_1	v_2	v_3
H	M	L
M	L	H
L	H	M

While majority voting delegates choice to the person whose preferences are median for the group, not all issues necessarily will have a majority motion. There may be cases in which a majority motion does not
exist, and even if it does, not all voting procedures will necessarily produce
that motion as its outcome. For example, De Meyer and Plott estimate
that with three motions, the probability that a majority motion does not
exist approaches 9 percent as the number of voters becomes large.[15]

Consider the case in which there are three voters—v_1, v_2, and v_3,
and three motions on the amount of public spending—a large budget (H),
a medium budget (M), and a low budget (L). Table 3-1 shows the preference ordering of the motions for the three voters. Thus, v_1 prefers a large
budget to a medium budget to a small budget; v_2 prefers a medium budget
to a low budget to a large budget; and v_3 prefers a low budget to a large
budget to a medium budget. While v_3's preference pattern may seem odd,
it may be reasonable in some instances, perhaps being encapsulated in the
adage "anything worth doing is worth doing well." One might prefer that
the activity not be performed at all, but that if it is going to be performed,
it should be done well. Thus, v_3 might prefer a low budget to a high budget
for sanitation services because he would like the government to require
that residents compact their trash, thus allowing twice weekly pickup to
be replaced by fortnightly pickup. The high budget may represent maintenance of twice weekly pickup, while the medium budget represents weekly
pickup. If v_3 feels that weekly pickup will allow the trash to stand too
long and thus attract rats, he may prefer twice weekly pickup to weekly
pickup even though he would prefer fortnightly pickup under different
conditions.

In such circumstances, a majority motion does not exist. Any motion
that is proposed can be defeated by some other motion. In a vote between
the high budget and the medium budget, the high budget will win. But
in a vote between the high budget and the low budget, the low budget
will win. And in a vote between the low budget and the medium budget,
the medium budget will win. When there is no majority motion, the out-

[15] Frank De Meyer and Charles R. Plott, "The Probability of a Cyclical
Majority," *Econometrica,* 38 (March 1970), 345–54.

TABLE 3-2
Preference Orderings: Five Voters and Five Motions

v_1	v_2	v_3	v_4	v_5
A	B	C	D	A
E	E	E	E	E
B	C	D	A	B
C	D	A	B	C
D	A	B	C	D

come depends on the order of voting. Suppose the rules of voting specify that initially, two of the three motions must be run off; the motion that wins is paired against the remaining motion; and the motion that prevails is declared the collective choice. If the first vote is between *H* and *M*, *L* will be the majority choice; if the first vote is between *H* and *L*, *M* will be the choice; and if the first vote is between *M* and *L*, *H* will be the majority choice.

Even if a majority motion exists, not all voting procedures will produce that motion as the victor. Only in a round robin vote, a procedure that pairs one motion against all alternatives, will the majority motion necessarily emerge victorious. Plurality voting, as an alternative system of voting, will not necessarily select the majority motion. With the preference schedules shown in Table 3-2, motion *A* would capture a plurality. Yet *E* is the majority motion.

Our analysis of budgetary choice can be illustrated by a numerical example. Consider three persons (m_1, m_2, m_3) with the following marginal valuation schedules for the collectively suplied service, x:

$$m_1: p_1 = 8 - x/3,$$
$$m_2: p_2 = 12 - 2x/3,$$

and

$$m_3: p_3 = 15 - x.$$

We shall treat these marginal valuation schedules as demand schedules, although they are really more restrictive than demand schedules are. All positions on a demand schedule represent attainable alternatives, but only the equilibrium position on a marginal valuation schedule is attainable. Because a marginal valuation schedule is derived by plotting the slopes of indifference curves as they intersect the budget line, a change in price will generate an entirely new marginal valuation schedule.[16] While an analysis based on marginal valuation schedules can be used to examine

---

[16] See Buchanan, *Demand and Supply of Public Goods*, pp. 37–46, for a discussion of the relation between demand curves and marginal valuation curves.

the characteristics of an equilibrium position, it cannot be used to locate that equilibrium position.

To provide a benchmark, let us first determine the Wicksellian-efficient rate of output under the assumption that marginal cost is $15 per unit of x. As described in Chapter Two, the efficient rate of output is found by solving:

$$[8 - (x/3)] + [12 - (2x/3)] + (15 - x) = 15,$$

which gives $x = 10$. The efficient distribution of marginal tax prices is found by substituting 10 for x in the three marginal valuation functions, which gives $p_1 = \$4.67$, $p_2 = \$5.33$, and $p_3 = \$5$. Now that we have established a Wicksellian-efficient benchmark, let us examine the properties of majority voting.

If we assume that fiscal choices are made by majority vote subject to the fiscal constraint that taxes are shared equally by the populace, what will be the collectively chosen rate of output of x? The first step in answering this question is to determine the most preferred rate of output for each person. This is determined by substituting $5 for p_1, p_2, and p_3. When the equation is solved, the individual preferences are $x_1 = 9$, $x_2 = 10.5$, and $x_3 = 10$. In this situation, m_3 has the median preference, so $x = 10$ will be the collective choice.

In this particular instance, fiscal choice under majority rule is identical to fiscal choice under unanimity. This result becomes understandable once we note that the magnitudes of disequilibrium for m_1 and m_2 are of equal absolute value. The marginal valuation of m_1 is $.33 less than the price, which is equal to the amount by which the marginal valuation of m_2 exceeds the price. When $x = 10$, individual preferences are distributed symmetrically about the median voter's preferences. Thus, the median preference is equal to the mean of the individual preferences; as long as this is true, majority voting will produce an efficient rate of output.

There is, of course, one significant difference between the outcome under majority vote and the outcome under unanimity. With majority vote, each person is paying a tax price of $5 per unit of x. With unanimity, marginal tax prices vary among the individuals, being $4.67, $5.33, and $5 for m_1, m_2, and m_3 respectively. With majority rule, only the person with median preferences is in equilibrium. Person m_1 is paying a price of $5 for something he values at $4.67, so he would like to see the budget contracted. In contrast, because m_2 values the service at $5.33 but pays only $5, he would like to see the budget expanded. Thus, only m_3 is in equilibrium; m_1 and m_2 are in disequilibrium in offsetting directions. A redistribution of income is taking place; income is being transferred from m_1 to m_2, for the former is paying more than he is willing to pay for the equilibrium rate of output while the latter is paying less. This redistribution, however, affects the allocation of resources between public and private uses only to the extent that there are second-order effect feedbacks on demands.

Let us see what happens if marginal cost is reduced to $9 per unit, which reduces per capita tax prices to $3 per unit. The Wicksellian-efficient level of output is now found by solving $[8 - (x/3)] + [12 - (2x/3)] + (15 - x) = 9$, which gives $x = 13$. But what will be the rate of output chosen by the collectivity? Substituting $3 for p_1, p_2, and p_3 in the marginal valuation functions and solving for x gives $x_1 = 15$, $x_2 = 13.5$, and $x_3 = 12$ as the most preferred rates of supply. Because the median voter in this instance is m_2, the equilibrium rate of output now will be 13.5, which is an inefficiently large rate of output.

When we assumed a marginal cost of $15, the efficient rate of output and the majority equilibrium rate of output coincided. But when we assumed a marginal cost of $9, the majority equilibrium rate of output exceeded the efficient rate of output. What difference in the second case makes majority voting produce an inefficient equilibrium? When $x = 13.5$, marginal valuations for the three persons are:

$$p_1 = \$3.50,$$
$$p_2 = \$3.00,$$

and

$$p_3 = \$1.50.$$

The marginal valuation of m_3 lies below the median valuation by more than the marginal valuation of m_1 lies above it. Preferences are distributed asymmetrically about the median preference when $x = 13.5$, for the marginal valuation of the median voter exceeds the mean of the marginal valuations.

Let us consider the situation at $x = 13$, the Wicksellian-efficient rate of output. At that position, marginal valuations for the three persons are:

$$p_1 = \$3.67,$$
$$p_2 = \$3.33,$$

and

$$p_3 = \$2.00.$$

While $x = 13$ may be an efficient rate of output, it is clearly not an equilibrium rate of output when all voters pay equal tax prices. When $x = 13$, both m_1 and m_2 find that the marginal value of x to them exceeds their share of the cost, $3. Majority rule equilibrium occurs when $x = 13.5$, for only then will it no longer be profitable for the members of the majority coalition to support an expansion in output.

We could introduce any number of more complex tax sharing rules and examine the outcomes. While tax institutions more complex than equal per capita sharing might seem more realistic, the essential thrust of the analysis would be unchanged. Let us examine fiscal choice under the assumption that public expenditures are financed by proportional income taxation. Analytically, the step from proportional income taxation to other forms of income taxation is small. Therefore, our analysis should suffice to show how an equilibrium budgetary choice can be determined from information about individual demands, the cost of the public services, and the tax institutions that are used to apportion the cost among the citizenry.

A rule of levying taxes proportionate to income fixes the distribution of tax prices proportionate to individual income. Let us assume that the taxable incomes of our three persons are:

$$I_1 = \$9,000,$$
$$I_2 = \$6,000,$$

and

$$I_3 = \$5,000.$$

Under this distribution of income, m_1 pays 45 percent of the cost of each unit of output, m_2 pays 30 percent, and m_3 pays 25 percent. Continuing with our assumption that marginal cost is \$9 per unit, the distribution of tax prices per unit now becomes:

$$p_1 = \$4.05,$$
$$p_2 = \$2.70,$$

and

$$p_3 = \$2.25.$$

Substituting these per unit tax prices into the individual marginal valuation or demand functions produces the most preferred rate of output units for the three individuals:

$$x_1 = 11.85,$$
$$x_2 = 13.95,$$

and

$$x_3 = 12.75.$$

In this instance, m_3 has the median preference, so the rate of output chosen under majority vote will be 12.75 units.

The Wicksellian-efficient rate of output is still $x = 13$, for it would be unchanged by the mere change in taxing rules. But the majority equilibrium under proportional income taxation is $x = 12.75$, which is an inefficiently small rate of output. The inefficient outcome is again traceable to the asymmetrical distribution of preferences. In this case, in contrast to the previous case, the median preference, 12.75, is less than the mean preference, 12.85. Efficiency is achieved when choice is based on the mean preference but actual choice is based on the median preference. Thus, when the median preference is less than the mean preference, the rate of output chosen under majority rule will be inefficiently small.

The efficient rate of output is independent of the particular fiscal institutions that are used to assign tax liability, for it depends only on preferences for the collectively supplied service and the cost of that service. Yet the rate of output that will be chosen by a collectivity operating under majority rule will depend on the particular taxing institutions that are used to assign liability for payment. Even if cost and preferences are unchanged, a change in the particular tax form used to finance public services may change the equilibrium fiscal choice.

Our analysis to this point suggests that unanimity is the appropriate benchmark for examining fiscal choice in much the same sense as pure competition is the appropriate benchmark for examining market choice. We have also seen that when preferences are distributed symmetrically about the median voter, majority voting will produce the same results as will unanimity voting. When preferences are distributed symmetrically about the median voter, then, majority rule also provides a benchmark that is analogous to that provided by pure competition.

Under what conditions should we expect a symmetrical distribution of preferences? Expenditures for services that benefit the population generally instead of for services that benefit some subset of the population are likely to be distributed fairly symmetrically. When such general expenditures are financed by general taxes, the distribution of preferences is likely to be symmetrical. A nonsymmetrical distribution of preferences can arise from two sources. First, marginal valuations can be nonsymmetrical. Marginal valuations for a national park, for instance, are likely to be asymmetrical: those living in close proximity to the park are likely to value the park more highly than those living in more distant places value it. The distribution of tax liability can also be nonsymmetrical, as we have seen above. Nonsymmetric preferences can arise, then, on both the taxing and the spending sides of the budget. A successful majority coalition can practice tax discrimination, expenditure discrimination, or both. In any event, price reductions to majority coalitions that result in marginal majority cost being less than marginal social cost will be subject to the standard Pigovian critique.

TABLE 3-3
Differential Intensity of Preference: Two Voters and Two Motions

Motion	Vote		Utility Scale		Utility Vote	
	Yes	No				
A	30	70	+100	−10	+3000	−700
B	30	70	+100	−10	+3000	−700

Before examining tax and expenditure discrimination, we might note that the case of symmetrical distribution of preferences corresponds to what has often been labeled a case of equal intensity of preferences. If preferences are of equal intensity and a motion passes under majority vote, the sum of the benefits must exceed the sum of the costs. This is not necessarily so under differential intensity of preferences, which corresponds to nonsymmetrical distribution of preferences.[17] Consider the case of differential intensity of preference shown in Table 3-3 above. There are two motions, *A* and *B*, and the yes and no votes are as indicated. For simplicity, we suppose that the supporters of *A* form a disjoint set from the supporters of *B*. Under the assumption of equal intensity, the utility figures entered for supporters and opponents would be the same. But here we have assumed that supporters are relatively more intense about the issue than opponents are. For each issue, the utility gain exceeds the utility loss, but both issues would fail under majority rule. We might note that both issues would pass if vote trading were allowed, but such considerations are deferred until the next section of this chapter.

Tax discrimination is one source of nonuniformity in the distribution of preferences. Assume that a community of 100 can supply themselves with sanitation crews at a monthly cost of $2,500. Let each citizen have the identical demand schedule $p = 50/x^{1/2}$. Further, assume that taxes are shared equally and each voter pays a monthly tax bill of $25 per crew. Under such circumstances, the number of sanitation crews desired per month by each voter is $x = 4$, which is found by solving $50/x^{1/2} = 25$. Each voter pays a monthly tax bill of $100, and the monthly community budget is $10,000. This represents the efficient supply of sanitation crews as well as the number that will be supplied under majority vote.

Now suppose a majority coalition of 51 members succeeds in revising the rules for assigning tax liability. Under the revised rules, the tax payments of the minority coalition decrease while the payments of the minority coalition increase. Suppose the monthly tax liability placed on the members of the majority coalition is reduced from $5,100 to $4,080, which

[17] A formulation in terms of equal and differential intensity of preferences is given in Buchanan and Tullock, *Calculus of Consent*, pp. 125–28.

entails a tax price of $20 per sanitation crew. This reduction requires an offsetting increase in the monthly tax liability of the members of the minority coalition from $4900 to $5920, which requires a tax price of $30.20 per crew. After this tax change, the members of the majority coalition no longer find themselves in equilibrium, for their marginal valuation of four sanitation crews, $25, now exceeds the marginal cost to them, $20. The majority coalition will approve the rate of output that satisfies $50/x^{1/2} = 20$, which is $x = 6.25$ crews per month. When the majority coalition is able to practice tax discrimination of this form, two things happen. First, income is transferred from the members of the minority to the members of the majority. Second, the public budget becomes excessively large, for public expenditure is the instrument by which the members of the majority are able to exploit the members of the minority.

Such blatant tax discrimination, however, is not the only possible form of tax discrimination. A situation in which people with identical demand schedules are charged unequal prices is essentially identical to a situation in which people with different demand schedules are charged equal prices. This latter case also qualifies as tax discrimination because all members of the collectivity, by the very nature of collective choice, must purchase the same quantity. This differs from market choice, where people with different demand schedules pay equal prices but are able to purchase the quantity that each individual prefers.

For example, suppose that the demand schedule for 60 citizens is $p_1 = 20/x$ and the schedule for 40 citizens is $p_2 = 10/x$. The monthly cost per sanitation crew is still $1,000. The Wicksellian-efficient rate of supply is given by equating the sum of the marginal valuation schedules to the cost. Solving $60(20/x) + 40(10/x) = 1000$ gives $x = 1.6$ crews per month. Substituting 1.6 for x in the marginal valuation schedules gives the efficient prices of $12.50 per unit for members of p_1 and $6.25 per unit for members of p_2. If these two sets of individuals were charged these tax prices per unit, the efficient rate of output would be chosen under either majority rule or unanimity.

But suppose all citizens are assessed equal tax prices of $10 monthly per crew. Members of the majority coalition would prefer that $x = 2$ crews per month, which is found by solving $10 = 20/x$. Members of the minority coalition would prefer that $x = 1$ crew per month, which is found by solving $10 = 10x$. The collective choice would thus be two sanitation crews per month. While the marginal cost of the second sanitation crew is $1,000 per month, the marginal value is only $800 [60(20/2) + 40(10/2)]$. Although the cost of the additional .4 crew exceeds its value, it is supplied nonetheless, for the majority coalition receives net benefits from the additional output.

The properties of tax discrimination in this instance are equivalent to those of Pigou's classic illustration of the smoke-spouting factory.[18] Because the factory does not include the damage caused by its smoke as one of its costs of production, the price of the factory's output will be excessively low. In addition to excessive output from the factory, there will be too much investment in laundering and too little output of other products. A majority coalition will be similar to the smoke-producing factory if it makes budgetary choices on the basis of a marginal cost to its own members that is less than the marginal social cost. Under such circumstances, the majority coalition, like the smoke-producing factory, will supply an inefficiently large amount of the service.

In his now classic critique, Ronald H. Coase exposed the shaky foundations on which the Pigovian tradition rests.[19] The right of the factory to spout smoke into the air is itself a factor of production, and to abridge that right is to destroy a productive input. Because the destruction of any factor of production costs us what the factor could have produced, we must ask whether our gain from destruction will exceed our loss. If the value of the additional product that is produced by using the more smoke-intensive means of production exceeds the loss in value that will result from dirtier clothes, it would be socially inefficient to reduce smoke emissions from the factory. Conversely, the amount of smoke would be excessive only if the value of the additional product were less than the other values destroyed by creating a dirtier environment. But even if the factory smoke were excessive and the factory had the legal right to pollute the air, the residents of the affected area could bribe the factory to reduce its smoke emissions. If the property rights were reversed, the factory could not buy the consent of the community to dump more smoke. However, the factory smoke will be reduced to efficient levels under assignment of property rights. As long as transaction costs are relatively low, the particular rules of liability may have little effect upon the allocation of resources. Relatedly, but in a different context that we shall examine more fully in the next section, Buchanan and Tullock have shown that majority voting will not generate budgetary inefficiency if votes can be bought and sold for money.[20] A prohibition on side payments is identical in its effect to a rise in transaction costs: it becomes more difficult to organize efficient trades. The existence of high transaction costs and the prohibition on side payments serve to prevent disintegration of inefficient outcomes.

[18] A. C. Pigou, *The Economics of Welfare,* 4th ed. (London: Macmillan & Co., 1932), pp. 183–84.
[19] "The Problem of Social Cost," *Journal of Law and Economics,* 3 (October 1960), 1–44.
[20] *Calculus of Consent,* pp. 147–69.

In our previous numerical illustration, tax discrimination generated an inefficiently large supply of sanitation services. If the distribution of preferences is reversed so that 60 persons have the demand function $p_1 = 10/x$ and 40 have the demand function $p_2 = 20/x$, majority rule will produce an inefficiently small budget. With this reversal in preferences, the output rate preferred by the majority coalition is one sanitation crew per month. We have seen that majority voting may generate either an excessive supply or an insufficient supply of some publicly supplied service. Whether the supply is excessive or insufficient depends on the particular majority coalition that happens to control the decision.

When fiscal discrimination takes place, income is transferred from members of the minority coalition to members of the majority coalition. Pure income redistribution is not inefficient for it is merely a movement among alternative Paretian-optimal positions. Nevertheless, the actions of the majority coalition are not purely redistributive because the majority coalition uses budgetary expansion as the vehicle for transferring income to itself. Social waste is the result of expansion in the size of the budget, not of the redistribution of income per se. Fiscal discrimination may be practiced on either the taxing or the spending side of the budget. Tax discrimination results when different people are charged different tax prices even though they have equal demands for the collective activity. Expenditure discrimination results when equal tax prices are charged to finance some activity for which demands differ among the members of the community. Although tax discrimination is conceptually distinguishable from expenditure discrimination, the two are indistinguishable for practical purposes. In some instances, it may be possible to specify fiscal rules that will preclude majority coalitions from making certain types of inefficient choices. We saw earlier, for instance, that if all members of the community had identical demand schedules, a fiscal rule of equal tax sharing would preclude majority coalitions from making inefficient budgetary choices. But demand schedules are unlikely to be identical, and they are not even likely to be distributed uniformly about the median. What do these considerations suggest in regard to the choice of fiscal rules that would preclude majority coalitions from making relatively inefficient choices?

Geography is one possible basis for the formation of tax choice coalitions. Tax discrimination will result if the residents in those areas that form a majority coalition reduce their tax prices relative to the tax prices of the remaining residents. With such tax discrimination, budgetary choice is based on a marginal majority cost that is less than marginal social cost. Therefore, inefficiently large budgets will be the result. While unanimity would prevent geographical tax discrimination, the added decision costs of unanimity may exceed the reduction in external costs. Nevertheless, the efficiency properties of unanimity may be achieved without incurring the costs of unanimity if the fiscal constitution requires geographical uniformity in taxation.[21]

Tax choices also may be exercised by majority coalitions that are constituted along functional lines. Suppose the population is divided into two groups of approximately equal size—for example, agricultural and commercial interests on the one hand and industrial interests on the other. If the members of the majority coalition are able to practice price discrimination against the members of the minority by such means as imposing special taxes on industrial property, budgetary choice will be based on a marginal majority cost that is less than marginal social cost, which will generate an inefficiently large budget. While horizontal equity—equal treatment for equals—has been treated as a principle of fiscal equity, to the extent that it prevents the emergence of functional coalitions on the tax side of the budget it also may be viewed as a fiscal rule that precludes majority coalitions from enacting certain types of inefficient choices.

Majority coalitions may also form along income lines, with one coalition containing the wealthier half of the population and the other coalition representing the poorer half. The coalition that contained the median voter would control the collective choice in this instance. If majority marginal cost is less than social marginal cost, budgetary inefficiency will result once again. Although supplementary fiscal rules can impose further constraints on the choices of majority coalitions, the appropriate fiscal rules are more difficult to design, as they are critically dependent on the prevailing income and price elasticities of demand for collective services.[22] Without introducing specific assumptions, the most reasonable a priori assumptions are unitary income and price elasticities. With unitary elasticities, a fiscal rule requiring proportional income taxation will produce Wicksellian-efficiency in collective choice. With a unitary income elasticity, an increase of 100 percent in income would generate an increase of 100 percent in the quantity of the public service demanded—at the initial tax price. But doubling the income would also double the tax price of the public service. With a unitary price elasticity, the quantity demanded of the public service would fall to its initial rate. With unitary price and income elasticities, a fiscal rule of proportional income taxation would preclude majority coalitions from making inefficient choices. With alternative income and price elasticities, alternative tax rate schedules would be required to preclude

[21] Article I, Section 8 of the U.S. Constitution has been construed as requiring geographical uniformity in national taxation. Similar requirements exist in the state constitutions. See David G. Tuerck, "Constitutional Asymmetry," *Public Choice,* 2 (1967), 27–44.

[22] Buchanan, "Fiscal Institutions and Efficiency in Collective Outlay."

inefficient outcomes. In any event the essential point is that inflexible tax institutions may preclude certain sources of budgetary inefficiency.

Majority coalitions also may practice fiscal discrimination on the expenditure side of the budget. Suppose tax uniformity prevails, but that preferences for some collective activity differ among the members of the community. Opportunity still exists for the majority coalition to practice fiscal discrimination, and the outcome will depend on whether the majority coalition has above average or below average preferences for the proposed object of expenditure. If the members of the majority coalition have above average preferences for the activity, an inefficiently large budget will be chosen. Conversely, if the members of the majority coalition have below average preferences for the activity, an inefficiently small budget will be chosen.

Geographical expenditure discrimination is widespread. The benefits from many national expenditures are highly localized, while the accompanying tax revenues are extracted from the entire nation. Some of the most rapidly expanding components of the national budget are those that entail significant geographical discrimination. Expenditures for urban-related activities are a prominent example. Funding for the relative handful of cities subsidized by the Model Cities program is by taxes levied on the entire national citizenry, yet a direct reduction in national tax rates for the residents of those select cities designed to produce the identical effect probably would be held in violation of the uniformity clause.[23]

In examining the budgetary consequences of geographical discrimination in public expenditure, it may be useful to construct a simple model. Consider a nation that contains three geographically distinct clusters of population of equal size that operate under a national requirement of geographically uniform taxation. The national legislature operates under simple majority voting, which is identical to a rule of two-thirds majority in our three-area model. Each area proposes the construction of an artifical lake in its vicinity. The characteristics of the budgetary equilibrium that will emerge within our given set of fiscal rules must be examined.

Any one area will succeed in getting its artificial lake constructed only if it secures the support of one other area. With geographical tax uniformity, however, the residents of the supporting area would bear part of the cost of the lake. To secure the needed support, the first area must somehow compensate the second. If side payments (buying votes) are prohibited, compensation must take the form of a vote trade on another issue, a trade to support construction of another artificial lake in our illustration.

---

[23] See Tuerck, "Constitutional Asymmetry" for a discussion of how expenditure discrimination can destroy the accomplishments of tax uniformity.

Thus, a majority coalition will form among two of the three areas, and two artificial lakes will be constructed. These two areas will choose a lake size for which the marginal cost *to them* equals their marginal valuation. But the majority coalition places part of the cost on the minority, for whom the lakes are practically valueless. The marginal majority cost of the two lakes is less than the marginal social cost, so public expenditure upon the artificial lake will be inefficiently large. Obviously, the conclusion about budgetary inefficiency does not require that the two majority regions supply themselves with descriptively identical projects. One region might sponsor construction of an artificial lake, the other some urban redevelopment project. Whatever the descriptive feature of the particular expenditure project, the essential feature required to produce overproduction is only that the beneficiaries be more concentrated geographically than are the contributors.

As budgetary processes unfold, a system of revolving majorities will transpire. The composition of the majority coalition will change over time; members of the minority on one issue will find themselves in the majority on some other issue.[24] In our model with three areas, revolving majorities produces results that make each of the three coalitions equally likely: each area would expect to be in the majority on two-thirds of the issues that arise. Income effects will sum to zero when there are revolving majorities, for the income gains from membership in majority coalitions will be offset by the income losses from membership in minority coalitions. Although income effects cancel over a sequence of coalitions, a price effect remains. A majority coalition exercises choice on the basis of the price to its members, which may be less than marginal social cost. The price effect of majority voting, not the income effect, produces budgetary inefficiency.[25]

Budgetary inefficiency would be eliminated if majority coalitions could be prevented from practicing geographical discrimination in public expenditure. A federal form of government may be viewed as a fiscal rule that constrains some sources of budgetary inefficiency by reducing the opportunities for expenditure discrimination along geographical lines. If the national government in our previous illustration had been federated into three states, with the provision of artificial lakes made a state function, the excessive investment in artificial lakes would have been prevented. If

[24] Gordon Tullock, "Some Problems of Majority Voting," *Journal of Political Economy,* 67 (December 1959), 571–79.

[25] Tullock's discussion, *ibid.,* of the inefficiency of majority voting confused income and price effects, and his illustrations of gross inefficiency are caused by his failure to allow for offsetting income effects. Anthony Downs, in "In Defense of Majority Voting," *Journal of Political Economy,* 69 (April 1961), 192–99, seems to have sensed the difficulty with Tullock's failure to allow for offsetting income effects, but he, in turn, failed to recognize that majority rule creates price effects.

the fiscal constitution prevents the national government from financing expenditures that are geographically concentrated, the divergence between marginal private costs and marginal social costs could vanish.[26] A federal form of government, then, may be viewed as a fiscal rule that substitutes for a more restrictive voting rule.[27]

LOGROLLING, SIDE PAYMENTS, AND FISCAL CHOICE

Our single issue model of fiscal choice is appropriate for referenda situations. But when more than one issue simultaneously is subject to choice, our analytical models must be modified. Political exchange becomes possible when multiple issues exists: it becomes possible for a person to give away his vote on one issue in exchange for someone else's vote on another issue. *Side payments* are a form of exchange in which votes on an issue are bought and sold for money. *Logrolling* is a form of political exchange in which support on one issue is exchanged for support on another issue. Logrolling may be either explicit or implicit. *Explicit logrolling* is a direct exchange of political support among issues. *Implicit logrolling* does not involve a direct agreement to exchange support on specific issues. Rather, it involves creating a package of issues that the various individuals can support. Political platforms, which represent the effort of political entrepreneurs to put together a winning package of issues, illustrate implicit logrolling. The trades, in this instance, are implicit in the package that is offered for electoral considerations.

Logrolling has attracted considerable attention from economists because of its similarity to ordinary market exchange. Buchanan and Tullock, for instance, observed that "because it does allow differentials in relative intensities to be reflected in results, logrolling, as an institution, makes ma-

---

[26] In Tullock's illustration of excessive investment in road repairing ("Problems of Majority Voting"), the source of the excessive investment in road repairing is that expenditure benefits (repair of one farmer's road) are more concentrated geographically than are the tax charges (levied upon all farmers). A federation that made each farmer responsible for the repair of his own road would eliminate the excessive investment.

[27] Given the lack of governments that cover regions larger than states, a requirement of geographical uniformity in public expenditure will sometimes perform poorly. For a discussion of some of these issues, see Robert G. Dixon, Jr., "Constitutional Bases for Regionalism," *George Washington Law Review,* 33 (October 1964), 47–88.

For an examination of federal government as a fiscal rule that may substitute for a more restrictive voting rule, see Wagner, *Fiscal Organization of American Federalism,* pp. 16–20.

TABLE 3-4
Demand Functions: Three Voters and Three Services

$p_{x1} = 20 - x$	$p_{y1} = 10 - y$	$p_{z1} = 6 - z$
$p_{x2} = 10 - x$	$p_{y2} = 6 - y$	$p_{z2} = 20 - z$
$p_{x3} = 6 - x$	$p_{y3} = 20 - y$	$p_{z3} = 10 - z$

jority voting rule more efficient."[28] And again, "Our analysis was aimed at demonstrating that [logrolling] . . . make[s] the whole process work 'better' rather than worse, by orthodox efficiency standards."[29]

The analogy between logrolling and ordinary trade has produced understandable partiality to the arrangement among economists. Unfortunately, as we shall see, this partiality lacks rational support. To gain an understanding of logrolling and side payments, we shall explore a simple numerical illustration along several dimensions.

Consider a community of three individuals, m_1, m_2, and m_3, that must collectively choose the rates of supply of three public services, x, y, and z. These services might represent library facilities, park facilities, and sanitation services. Let p_{x1} denote m_1's demand for x, let p_{y2} denote m_2's demand for y, and so on. The postulated demand functions are shown in Table 3-4.

The Wicksellian-optimal rate of supply for each service is found by summing the individual demand curves for that service, setting the sum equal to the marginal cost, and solving for the rate of supply. Assume that marginal cost equals average cost equals \$30 for x, y, and z. The optimal rate of output for x is found by solving $(20 - x) + (10 - x) + (6 - x) = 30$, which gives $x = 2$. Similarly, $y = 2$ and $z = 2$ are the optimal quantities of y and z.

Assuming that budgetary costs are shared equally by the three persons, what will be the rates of output chosen by the community when output decisions are made by referenda under majority rule? Under this decision procedure, a motion is proposed and a vote taken. If that motion secures a majority, a motion supporting a greater output is advanced. The highest motion to secure a majority becomes the output decision. Simple inspection of our demand functions shows that the identical voting results will occur for any service. Thus, we need examine only one service. Consider an initial motion that $x = 1$ per month. This motion will secure majority support, for both m_1 and m_2 will support the expansion from zero to one. The motion that $x = 2$ will fail, however, for only m_1 will support

[28] James M. Buchanan and Gordon Tullock, "Gains-From-Trade in Votes," *Ethics*, 76 (July 1966), 305–06.
[29] *Ibid.*

it. Thus $x = 1$, $y = 1$, and $z = 1$ will be the rates of supply chosen collectively by referenda under majority vote.

Now consider logrolling under unanimous consent. Clearly, it is possible for all three persons to make a package agreement of the sort that m_2 and m_3 agree to support two units of x, m_1 and m_2 agree to support two units of y, and m_1 and m_3 agree to support two units of x. Each of the three persons will prefer the combination $(2,2,2)$ to the combination $(1,1,1)$. Consider the situation faced by m_1, who wants to have the supply of x expanded, but must pay for it by agreeing to have the supply of y and z expanded also. Since m_1's marginal valuation on the second unit of x is \$18 while his cost is only \$10, his net gain on the second unit of x is \$8. The marginal cost of the second unit of y and z is \$10 each, or \$20 total, but m_1's marginal valuation of these units is only \$8 and \$4 for y and z respectively, or \$12 total. He thus loses \$8 on the expansion of y and z. At the margin, the package is efficient for m_1, for the marginal gain exceeds the marginal loss until the point $(2,2,2)$, is attained. In this instance, logrolling, the exchange of votes for other votes, increases the efficiency with which collective choices are made.

But what happens when logrolling takes place under majority rule? Among the three equally likely majority coalitions (m_1, m_2), (m_1, m_3), and (m_2, m_3), consider the coalition between m_1 and m_3 over the provision of x and y. Take the Wicksellian-efficient output $(2,2,2)$ as a starting point. This output bundle clearly is not an equilibrium under majority rule. It will be profitable for the coalition (m_1, m_3) to support an expansion in the output of x and y. Consider a proposal to change from $(2,2,2)$ to $(3,3,2)$. The marginal cost of this expansion of output is equal to \$20 for each member of the coalition. The marginal benefit of such an expansion of \$26 $(18 + 8)$ for m_1 and \$22 $(4 + 18)$ for m_3. So both members of the coalition will receive net gains from an expansion in output to $(3,3,2)$. At the output bundle $(3,3,2)$, the marginal cost of m_1 and m_3 of expanding output to $(4,4,2)$ is still \$20. The marginal benefit of this expansion is \$24 $(17 + 7)$ for m_1 and \$20 $(3 + 17)$ for m_3. While m_1 would support even more expansion, m_3 would not, so $(4,4,2)$ is an equilibrium pattern of agreement for the coalition. In this instance, logrolling under majority vote produces an overexpansion in those activities supported by the majority coalition.

Logrolling is a form of trading, but of votes rather than of ordinary commodities. By the nature of collective activity, all members of the collectivity share in the cost of services that are supplied collectively. Yet the agreement is made only among a majority of the collectivity, which enables the majority to impose external costs on the minority. A situation in which two people agree to finance something, with part of the cost being paid by a third party, is equivalent to a situation in which producers do not account for all of the costs of their activities. The standard Pigovian critique about the divergence of private costs from social costs thus applies to the actions of majority coalitions.

Majorites will revolve over time: a member of a majority coalition today may be in the minority coalition tomorrow, and a member of the minority coalition today may be in the majority coalition tomorrow. With revolving coalitions, income gain will tend to cancel income losses from the perspective of any single person. But this does not mean that the in-

FIGURE 3-3
Logrolling and Inefficiency in Budgetary Choice

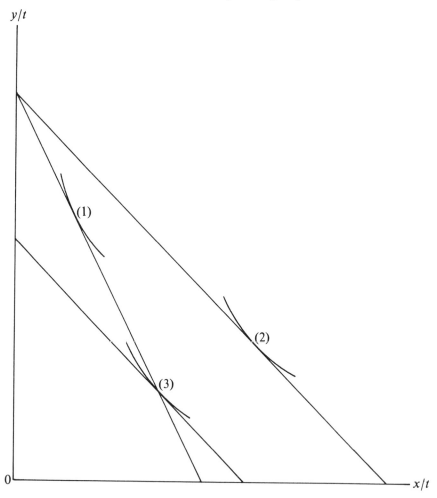

efficiency will evaporate. Figure 3-3 illustrates the issue for the median voter. Let x denote publicly supplied services and y denote privately supplied services. Given the indicated transformation schedule and preference pattern, the efficient allocation of resources that would result under unanimity is indicated by position (1). Without an offsetting membership in a minority coalition, membership in a majority coalition, reduces the price of x and produces an income gain that moves the median vote to such a position as (2). When the loss of income resulting from membership in a minority coalition is introduced, however, the median voter attains such a position as (3), which is revealed to be inferior to (1) because of the inefficiently large supply of public services x.

Nevertheless, unanimity will not ensure that logrolling will be efficient. Budgets will not be excessive, but they might be insufficient. Under unanimity, logrollling will exploit some, but not all, gains from trade. Consider the data shown in Table 3-5. The Wicksellian-efficient rates of output are $x = 20$, $y = 13.33$, and $z = 6.67$—assuming again that marginal cost and average cost are equal to $30 per unit.

Consider the situation of (19, 12.33, 5.67), which is a pattern of output in which all three variables are each one unit short of their optimal rates. Will all three persons support a trade of votes to secure a one unit expansion in all three variables? Such an agreement will cost each individual $30. The gain to m_1 is $53 ($51 - 2.33 + 4.33$), so he will support the proposed vote trade. The gain to m_2 is $33 ($-9 + 37.67 + 4.33$), so he too will support the proposed vote trade. The gain to m_3, however, is only $13 ($-9 - 2.33 + 24.33$), so he will oppose the agreement. Thus, logrolling under unanimity can result in an equilibrium in which not all efficiencies from budgetary expansion are exploited.

Under majority voting, a coalition between m_1 and m_2 could form, which would pass the output (21, 13.33) for x and y. But at that position, the gains from further budgetary expansion are $46.67 ($50 - 2.33$) for m_1 and $26.67 ($-10 + 36.67$) for m_2. For both persons, the gains from further expansion exceed the costs of $20. Thus, when majority voting replaces unanimity, budgetary expenditures will be pushed beyond efficient levels.

Side payments are an institution by which votes are bought and sold

TABLE 3-5
Demand Functions: Three Voters and Three Services

$p_{x1} = 70 - x$	$p_{y1} = 10 - y$	$p_{z1} = 10 - z$
$p_{x2} = 10 - x$	$p_{y2} = 50 - y$	$p_{z2} = 10 - z$
$p_{x3} = 10 - x$	$p_{y3} = 10 - y$	$p_{z3} = 30 - z$

for money. Consider the above illustration of logrolling in which the Wicksellian-efficient set failed to secure passage under unanimity on the one hand and x and y were supplied at inefficiently large levels under majority rule on the other. Table 3-6 shows for all three services the net gains that each person would receive from one-unit expansion from the output set (19, 12.33, 5.67). The net gain to m_1 for a one-unit expansion in x, for instance, would be $41 (51 — 10).

Person m_1 wants to buy the votes of m_2 and m_3 on the motion that $x = 20$. Similarly, m_2 wants to buy the votes of m_1 and m_3 on the motion that $y = 13.3$, and m_3 wants to buy the votes of m_1 and m_2 on the motion that $z = 6.67$. Can these purchases be effectuated? Consider the case of m_1 buying votes on x; the same reasoning applies to the other two cases. Person m_1 is willing to pay a *maximum* price of $41 for the votes of m_2 and m_3 on the motion $x = 20$. To be willing to sell their votes, m_2 and m_3 must each receive a *minimum* price of $19 each. Thus, the maximum price that m_1 is willing to pay exceeds the minimum prices that m_2 and m_3 together must receive to be willing to sell. A $3 bargaining range thus exists within which all participants would prefer to reach some agreement concerning the sale of the votes.

What about side payments under majority rule? Consider a coalition between persons m_1 and m_2 proposing the inefficiently large motions $x = 21$, $y = 14.33$. The net gain from the increase in x is $39, —$21, —$21 to m_1, m_2, and m_3 respectively. Similarly, the net gain from the increase in y is —$14.33, $25.67, and —$14.33 to m_1, m_2, and m_3 respectively. In both cases, then, the net gain for the entire group is —$3. Yet there is a gain to the majority coalition. For m_1, the net gain is $24.67 (39 — 14.33), while for m_2 it is $4.67 (—21 + 25.67). By contrast, m_3 suffers a net loss of —$35.33 (—21 — 14.33).

But m_1 would be unable to buy m_2's vote on the motion $x = 21$. Likewise, m_2 would be unable to buy m_1's vote on the motion $y = 14.33$. The maximum amount that m_1 is willing to pay to m_2 for the latter's vote on $x = 21$ is $39. If m_2 makes this sale, his net gain is $18 (39 — 21). But m_3 would lose $21 if the sale were made, and this is the maximum

TABLE 3-6
Net Gain from One-Unit Expansion in Output

Person	Service		
	x	y	z
1	41	−12.33	−5.67
2	−19	27.67	−5.67
3	−19	−12.33	14.33

amount he would be willing to pay to buy m_2's vote. Thus, the vote would be sold to m_3 rather than to m_1. A similar situation holds with respect to the sale of m_1's vote on the motion $y = 14.33$.

Even under majority rule, then, side payments will prevent budgetary inefficiency. Side payments will both prevent the passage of inefficient proposals and ensure the passage of efficient proposals that would otherwise fail. But with side payments under majority rule, a vast redistributive game can result. Unless certain types of issues can be prevented, side payments under majority rule could degenerate into a form of collectively sanctioned blackmail. Inefficient motions could be made by majority coalitions, not with the objective of securing passage, but with the objective of collecting side payments. Income redistribution is ordinarily thought of as being zero sum, but to the extent that people invest resources in trying to escape re-distributive losses and to secure redistributive gains, such redistribution will generate social losses.[30]

[30] See Gordon Tullock, "The Welfare Costs of Tariffs, Monopolies, and Theft," *Western Economic Journal,* 4 (June 1967), 224–32.

4. Fiscal Choice with Multiple Governments

Up to this point, we have examined the public economy under the implicit assumption that one government unit exists in isolation from all others. We shall now relax this assumption and consider fiscal choice in a state in which there are a multiplicity of governments.[1] When we drop our assumption of an isolated state, we drop it in two dimensions. On the one hand, a subnational government will face competition from other subnational units of government. By introducing such elements as competition for tax base, such horizontal competition constrains the actions of a political unit vis-á-vis those of its equals. On the other hand, there also will be a hierarchy of governments, and such vertical relations will influence the process of fiscal choice. In the American federal state, for instance, there is one national government, but there are 50 state governments, and each state government contains a large number of local governments. The peculiarities introduced by the hierarchical organization of governments also must be examined. Thus, when we leave the context of an isolated state, we must modify our analysis in both vertical and horizontal dimensions.

THE FISCAL ORGANIZATION
OF A FEDERAL STATE

A federal state faces two primary issues of fiscal organization.[2] First, there is the vertical problem: which public services should be supplied by which levels of government? Second, there is the horizontal problem: in what

[1] Much of the discussion in this chapter is based on Richard E. Wagner, *The Fiscal Organization of American Federalism* (Chicago: Markham, 1971).

[2] We shall use the term "federal state" synonymously with "decentralized" state." While this usage of "federalism" is broader than that used by political scientists, it is a more fascile terminology than is "decentralism." Federal government is used synonymously with decentralized government in Wallace E. Oates, *Fiscal Federalism* (New York: Harcourt Brace Jovanovich, 1972).

manner should some geographical area be divided into units of government? The first issue has been construed primarily as a matter of the range of benefit spillover from public services. The provision of an army benefits the entire nation; therefore, an army should be supplied by the national government. In contrast, the provision of fire protection benefits only the local area and should be supplied by local governments. The second issue has been construed primarily as a matter of economies of scale. If fire protection should be supplied by local governments, what size should these localities be?

Support for a federal form of government rests on two foundations. On the one hand, it may constrain the set of budgetary choices available to majority coalitions so as to preclude certain inefficient outcomes from the choice set. On the other hand, a federal form of government can accommodate differences in individual preferences for public services more fully than can a unitary form of government.

Remember our discussion in Chapter 3 pp. 51–53. If preferences for some collective activity differ among the members of the community, opportunity may exist for the majority coalition to practice expenditure discrimination, and the particular outcome that results will depend on whether the majority coalition has above-average or below-average preferences for the proposed expenditure. Both the constitutional requirement of geographical tax uniformity and the general acceptance of the principle of horizontal equity impose considerable constraint on effective tax discrimination. But similar constraints do not impinge on the ability of majority coalitions to practice expenditure discrimination. There is little notion of principles of equity in the distribution of public expenditure. Moreover, geographical uniformity in public expenditure is not a requirement. In effect, the U.S. Supreme Court, in its decision in the companion cases of *Frothingham v. Mellon* and *Massachusetts v. Mellon,*[3] ruled that congressional majorities can spend public monies in almost any manner they choose. Geographical expenditure discrimination is permitted. Benefits from many national expenditures are highly localized, while the accompanying tax revenues are extracted from the entire nation. Tuerck has shown how expenditure discrimination can offset tax uniformity, thereby promoting fiscal inefficiency.[4] A federal form of government can be viewed as a fiscal rule that requires public services with geographically concentrated benefits to be financed by the benefited areas. By reducing the scope for expenditure discrimination, effective federalism precludes certain ineffi-

[3] 262 U.S. 447 (1923).
[4] See David G. Tuerck, "Constitutional Asymmetry," *Public Choice,* 2 (1967), 27–44, for a discussion of how expenditure discrimination can destroy the accomplishments of tax uniformity.

cient outcomes from the choice set confronted by majority coalitions at the national level.

Budgetary choices ordinarily are subject to continuous variation over quantity. However, many collective choices are primarily binary, being an either-or choice among competing motions. The efficiency basis of federal government also holds for these binary choices, as has been shown by J. Roland Pennock.[5] Consider a community of 100,000 that must choose between A and B. If 55,000 prefer A and 45,000 prefer B, A will be the collective choice, and the desires of 45 percent of the population will be frustrated. Now suppose that federation takes place. There are now two communities, each with 50,000 population. Let community X prefer B to A by a vote of 30,000 to 20,000, and let community Y prefer A to B by 35,000 to 15,000. In total, A still collects 55,000 votes and B gets 45,000, but the public policy desires of only 35 percent of the population are being frustrated. At the very worst, federation would have zero impact on a reduction in frustration, which would occur if each lower level of government had a majority for the same issue.

It may be objected that because the issues are of a sort for which there is a potential value consensus, it is meaningful to speak of correct policies, not just preferred policies. Even this objection does not alter the efficiency attributes of federal government. Suppose there are just two possible policies, "correct" and "incorrect." Consider two institutional settings, one in which a single national policy is chosen and one in which each state makes a policy choice. If each political unit faces the same probability of choosing correctly, the expected value to any individual of living under a "correct" policy would be the same in both institutional settings. But because the variance will be less if choice is exercised by the states, principles of risk avoidance suggest that federalization is superior to nationalization. Of course, it takes time to locate the "correct" policy. Any policy that is chosen will remain in effect for some period of time before it is changed. We would expect the "correct" policy eventually to emerge everywhere, regardless of whether it was federalized or nationalized. But the expected total cost of choosing incorrectly, the difference between the payoff of the correct policy and the payoff of the actual policy, will be lower if the policy choice is left to the states rather than to the national government. Thus, there are strong efficiency attributes in the greater experimentation in a federal system, which has been duly noted in Justice Brandeis' "laboratory of the states" support of federal government.[6]

[5] "Federal and Unitary Government—Disharmony and Frustration." *Behavioral Science*, 4 (April 1959), 147–57.

[6] A thorough defense of federal government would have to become involved in such considerations as the decentralization of power: the national government is the only unit of government that does not face competition from other units of government. Such issues, however, would lead us too far afield for our purposes.

In several respects, an individual's choice of a community in which to reside is similar to his market choice of a bundle of goods and services. There is considerable variation in individual preference for different types of activities and services, both private and public. We should expect the communities within a metropolitan area to reflect these differences.[7] The operation of a system of local government in a metropolitan area may resemble the operation of a system of competitive markets. Competition among governments in a metropolitan area may have efficiency properties similar to competition among firms as long as three conditions are met: first, there must be several competing governments in the metropolitan area; second, each competing government must supply a significantly different bundle of services; and finally, individuals in the area must be reasonably aware of the available alternatives and their costs.[8] As a result of this competitive process, there will be some tendency for the budgetary choices of local governments to be Pareto-efficient.[9]

INTERGOVERNMENTAL SPILLOVERS AND FISCAL EFFICIENCY

Even in the absence of spillovers across government boundaries, the budgetary equilibrium attained by a system of localities generally will not be Wicksellian-efficient, as Buchanan and Goetz have shown.[10] Intergovernmental spillovers, however, generally are considered to be the most significant source of budgetary inefficiency in a system of local government. Budgetary decisions within any locality will be based on a comparison of the cost and the benefit of its own activities to its own residents—more specifically, to the median voter. If some of the cost is transferred to other localities, the action-taking locality will not consider the full cost of its choice in making a budgetary decision, so its budget will tend to be inefficiently large. If, by contrast, some of the benefit is transferred to other states, the action-taking state will not consider the full benefit of its choice in making a budgetary decision, so its budget will tend to be inefficiently small. Although McLure has estimated that about 25 percent of state and

[7] For an interesting description of such variations in preference for public services, see Thomas R. Dye, "City-Suburban Social Distance and Public Policy," *Social Forces,* 44 (September 1965), 100–6.

[8] Charles M. Tiebout, "A Pure Theory of Local Expenditures," *Journal of Political Economy,* 64 (October 1956), 416–24; Vincent Ostrom, Charles M. Tiebout, and Robert Warren, "The Organization of Government in a Metropolitan Area," *American Political Science Review,* 55 (December 1961), 831–42.

[9] The limitations within which this tendency operates are examined in James M. Buchanan and Charles J. Goetz, "Efficiency Limits of Fiscal Mobility: An Assessment of the Tiebout Model," *Public Economics,* 1 (Spring 1972), 25–43.

[10] *Ibid.*

local taxes are exported across state boundaries,[11] most diagnoses of federal fiscal inefficiency are based on the assumption that expenditure spillover dominates cost spillover.

Under majority voting, public expenditure within a locality will be expanded until the marginal cost of the public service to the median voter equals his marginal valuation. At the budgetary outlay that conforms to the most preferred position of the median voter, offsetting numbers of residents will desire larger and smaller expenditures. If the preference of the median voter is also the mean preference within the locality, the budgetary choice will be fully efficient. Because we are interested in inefficiency caused by spillovers rather than those attributable to imperfect voting rules, we shall assume that the preference of the median voter is also the mean preference.

Let us construct a simple model of federal fiscal choice under conditions of expenditure spillover. The national government, A, contains two localities, A_1 and A_2. To supply descriptive concreteness, we may assume that A_1 provides a park that is made freely available to all users and that A_2 subsidizes hospitals by charging all users the same, below-cost, price regardless of residence. The implications can be seen most clearly if we assume that spillovers are equal in both directions; therefore, we shall assume that the value of park services received by residents of A_2 is equal to the value of hospital subsidies received by residents of A_1. In contrast, if we assume that the spillovers are unequal, residents of one locality enjoy a net subsidy while residents of the other locality suffer a net cost, and these income effects would have to be incorporated into our analysis. Yet the income effects must sum to zero for both localities combined, so assuming that the income effects are zero for each locality taken separately simplifies the analysis considerably and maintains its validity as an expression of central tendency.

Figure 4-1 depicts the budgetary choice of the median voter. Let X denote the public service and Y the residual bundle of private services. Without spillovers, the median voter faces the attainable set of consumption possibilities that lie along $Y_0 X_0$. Given the price of X, Y_0/X_0, the median voter selects the bundle of services indicated by b_0. The amount of X contained in b_0 will be the amount of X chosen by the median voter for the locality.

With spillovers, however, the locality's residents, including the median voter, must pay a higher price for the public service. The provision of some fixed number of hospital beds for A_2's residents requires that A_2 supply a greater number of beds to accommodate residents of A_1. Similarly,

FIGURE 4-1
Intergovernmental Spillover and Budgetary Inefficiency

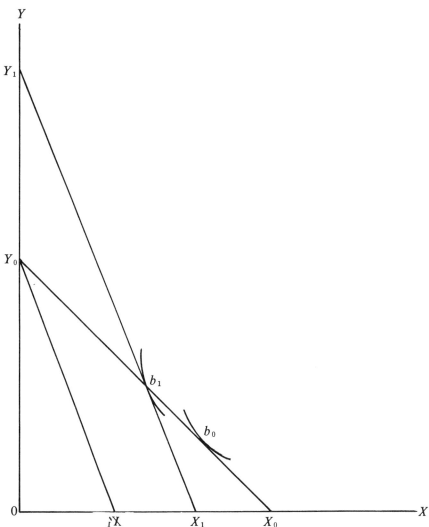

the provision of some fixed number of acres of park for the residents of
A_1 requires that A_1 supply an additional number of acres when residents
of A_2 also use the park. In Figure 4-1, we assume that a constant percentage of each locality's output, $X_1 X_0 / O X_0$, is used by residents of the
other locality. $Y_0 X'_1$ then indicates the higher price paid by the median
voter after the spillout. Because we have assumed that spillins equal spillouts, however, income effects are cancelled, and the median voter of each
locality still consumes along the opportunity set $Y_0 X_0$. Consumption now

takes place at the point b_1, where the new price set, Y_1X_1, which entails the higher price of X, intersects Y_0X_0. Since b_1 could have been purchased when spillouts were absent but was rejected in favor of b_0, b_1 is revealed inferior to b_0. Expenditure spillout clearly reduces fiscal efficiency, even when the value of spillout is offset by the value of spillin.

In terms of Figure 4-1, federal fiscal efficiency requires that the median voter choose b_0 rather than b_1. The attainment of federal fiscal efficiency through conditional grants can be conceptualized as a two-stage process. In the first stage the national government levies an income tax upon both localities in an amount sufficient to collapse the budget constraint from Y_1X_1 to $Y_0X'_1$. In the second stage the national government uses the proceeds to pay each locality X'_1X_0/OX_0 percent of its total expenditure upon X. This conditional grant lowers the price of X such that the budget line Y_0X_0 is attained and b_0 is chosen once again. It should be noted that the grant does not entail the distribution of some fixed sum, but is open-ended, with the size of the grant residually determined as the product of the locality's expenditure decision and the rate of matching.[12]

We can construct a rationale for conditional grants-in-aid easily, but are we justified in concluding that conditional grants actually perform in the manner described by this rationale? A median voter will prefer national provision of some service to local provision if the tax price charged by the national government is less than the tax price charged by the local government. It does not follow, however, that the resulting change of governmental mix is efficient. We must distinguish two sets of circumstances under which a median voter will prefer national provision. In the first instance, the tax price of the service at the local level exceeds the marginal cost while the tax price at the national level equals marginal cost. In the second instance, the tax price at the local level equals marginal cost while the tax price at the national level is less than marginal cost. In both cases the median voter faces a lower tax price at the national level. Only in the first instance, however, is national provision the more efficient alternative. Before choosing one of these alternatives, we must determine which relation between tax price and marginal cost is more likely, which in turn requires that we examine the demand for and the supply of conditional grants.

Within wide limits, it is individually rational for local politicians to demand conditional grants. Local politicians face the choice of either financing some activity wholly from taxes levied on their constituents or securing conditional grant financing from the national government (which

---

[12] For an examination of such optimizing conditional grants, see George F. Break, *Intergovernmental Fiscal Relations in the United States* (Washington, D.C.: Brookings, 1967), pp. 77–79.

would, on the average, finance two-thirds of the cost). Thus, conditional grants enable local politicians to offer public services at reduced prices, but on the average, the national taxes levied to finance the entire package of conditional grant programs offsets a locality's direct benefit from the price reduction it receives from the grant. This offsetting income effect is accepted as part of the fiscal environment, as no locality directly can control the grant-related activities of other localities.

The desire of national politicians to supply conditional grants is more constrained than is the desire of local politicians to accept them. Although grants may be virtually costless to local politicians, national politicians must levy the taxes to finance the grants. Obviously, conditional grants also provide benefits, and every national politician will have some preferred grant policy that balances the costs and the benefits to him, as he sees them. Constitutional restrictions generally limit the national government to responsibility for military and foreign affairs and other general benefit activities. These general benefit activities offer little opportunity for national politicians to deliver particular benefits for their constituents. It is another manifestation of the free-rider dilemma that special benefit legislation generally offers greater opportunity for political profit. Because the activities of any one congressional district have an imperceptible impact on the supply of general benefit expenditures, it is rational for individual legislators to devote particular attention to special benefit activity.[13] Conditional grant programs are a vehicle by which the national politician can invade this lucrative vote market without directly violating the constitutional assignment of responsibilities.

Generally, American courts have interpreted the Constitution as requiring that national taxes be geographically uniform; a national tax must be applied at the same rate throughout the nation. As a result of the Supreme Court's decision in *Frothingham v. Mellon* and *Massachusetts v. Mellon*,[14] congressional majorities are considered to be the sole judge of the activities that may be pursued through conditional grants. Thus, geographical uniformity is required for national taxation, but not for national expenditure.[15] This fiscal asymmetry—the combination of tax uniformity with expenditure nonuniformity—often produces budgetary inefficiency, with expenditures sometimes being too large and sometimes too small.[16]

[13] See Mancur Olson, Jr., *The Logic of Collective Action* (Cambridge: Harvard University Press, 1965).

[14] 262 U.S. 447 (1923).

[15] For an examination of this fiscal asymmetry, see Tuerck, "Constitutional Asymmetry."

[16] For an early recognition that either type of budgetary inefficiency may result (1896), see Knut Wicksell, "A New Principle of Just Taxation," in Ricahrd A. Musgrave and Alan T. Peacock, eds., *Classics in the Theory of Public Finance* (London: Macmillan & Co., 1962), 72–118.

If a proposed grant program supplies benefits to only a few localities, it may fail to secure majority support even if the grant is potentially efficient. Under the constitutional requirement of tax uniformity, the proposed grant program would produce negative net returns for the majority of the localities, as they would contribute their share of tax payments without receiving benefits. Fiscal inefficiency of this form is the result of insufficient flexibility in cost-sharing arrangements. Under more flexible cost-sharing arrangements, the beneficiaries could be charged for the project, and majority opposition to the otherwise efficient project would cease. This type of inefficiency may have particular relevance in dealing with regional problems, where the benefits from joint action are concentrated within relatively small areas.[17]

Suppose, however, that a proposed grant program gains acceptance by a majority coalition and is enacted by the national legislature. Because the tax revenues required to finance the grant will be levied uniformly over the nation, the majority coalition will place some of the cost of the grant program on the minority nonbeneficiaries. In the extreme limiting case, only one-half of the localities will receive benefits but all will contribute to the cost. Furthermore, the price of the grant program to the members of the majority coalition will be only one-half the marginal social cost of the grant. The national provision of geographically nonuniform expenditure financed by geographically uniform taxation is really another form of cost exporting. Of course, majorities will revolve through time and, because the composition of majority and minority coalitions changes continually, the income effects of particular grant programs tend to cancel. But the price effects remain. Each majority coalition makes its choice on the basis of majority or private marginal costs that are less than social marginal costs, and those grant proposals that secure majority support will tend to become inefficiently large.

Political competition seems subject to what may be called a Gresham's law of politics—an inefficient set of policies will tend to defeat an efficient set of policies if constitutional rules permit majority choice among the two sets.[18] Under conditions of geographical uniformity in taxation, conditional grant programs that receive majority support will tend to become inefficiently large. Yet, as we have already seen, it remains individually rational for state politicians to demand conditional grants, so the negative-sum game has positive survival value. If the set of conditional grants is efficient, some majority coalition will find it profitable to support

---

[17] R. G. Dixon, Jr., "Constitutional Bases for Regionalism," *George Washington Law Review*, 33 (October 1964), 47–48.

[18] This is similar to the proposition that a party that proposes a Pareto-optimal set of policies will be defeated by one that proposes a nonoptimal set. See Anthony Downs, *An Economic Theory of Democracy* (New York: Harper, 1957), 177–82.

an additional set of inefficient grants, at least as long as nonuniform expenditure may be financed by uniform taxation.

SPILLOVERS, POLITICAL COMPETITION, AND FISCAL EFFICIENCY

In the model described by Figure 4-1, the median voter of each locality prefers b_0 to b_1. If each state acts independently, however, b_1 is attained. In effect, a conditional grant forces the localities to act jointly, which enables them to attain b_0. Intergovernmental negotiations also can lead to attainment of b_0. The greater the rate of spillover, the greater the gain in utility the median voter would experience if b_0 should somehow be reestablished: as the rate of spillover increases, it becomes more profitable for some politician in each locality to campaign on a platform that promises joint action to increase the supply of X to b_0. To change the focus, it becomes more likely that politicians in office will produce some joint action in an attempt to capture the political profit in voter support that such joint action would produce. Regardless of which focus is chosen, however, b_1, although clearly inefficient, is a position of disequilibrium because opportunities for political profit remain exploited as long as b_0 is not attained. In fiscal theory, which lies along the boundaries of economics and politics, it is vital that the formulations of equilibrium be extended to include the competition among politicians for voter support.[19]

It may be helpful to reexamine our preceding discussion with reference to a numerical illustration. Although the magnitudes of the illustration are arbitrary, as must be the case with any illustration, the essential features under examination are not compromised by the use of a specific illustration. Let us assume that locality A supplies library services, X, and that locality B supplies park services, Y. The following data describe the situations faced by the median voters in each locality: $C_X = 25X$; $V_{AX} = 100X^{1/2}$; and $V_{BX} = 50X^{1/2}$; $C_Y = 25Y$; $V_{BY} = 100^{1/2}$; and $V_{AY} = 20Y^{1/2}$. (C_X denotes the total cost of supplying X; V_{AX} is the total valuation placed upon X by residents of A; and V_{BX} is the total valuation placed upon X by residents of B. Similar notation applies to C_Y, V_{BY}, and V_{AY}.) If each locality acts wholly on its own, equilibrium results when $C'_X = V'_{AX}$ and $C'_Y = V'_{BY}$. Under these conditions, the rates of supply will be $X = 4$ and $Y = 4$ where the units refer to some normalized measure of quantity. The rates of output chosen under independent action are clearly inefficient.

[19] Albert Breton, "A Theory of the Demand for Public Goods," *Canadian Journal of Economics and Political Science,* 32 (November 1966), 455–67, is an exception that recognizes the need to modify the orthodox list of parameters so that political phenomena are treated as variables.

Wicksellian-efficiency results only when $C'_X = V'_{AX} + V'_{BX}$ and $C'_Y = V'_{BY} + V'_{AY}$, which requires a rate of supply of $X = 9$ and $Y = 5.77$.

The output set $(X = 4, Y = 4)$ is clearly inefficient, but it is *not* an equilibrium position. Let us first examine the supply of X by locality A. We want to understand why the equilibrium position is $X = 9$, which is the efficient position, not $X = 4$, which is the commonly denoted position of inefficient equilibrium. When $X = 4$, residents of A pay the entire cost, but residents of B also enjoy greater library services. Although total per capita valuation of four units of X is \$200 for residents of A and \$100 for residents of B, residents of A pay the entire cost of \$100. Some people argue that this position is inequitable—that equity requires that B pay \$33 and A only \$67. The issue of inequity, however, is separable from the issue of inefficiency, and $X = 4$ is clearly a disequilibrium rate of output. Although residents of B enjoy the services of four units of X without cost to themselves, they would be willing to contribute something to induce locality A to *expand* its supply of X. B's demand for X is $V'_{BX} = 25X^{-1/2}$. To supply additional X, locality A must receive at least the amount by which its cost of supply exceeds its demand for the service. Locality A thus has a marginal supply price for X of $C'_X - V'_{AX} = 25-50X^{-1/2}$. The potential gains from trade from expansions in output are shown in Table 4-1. When $X = 4$, B's demand price exceeds A's supply price by \$12.50, so the rate of output will rise. Equilibrium will be attained only when $X = 9$, which is also the fully efficient solution.

The same conclusions hold for the supply of Y by locality B. The equilibrium rate of output will be $X = 5.77$, not $X = 4$. When $X = 4$, residents of A enjoy a free ride as they use the parks supplied by residents of B, but this issue of equity does not have direct efficiency consequences. Locality A would be willing to pay up to $V'_{AX} = 10Y^{-1/2}$ for additional Y, while B would be willing to supply additional Y as long as it will receive at least $C'_X - V'_{BY} = 25-50Y^{-1/2}$. As with the supply of X by A, incentives

TABLE 4-1
Intergovernmental Spillover and Gains from Trade

Output of X	B's Demand for X	A's Supply of X
4	\$12.50	\$0.00
5	11.16	2.68
6	10.20	4.60
7	9.43	6.14
8	8.83	7.34
9	8.33	8.33
10	7.91	9.18

exist for negotiation when $Y = 4$, and equilibrium in the supply of Y is attained only when $Y = 5.77$.[20]

Political competition, then, will tend to produce negotiated agreements concerning the size and financing of the park and library. Ordinary pronouncements of inefficiency under spillover fail to consider the full range of competitive processes. Inefficiency implies the existence of unexploited gains from trade, so negotiated settlements that alleviate the inefficiency will produce political profit in the form of voter support. If these settlements operate perfectly, both conditional grants and intergovernmental negotiation will produce the same outcome.

Political competition, like market competition, may work imperfectly in some instances. Intergovernmental negotiation is a rule of unanimity, and the costs of securing unanimous consent are likely to increase dramatically as the number of participants becomes large.[21] The significance of negotiation costs in preventing efficiency should not be overestimated, however, for usually we are concerned with negotiations among a limited number of political units. The primary obstacle to the attainment of federal fiscal efficiency through intergovernmental negotiation seems to be associated more with a dilution of the incentives to enter into negotiation than with the existence of excessively high costs of negotiation. Suppose that joint action among two localities offers some profitability because of the existence of unexploited economics of scale. Some particular service may be supplied by the independent action of each locality at an annual cost of $200 per resident or by the joint action of both localities at an annual cost of $100 per resident. An intergovernmental agreement by which one locality agrees to supply the service to both localities in exchange for compensating payment would reduce the annual cost for residents of each locality by $100. As a first approximation, we should expect such an agreement to emerge through the ordinary processes of political competition. Because a party that runs on a platform of joint action can offer to reduce

---

[20] Issues of equity are perhaps more legitimate here than are issues of efficiency. Although we have previously touched on some issues of equity, a modification of an earlier illustration may focus the issues more sharply. Suppose we modify the value received by B from library services in A to $V'_{BX} = 50X^{1/2} - 12.5X$. When A produces the rate of output $X = 4$, we now find $V'_{BX} = \$0$. B is receiving benefits from the library service that is provided by A, as B places a total valuation of $50 upon the four units of X. Yet B places a value of zero upon *increases* in the rate of output beyond $X = 4$; residents of B feel that additional units of X have no value to them. Although many people would find it objectionable if B did not contribute to A's cost of supply, analytical clarity can be achieved only if we separate issues of equity from issues of efficiency. Moreover, as we shall see below many discussions of city and suburb similarly fail to distinguish issues of equity and issues of efficiency.

[21] See James M. Buchanan and Gordon Tullock, *The Calculus of Consent* (Ann Arbor: University of Michigan Press, 1962), pp. 97–116.

taxes by $100 per resident without lowering the level of public service, a platform of joint action would defeat a platform of independent action.

Of course, environmental changes must be of some finite magnitude before their impact is felt; a price reduction must be of some minimal amount before an individual will feel its effects.[22] If the efficiency saving that is potentially offered by intergovernmental negotiation is not large enough to bridge the threshold of perception, competitive processes will not elicit such agreements. In terms of a single-service budget, the issue of the efficiency of intergovernmental negotiation is primarily an empirical one that depends on the relation between the size of the threshold and the profit from the intergovernmental agreement. More significant issues can be raised, however, if we examine the consequences of expanding the list of activities undertaken by a government unit.

It seems a reasonable approximation that the size of the threshold will be some constant percentage of the amount paid for the service. If the threshold is ten percent, for instance, an object that initially sells for $10 must sell for more than $11 before the rise in price will be perceived. Similarly, an object that initially sells for $10 must sell for less than $9 before the decrease in price will be perceived. A public budget offers taxpayers a multicomponent bundle of services. Because the individual components of the budget are not separately priced, the only price signal an individual receives is his total tax contribution. A single-service budget is a useful benchmark, as changes in the size of the budget are identically equal to changes in the price of the single service. In a multi-service budget, however, changes in the size of the budget are smaller than changes in the price of a particular service. Suppose, for instance, that the budget contains ten components of equal size. If some intergovernmental agreement on the supply of one of the services should reduce its price by 20 percent, the taxpayer would perceive only a 2 percent reduction in the price of the package of collective services. Although an intergovernmental agreement would reduce the price of the service by 20 percent, taxpayers would sense a difference of only 2 percent, provided that two percent bridges the perception threshold. The greater the number of services supplied by a single government, the less the sensitivity of taxpayers to changes in the price of collective services. The implications of the analysis run contrary to the widely held belief that massive governmental consolidation is required for fiscal efficiency. The greater the number of services provided within a single budget, the more significant must be any change in a single component before a budgetary change will be perceived, thus reducing the effectiveness of political competition.

[22] For some implications of threshold sensitivity, see Nicos Devletoglou and P. A. Demetriou, "Choice and Threshold," *Economica*, 34 (November 1967), 351–71.

In the customary explanations of the function of conditional grants, intergovernmental negotiation is ignored as an alternative institution of federal fiscal adjustment. It is tacitly assumed that we must choose between (1) efficient conditional grants and (2) inefficient intergovernmental negotiation. In this situation, of course, there is really no choice at all. Nevertheless, there is no reason why we could not be presented with a choice between (1) efficient intergovernmental negotiation and (2) inefficient conditional grants. Should this situation prevail, conditional grants will play no role in securing federal fiscal adjustment; this choice situation, of course, is also really no choice at all. It is illegitimate to choose among institutions by comparing an existing inefficient situation with an unattainable efficient situation. Rather, choice must be based on a comparison of the actual workings of grants and negotiation within a system of political competition.[23]

CITIES, SUBURBS, AND INTERGOVERNMENTAL COMPETITION

A system of intergovernmental competition will perform imperfectly if such competition generates substantial external effects, unless there is a market in such external effects. The competition among suburban communities and central cities in metropolitan areas is often suggested as an instance in which intergovernmental competition performs badly because such external effects are substantial while no market exists to internalize them. Many suburban residents earn their livings in the central city, using such city services as roads and police in the process, but pay the major portion of their local taxes, primarily property taxes, to the suburbs where they reside. These observations frequently stimulate the suggestion that suburban residents be required to contribute to the support of central cities. There are grounds for claiming that resources will be allocated inefficiently if the suburban resident does not pay for his use of city services. Because the social cost of city residency will be overstated, there will be too few people residing in the cities and city budgets will be inefficiently small. Conversely, there will be too many suburban residents, and suburban bud-

---

[23] For two papers devoted largely to this theme, see Roland H. Coase, "The Problem of Social Cost," *Journal of Law and Economics,* 3 (October 1960), 1–44; and James M. Buchanan, "Politics, Policy, and the Pigovian Margins," *Economica,* 29 (February 1962), 17–28.

We should perhaps note here that a corollary of Gresham's Law of Politics is that the mere availability of conditional grants as a form of intergovernmental fiscal adjustment will reduce the incentive for governments to attempt to negotiate some agreement.

gets will be inefficiently large. If suburban residents were charged for their use of city services, the price of city residency relative to suburban residency would fall and the relative amount of city residency would increase.

In their travels to the city to work, to shop, and to play, obviously, suburban residents use public facilities supplied by city residents, primarily road and police services. But suburban residents may also contribute to the support of those services. Even if suburban residents make no direct contribution to the cost of city services, they may contribute indirectly. By working, shopping, or playing in the central city, the suburbanites increase the value of city businesses, which increases the city's tax base. The provision of free public services to suburban residents may be looked on as an investment by the city that is essential to the prosperity of city-based industries. As an extreme illustration, suppose a city refused to let suburban residents use city services. There would no longer be any opportunity for suburban exploitation of city residents. But if suburban residents cease working, shopping, and playing in the central city, the level of the city's prosperity would fall sharply. Many city businesses would become bankrupt. Employment in the city would fall, inducing out-migration in search of better employment opportunities. Each of these events would destroy some of the city's tax base. Many city services that are used by suburban residents are more appropriately viewed as productive inputs than as consumption goods. Such services as highways and police and fire protection are not consumption goods to suburban residents, but rather are productive inputs used by commercial and industrial facilities within city boundaries. Within this context, an observation that the central city is exploited by its suburbs is nothing more than an observation that the city has invested unprofitably, that the net rate of return on its investment is negative. Hence the issue is one of inefficiency rather than one of inequity.[24]

The amount of direct contribution to the cost of city services made by suburban residents depends on the form of taxation used by the central city. If the city collects all its revenues from a personal property tax, only those suburban residents who operate businesses in the central city will

---

[24] For a careful empirical examination of such issues within an inequity-exploitation framework, see William B. Neenan, "Suburban-Central City Exploitation Thesis: One City's Tale," *National Tax Journal,* 23 (June 1970), 117–39. For an expanded examination, see Neenan's *Political Economy of Urban Areas* (Chicago: Markham, 1972), pp. 53–139. John C. Weicher, "The Effect of Metropolitan Fragmentation on Central City Budgets," in David C. Sweet, ed., *Models of Urban Structure* (Lexington, Mass.; D. C. Heath, 1972), pp. 177–203, showed that existing conceptual frameworks are inadequate, and using an alternative framework showed that suburban residents are exploited by city residents. While Weicher's conceptual framework seems superior, it too construes the issue within a consumption-equity framework.

make any direct city tax payments. If the city collects some of its revenues from a sales tax, suburban residents who work or spend money in the city will contribute directly to the provision of city services. If the link between purchase and tax payment is broken, suburban residents might be forced to contribute even more to city revenues. This link could be broken through the use of either an income tax based on origin or a payroll tax. At sufficiently low rates of taxation, such taxes would contribute to the tax base of the city, but they would raise the price required to induce a sub-urbanite to work in the city. As this price differential increases, and as the time from its inception lengthens, migration of firms to the suburbs in response to the competitive pressures exerted by the lower price of sub-urban labor will increase.

The average metropolitan area contains over 100 government units, and such government fragmentation is usually designated as the major source of metropolitan fiscal imbalance. The Committee for Economic Development reflected this prevailing diagnosis when it recently suggested that a solution to the fiscal problems of metropolitan areas must entail, among other things, an 80 percent reduction in the number of local governments.[25] Frequently, the claim is raised that governmental fragmentation both prevents the full exploitation of the economies of scale in supplying public services and generates significant uncompensated externalities. As we noted above, however, there is a tendency for negotiated settlements to internalize externalities and to exploit economies of scale. If it costs less per resident for two cities to supply one public service jointly than it would cost to supply that service separately, effective political competition will tend to produce an outcome of joint supply. Contrary to the opinion held by many people, however, joint supply does not require government consolidation. One city might supply the service for both cities, while the other city would pay for the service it received. This, of course, is the essential feature of the Lakewood Plan, which is characterized by more than 1,500 such contracts.[26]

The greater the difference among localities in their preferences for some public service, the greater the likelihood that a negotiated settlement will be more efficient than will consolidation. This may be illustrated with a simple example. Consider two cities, A and B, with populations of 10,000 and 20,000 respectively. Let each resident of A desire twice as much of some public service, X, as each resident of B desires. Each city thus produces the same rate of output, 20,000X, which entails a per unit

[25] Committee for Economic Development, *Modernizing Local Government* (New York: Committee for Economic Development, 1966).

[26] For a brief description of the Lakewood Plan, see Robert L. Bish, *The Public Economy of Metropolitan Areas* (Chicago: Markham, 1971), pp. 81–83.

cost of, say, $10. Thus, residents of A pay $20 for their consumption of $2X$ and residents of B pay $10 for their consumption of X. Assume that because of economies of scale in the supply of X, $40,000X$ could be supplied at a per unit cost of $9. As usually it is felt that considerations of equitable treatment dictate that equal tax rates apply to all citizens after consolidation (geographical variation in tax rates is prohibited), both a common rate of output and a common rate of taxation must be chosen. If, for purposes of illustration, we hold the total rate of production constant, each person will consume $1.33X$. If the residents of B are unwilling to pay an additional $2 for an additional $0.33X$, they will reject consolidation.

An intergovernmental agreement, however, can substitute for consolidation. Residents of both cities would benefit from an agreement that enabled the residents of B to use the larger facility of A, with B making some compensating payment. A can produce the 40,000 units of X at an average cost of $9. Residents of both cities would be better off if A produced all the X and sold 20,000 units to B at any price between $8 and $10 per unit. Negotiation introduces considerable flexibility into the terms at which output and cost are shared. By contrast, consolidation requires uniformity in treatment, so it cannot give expression to differences in individual preferences toward various activities.[27]

INTERGOVERNMENTAL DIFFERENCES IN FISCAL CAPACITY

Modern discussions of metropolitan crises frequently are confounded with discussions concerning the distribution of personal income. Central cities contain an above-average number of citizens with below-average incomes. Many suburbs face the reverse situation, and it is perhaps reasonable to interpret much of the discussion and quarrel about the "problem of metropolitan areas" as a distributive struggle over alternative points along the Pareto-efficiency surface. The struggle over metropolitan government seems to be one of taking away from some and giving to others rather than one of making more available to all.

[27] Although there are several specific institutional forms for achieving some fiscal adjustment in a metropolitan area, negotiation and consolidation may be looked on as the two polar types. Negotiation, along with service contracts and municipal federalism under provisions for contracting-out, enables each participating suburb to maintain its essential identity, as the suburb reserves the option of reverting to the *status quo ante*. By contrast, consolidation, either jurisdictional or functional, along with single- or multiple-purpose regional authorities destroys the essential identity of the participating suburbs, as the suburb gives up the option of reverting to the *status quo ante*.

Considerable variation in per capita income exists among localities and among states. In 1969, the national per capita income was $3,687, with Connecticut having the highest, $4,595, and Mississippi the lowest, $2,218. Only if the tax rate in Mississippi is about twice as high as the tax rate in Connecticut will residents of Mississippi be able to supply themselves with the same quantity of public services as do residents of Connecticut. Or if the tax rate is the same in both states, residents of Mississippi will be able to supply themselves with only one-half as many public services as will residents of Connecticut. People who feel that differences in per capita income among states violates feelings of equity have proposed that subsidies be given to states with low per capita incomes. A program of aid to poor states is thus viewed as a complement to a program of aid to poor persons.

The presence of low-income states in a federal system may also create problems of allocative efficiency. States with low per capita incomes will provide a bundle of public services inferior to that provided by states with high per capita incomes. Interstate differences in public service standards will create few problems as long as people do not migrate among the states. When migration takes place, however, interstate differences in the quantity and quality of public services may generate sources of strain. Because Connecticut, with its higher per capita income, can afford a better educational system than Mississippi can, a typical resident of Mississippi will receive an education inferior to that of the one received by a typical resident of Connecticut. Most migration from Mississippi to Connecticut, or from any other low-income state to a high-income state, will lower the average educational level within the higher income state. Yet states cannot restrict the free migration of individuals, so a state cannot avoid the external costs it suffers when it receives in-migrants with poor educational backgrounds. Such considerations as these prompt most of the agitation for the creation of minimal standards for the provision of some public services.

Considerable support exists for using federal grants to achieve some equalization in the distribution of per capita income among states. Several conditional grants specify that states with below-average per capita incomes shall receive above-average grants, other things equal. Other conditional grants, while not varying the size of the grant with per capita income, require lower rates of matching from states with lower per capita incomes. Moreover, almost all proposals for federal revenue-sharing advocate that revenue-sharing be used to achieve some equalization in the distribution of per capita income among states.

Advocacy of fiscal redistribution among political units, however, seems to be based on some fundamental misconceptions about the consequences of the policies being advocated. Suppose the per capita income of state A exceeds that of state B, and that each state contains one million residents. Consider a hypothetical revenue transfer of $10 million from A to B. The $10 million transfer will be distributed within B through some form of public expenditure. A simple one-man one-vote hypothesis produces the expectation that each resident of B will receive $10 in benefits as his share of the transfer.

Political units can neither enjoy benefits nor bear costs. Like any organization, they are inanimate. Only persons can enjoy benefits and bear costs. Therefore, it is illusory to speak of income as being redistributed among political units. Income can be redistributed only among individual persons residing in those units. If the usual variation exists in the distribution of personal incomes, there will be considerable overlapping in the incomes of the residents of the two states. Although the per capita income of A exceeds that of B, many residents of B will have personal incomes greater than the average income in A and many residents of A will have personal incomes less than the average income in B.

We may use Table 4-2 to illustrate some of the issues created by policies of fiscal redistribution. Assume that two states, A and B, each have five residents. Initial personal income is shown in column (1). Per capita income is $6,400 in A and $8,000 in B. The coefficient of variation among individual incomes is $V_2 = 41.1$ percent, and among state per capita incomes it is $V_1 = 11.1$ percent. In all cases, we shall assume that $4,000 is transferred, as this is the amount of intergovernmental transfer

TABLE 4–2
Impact of Alternative Forms of Income Redistribution

Individual	Initial Income Personal (1)	$4,000 Redistribution Among Governments		$4,000 Redistribution Among Individuals	
		Maximum Equali- zation (2)	Standard Case (3)	Maximum Equali- zation (4)	Standard Case (5)
A-1	$ 3,000	$ 5,500	$ 3,800	$5,000	$ 3,800
A-2	4,000	5,500	4,800	5,000	4,800
A-3	6,000	6,000	6,800	8,000	6,800
A-4	8,000	8,000	8,800	8,000	7,348
A-5	11,000	11,000	11,800	9,000	10,100
B-1	4,000	4,000	3,600	5,000	4,800
B-2	6,000	6,000	5,400	6,000	6,800
B-3	8,000	8,000	7,200	8,000	7,348
B-4	10,000	9,000	9,000	9,666	9,184
B-5	12,000	9,000	10,800	9,667	11,020
V_1	11.1%	0.0%	0.0%	6.5%	8.8%
V_2	41.1%	28.2%	37.7%	26.7%	31.2%

that will fully equalize the per capita incomes of the states. In columns (2) and (4), we present the maximum possible equalization of personal incomes that is compatible with the assumptions of the illustration; high incomes are paired down from the top and low incomes are built up from the bottom. In columns (3) and (5), we present our "standard case"; those who provide the subsidy are taxed in proportion to their incomes, and those who receive the subsidy receive an equal share of the subsidy.

A transfer of $4,000 from state *B* to state *A* will produce perfect equality in the per capita incomes of the states. Thus the coefficient of variation about $7,200 is $V_1 = 0.0$ percent. Under the hypothesis of maximum equalization (column (2)), the coefficient of variation among personal incomes is $V_2 = 28.2$ percent. In the standard case illustrated in column (3), residents of state *B* are taxed at 10 percent of their incomes and each resident of state *A* receives a subsidy of $800. Although we still have $V_1 = 0.0$ percent, we now have $V_2 = 37.7$ percent, which indicates that in spite of the complete equalization of state per capita incomes, the transfer has accomplished little equalization in the distribution of personal income.

Suppose we assume that $4,000 is redistributed among individuals. The maximum equalization, which is shown in column (4), results when the entire $4,000 is extracted from the three wealthiest individuals, leaving each of them with net incomes of $9,666.67, and given to the poorest three individuals, giving each of them net incomes of $5,000. Although the coefficient of variation among state per capita incomes has *increased* from 0.0 percent to 6.5 percent, the coefficient of variation among personal income has *fallen* from 28.2 percent of 26.7 percent. Although less intergovernmental equalization takes place, more interpersonal equalization is achieved. In the standard case shown in column (5), we assume that the $4,000 is raised by levying a proportional tax of about 8.2 percent on the five individuals with above-average personal incomes. We also assume that each individual with a below-average income receives a transfer of $800. We see that $V_1 = 8.8$ percent and $V_2 = 31.2$ percent. Once again, as contrasted with income redistribution among governmental units, the inequality in the distribution of state per capita income has increased while the inequality in the distribution of personal income has fallen.

Although numerical illustrations are sometimes misleading, the principles we have illustrated are generally applicable. Because income redistribution can take place only among individuals, fiscal policies that return disproportionately large revenue shares to states with low per capita incomes must be evaluated in terms of their contribution to the equalization of personal incomes. Any transfer from a political unit with an above-average per capita income to one with a below-average per capita income will produce substantial transfers from poorer citizens residing in the wealthier state to wealthier citizens residing in the poorer state. Intergovernmental income redistribution, then, is an inefficient means of narrowing the variations in personal income among individuals. Any amount of equalization of personal income that results from some program of intergovernmental redistribution can be achieved at a lower budgetary outlay if the transfers take place only among individuals. Or, for the same budgetary outlay, greater income equality can be achieved through a program of interpersonal income redistribution.[28]

FISCAL IMBALANCE IN A FEDERAL STATE

It is frequently alleged that the American federal system exhibits a serious fiscal imbalance. The public services that are most in need of additional financial support—education, health and welfare, public safety, recreation, and transportation, for instance—traditionally fall within the domain of our state and local governments. But the national government seems to have command over the most productive sources of revenue—especially the taxes on personal and corporate incomes. The result is a fiscal imbalance: the national government has an excess supply of revenue while the state and local governments have an excess supply of needs.[29]

Assume that the numerical projections of an expected deficiency of state-local revenue are correct. What would this tell us? How should we interpret such figures? Do they really indicate that there is something pathological in the fiscal organization of state-local government? Or do they merely indicate the universal budgetary problems of life—living within one's means? All units, whether they are individuals, corporations, clubs, schools, churches, or governments continually face a "fiscal crisis" in that they face some budget constraint that they wish were not so constraining. In a revealing survey conducted several years ago, over 50 percent of those interviewed indicated that they would like to see public spending increased on (1) aid for the elderly, (2) aid for the needy, (3) education, and (4) hospital and medical care. The question that was asked of the participants was essentially of the form: "If additional public spending cost you nothing, on which of the following programs would you like

---

[28] By inducing changes in individual behavior, any tax institution except a lump-sum tax generates excess burden. Since the amount of equalization of personal incomes achieved by fiscal redistribution among political units can be duplicated at a lower budgetary outlay by income redistribution among individuals, intergovernmental redistribution will always generate greater excess burden than will interpersonal redistribution.

[29] This theme is presented clearly in James A. Maxwell, *The Fiscal Impact of Federalism in the United States* (Cambridge: Harvard University Press, 1946), pp. 25–40.

to see spending increased?" But when the participants were made aware that to have more of one thing requires that they give up something else, not a single program received majority support for additional spending.[30] It is important to distinguish feelings of fiscal imbalance that merely reflect the universal existence of a budget constraint and feelings of fiscal imbalance that arise because there is something perverse in the operation of our federal fiscal system.

It is commonly claimed that ordinary economic growth creates a fiscal bias against state and local government. Because of progressive income taxation, a 1 percent growth in national income generates a 1.7 percent growth in national tax revenue. A 1 percent growth in national income, however, generates only a 1 percent growth in state-local tax revenue. Yet the most rapidly growing demands for public services lie in areas traditionally supplied by state and local governments. Thus, we have a fiscal imbalance; the national government tends to get more revenue than it needs for the performance of its traditional functions while state and local governments tend to get less. The problem of imbalance is not so much that state-local government is poor in some absolute sense as that it is poor relative to the fiscal position of the national government.

For purposes of discussion, we shall accept as correct the evidence on which claims of fiscal imbalance are based. But how can a fiscal imbalance exist? Or if it exists, how can it persist? It would seem that a fiscal imbalance can exist, or persist, only if there is significant imperfection in the operation of our federal democracy. Otherwise, we should expect political competition to produce changes in national and state-local tax rates that would rectify any fiscal imbalance. Suppose that both state-local and national tax structures have been generating revenues just sufficient to satisfy the demands of their citizens for public services. Now assume that an increase in the demand for public services supplied by state-local governments is exactly offset by a fall in the demand for public services supplied by the national government. As time elapses, we would find that at the prevailing prices of public services, citizens desire more state-local public services and fewer national public services. If political competition operates effectively, we should expect this change in demand to be accommodated through increases in state-local taxes and reductions in national taxes. A federal fiscal imbalance can be only a transitory phenomenon in a democracy that is working well. If a claim of federal fiscal imbalance is to be considered as something besides mere political rhetoric, then there must exist significant imperfections in the processes through which demands are expressed for public services.

[30] Eva Mueller, "Public Attitudes Toward Fiscal Programs," *Quarterly Journal of Economics,* 77 (May 1963), 215.

The difference in revenue elasticity of national and of state-local tax structures is frequently cited as a major source of federal fiscal imbalance.[31] Revenue elasticity shows the responsiveness of tax yields to growth in national income; it is the percentage increase in tax revenue collected from an unchanged tax structure and divided by the percentage increase in national income. To illustrate the following discussion, we shall assume a state-local revenue elasticity of 1.0 and a national revenue elasticity of 1.5. A growth of 10 percent in national income, then, will yield increases of 10 percent in state-local tax revenue and 15 percent in national tax revenue, assuming that revenue structures remain unchanged. To generate a condition of fiscal imbalance, let us assume that the income elasticity of demand is 1.25 for both national and state-local public services.

As income grows, national revenues will grow more rapidly than will the demand for national services, while state-local revenues will grow less rapidly than will the demand for state-local services. By contrast, if both revenue and income elasticities of demand were 1.25 for each level of government, federal fiscal balance would prevail continuously. With the 1.5–1.0 configuration of revenue elasticities, however, federal fiscal balance can be maintained only through conscious modification of both state-local and national tax rates. A federal fiscal imbalance may result from intergovernmental differences in the relations between subjective and objective cost. Objective cost is the cost flow visible to an external observer, usually monetary payments. Subjective cost is the obstacle to decision felt by the chooser: it is his subjective evaluation of the externally visible flows.[32] Take the 1.5–1.0 configuration of revenue elasticities and consider an individual who has an initial income of $10,000 and a tax liability of $1,000 to each level of government. If we let his income double to $20,000, his national tax is assessed at $2,500 and his state-local tax at $2,000. The national tax rate has increased to 12.5 percent while the state-local tax rate has remained constant at 10 percent. Considerations of subjective cost may enter here. People may *feel* that $2,500 of national expenditures are less costly than $2,500 of state-local public expenditures. An expenditure of $2,500 for the state-local level could be attained only if state-local taxes were raised to 12.5 percent. The national tax rate, by contrast, rises to 12.5 percent without conscious action, so the rise would be perceived as less costly.

[31] For one instance, see Walter W. Heller, "Strengthening the Fiscal Base of our Federalism," *New Dimensions of Political Economy* (Cambridge: Harvard University Press, 1966), p. 127.

[32] See James M. Buchanan, *Cost and Choice* (Chicago Markham, 1969); and James M. Buchanan, "Public Debt, Cost Theory, and the Fiscal Illusion," in James M. Ferguson, ed., *Public Debt and Future Generations* (Chapel Hill: University of North Carolina Press, 1964), pp. 150–63.

Although the fiscal environment is best described by the existing *rate of tax,* at least partially, individuals are likely to incorporate the existing *rate structure* into their perception of the fiscal environment. Under a progressive tax structure, increases in personal income produce automatic increases in the average rate of tax, even though the entire rate structure remains unchanged. Empirical evidence suggests that people tend to confuse the rate structure with the rate of tax. In his study of individual awareness of income tax payments, Wagstaff found that people with below-median incomes systematically overestimated the taxes they paid while people with above-median incomes systematically underestimated their tax payments.[33] Wagstaff's evidence implies that as an individual's income increases, his estimated additional tax payments would be less than his actual additional tax payments. He would underestimate the impact of the "natural" tax increase produced by progressivity in the rate structure; he would tend to incorporate the rate structure rather than the rate of tax into his perception of his fiscal environment.[34]

There also is a large body of casual evidence supporting the existence of faulty fiscal perception. Whenever a legislative assembly considers changes in tax rates, tortuous discussion takes place and considerable publicity is given to the deliberations. Yet no similar agonizing takes place over the continual, automatic increase in tax rates that is produced by progressivity in the national tax structure. Everyone is aware of a consciously enacted tax surcharge; a similar surcharge is enacted each year when income grows under progressive taxation, but this surcharge is not consciously perceived.[35] This faulty perception, which is a form of imperfect knowledge, introduces imperfection into our system of political competition. It thus becomes possible for federal fiscal imbalance to result from intergovernmental differences in revenue elasticities.

It does seem appropriate to claim that the American federal system suffers from a fiscal imbalance. The fiscal crisis of state-local government

[33] J. Van Wagstaff, "Income Tax Consciousness Under Withholding," *Southern Economic Journal,* 32 (July 1965), 73–80.

[34] This argument implies that a reduction in the rate of progressivity would reduce tendencies toward both underestimation and overestimation. Under a proportional tax, there would be no tendencies toward faulty tax estimation. With regressive taxation, individuals with below-median incomes would underestimate their taxes and individuals with above-median incomes would overestimate their tax payments.

[35] For an empirical assessment of this unconscious surcharge, see Charles J. Goetz and Warren E. Weber, "Inter-temporal Changes in Real Federal Income Tax Rates, 1954–70," *National Tax Journal,* 24 (March 1971), 51–63.

It is possible to design a progressive income tax in which nominal rates are reduced as income grows such that tax collections rise in proportion to income. See John O. Blackburn, "Implicit Tax Reductions with Growth, Progressive Taxes, Constant Progressivity, and a Fixed Public Share," *American Economic Review,* 57 (March 1967), 163–69.

results, however, not so much because state and local governments are poor in some absolute sense as because they are less wealthy than is the national government. An understanding of our federal fiscal crisis lies not in an examination of projections of state-local revenue and expenditure, but in an examination of the operation of democratic competition for political office. State and local politicians are subject to more intensive and more restrictive fiscal presures than are national politicians, and it is this differ ential in fiscal pressure that ignites the cries of state-local fiscal crisis. State and local politicians seem to face greater uncertainty in their efforts to continue their political careers than do national politicians; national politicians seem to be more insulated from latent taxpayer discontent than are state-local politicians.

Actions of the national government probably affect the survival prospects of state and local officials to a much greater extent than actions of state and local governments affect the survival prospects of national officials. Lower levels of government will be at a fiscal disadvantage relative to higher levels; the mere existence of a higher level of government will tend to reduce the fiscal capabilities of lower levels. If the national, state, and local fiscal systems all satisfy the Wicksellian conditions for fiscal efficiency, fiscal balance will characterize the federal system. But real-world fiscal systems are not fully efficient. The national government is a fiscal monopolist, while state and local governments are fiscal competitors. As a result, majority coalitions will be better able to extract redistributive gains through budgetary expansion at the national level than at the state-local level. Thus, national expenditures will be inefficiently large, which implies that state-local and private expenditures will be inefficiently small.

Suppose that a feeling develops among the residents of some state or local government that national taxes are too high, which, in a general equilibrium setting, implies an offsetting increase in demand for the composite bundle of private and state-local services. A reduction in national taxes will be achieved only if a majority of all state and local governments supports a reduction in national taxes. In contrast, a tax reduction within any single state or local government reduces the support of only a majority within that single political unit. Even though the residents of some political units desire a reduction in national taxes, a majority may not support a reduction. But even if such a majority should exist, ordinarily, it will usually be more costly to organize the national coalition than it would be to form a state or local coalition from the viewpoint of residents of any lower level of government. Under such circumstances, a reduction in state-local taxes may very well be the response to a desired reduction in national taxes, either because a national majority does not exist or because such a majority seems too costly to organize.

The failure of voters to approve school-bond issues may sometimes express the feeling that national taxes are too high rather than the feeling that the bond issue itself is not worthwhile. But given the greater cost of organizing national coalitions, a reduction in state-local taxes emerges as a second-best response. The local voter may feel that the school-bond issue would be worthwhile if national taxes were at a desirable level, but as they are not, his second-best response is to oppose the bond issue. State and local politicians generally are subject to stronger fiscal pressures than are national politicians; high national tax rates impinge more strongly on the taxing ability of state and local governments than state and local taxes impinge upon the taxing ability of the national government.

5. Budgetary Concepts and Budgetary Processes

When compared with a description of the way in which budgetary choices are made, the models of fiscal choice described in Chapter Three are strikingly unrealistic. It would seem a crude approximation at best to claim that budgetary choices are made by the median voter, for actual budgetary processes are vastly more complex than is indicated by the simple models presented in Chapter Three. Individuals do not vote directly on budgetary proposals; rather, they vote only for legislators who, in turn, are responsible for making budgetary choices. All analyses, of course, proceed by simplification through abstraction, and an analysis of budgetary choice must necessarily be based on simplified abstractions from actual budgetary processes. Nevertheless, the primary issue concerns not the fact of simplification, but whether the outcomes of actual budgetary processes are predicted with sufficient accuracy by the simplified models. We shall first describe the existing process of budgetary choice. Then we shall examine whether predictions based on our simple models correspond to the results of actual budgetary processes. To conclude this chapter, we shall relate the possible uses of budgetary data to the problem of choosing among alternative budgetary concepts.

THE INCREMENTAL NATURE OF BUDGETARY DECISIONS

The process by which budgetary decisions are made is clearly an incremental one in which current choices are relatively small modifications of past choices. An agency's budget for next year will tend to be some percentage markup from its budget for this year. Table 5-1, which shows the percentage increase in annual budgetary appropriations for 37 bureaus

TABLE 5-1
Distribution of Annual
Percentage Increases in
Budgetary Appropriations

Incremental Increase	Number
0 - 5%	149
6 - 10	84
11 - 20	93
21 - 30	51
31 - 40	21
41 - 50	15
51 -100	24
101+	7

over a 12-year period, illustrates the incremental nature of the budgetary process.[1] In nearly 35 percent of the 444 cases, the appropriation increased between 0 percent and 5 percent over the preceding appropriation. This annual increment ranged between 6 and 10 percent in 20 percent of the remaining cases, and between 11 and 20 percent in another 20 percent of the cases. The empirical record suggests that an agency's budget for next year will tend to be some percentage markup from its budget for this year. Budgets are not made *de novo* each year. Next year's budget will be primarily a revision of this year's budget; this year's budget is used as a base from which modifications are made to generate next year's budget.

The process of executive formulation of a budget, as well as the process of legislative authorization and appropriation, expresses the incremental nature of the budgetary process. It takes about 15 months to prepare and enact the national budget: 9 for executive preparation and 6 for legislative authorization and appropriation. The budget for Fiscal Year 1972 began on July 1, 1971 and concluded on June 30, 1972. While this budget was submitted by the President to Congress in January 1971, it began to take shape early in 1970, when the various bureaus within the larger cabinet departments formulated initial budgetary plans.[2] During the spring of 1970, the budget offices in the various cabinet departments and administrative agencies worked with their subordinate bureaus in formulating preliminary budget estimates. These estimates were then submitted to

[1] Aaron Wildavsky, *The Politics of the Budgetary Process* (Boston: Little, Brown, 1964), p. 14.
[2] Each cabinet department contains a number of bureaus, and each possesses substantial autonomy. The Department of the Interior, for instance, contains the Bureau of Land Management, the Bureau of Indian Affairs, the National Park Service, the Bureau of Mines, the Bureau of Reclamation, and the Fish and Wildlife Service, to name only a few.

the Office of Management and Budget for a preliminary review in light of guidelines announced by the President. During the summer of 1970, the departments and independent agencies revised their budget requests in conformance with these guidelines. The revised estimates were then submitted to the Office of Management and Budget, which reviewed departmental requests in detail, held hearings on the requests, and then compiled the overall budget document for submission to the President. The President reviewed the budget during November and December, made changes where he so desired, and submitted the budget to Congress in January 1971—a lapse of about nine months from initiation of the proceedings, and six months before the start of the new fiscal year.

The second phase of the budget cycle begins when Congress receives the budget. The House of Representatives initiates the action by submitting the budget to the House Appropriations Committee. This committee has 13 subcommittees, organized along such functional lines as military services, public works, agriculture, and education and labor. Each subcommittee examines those portions of the budget that are relevant to it and, eventually, makes its report to the full appropriations committee, which in turn reports out the bill to the House of Representatives. After approval by the House, the Senate acts on the budget, following a procedure similar to that followed by the House: subcommittees of the Senate Appropriations Committee examine the House appropriation bills, then the Senate Appropriation Committee reports to the Senate. Differences between the House and Senate appropriations bills are reconciled in a conference committee, and the resulting bill is sent to the President, where it may be either vetoed or approved.

The incremental nature of the budgetary process, which is evident in a description of the budgetary process, was demonstrated strikingly in two empirical studies by Davis, Dempster, and Wildavsky.[3] The budgetary process may be factored into two salient stages: (1) the President requests an appropriation for each agency; and (2) the Congress approves an appropriation for each agency. Davis, Dempster, and Wildavsky formulated two simple decision rules that explained most budgetary choices quite well. Let X_t denote the appropriation requested for some bureau by the President and Y_t denote the appropriation approved for that bureau by the Congress. The budgetary process follows a two-step sequential pattern. The President, with full knowledge of Y for year $t-1$, first states X for year t. The Congress, with full knowledge of X for year t, then states Y for year t.

[3] Otto A. Davis, M. A. H. Dempster, and Aaron Wildavsky, "On the Process of Budgeting: An Empirical Study of Congressional Appropriation," *Public Choice,* 1 (1966), 63–132; and Otto A. Davis, M. A. H. Dempster, and Aaron Wildavsky, "A Theory of the Budgetary Process," *American Political Science Review,* 60 (September 1966), 529–47.

One very simple set of bureau and congressional decision rules is suggested by incrementalism, a set that performed quite well in the empirical examination. For the set of sample bureaus, Davis, Dempster, and Wildavsky estimated the relation $X_{it} = \beta Y_{it-1} + \epsilon_{it}$, where ϵ_{it} is the disturbance term. That is, the President's request for any bureau, i, is equal to the appropriation made by Congress in the preceding year, Y_{it-1}, multiplied by some constant factor, β. If $\beta = 1.1$, for instance, the rule states that the President will request 10 percent more for the bureau this year than the Congress appropriated last year.

Similarly, Davis, Dempster, and Wildavsky estimated the relation $Y_{it} = \alpha X_{it} + \eta_{it}$, where η_{it} is the disturbance term and α is some constant coefficient. In this formulation, the congressional appropriation for bureau i for the current year is some multiple of the Presidential request for that same year. If $\alpha = .95$, for instance, the Congressional appropriation will equal 95 percent of the Presidential request.

While Davis, Dempster, and Wildavsky experimented with two more complex equations for Presidential requests and two more complex equations for congressional appropriations, the two equations shown here had the most explanatory power.[4] To test their empirical formulation, Davis, Dempster, and Wildavsky used time series data for 58 nondefense agencies of the national government over the period 1947–63. The appropriations for these agencies in 1963 were approximately 27 percent of nondefense spending for that year.

As we noted earlier, the budgetary data seemed to be explained fairly well by these simple linear decision rules. In 36 of 58 cases, the two linear decision rules shown above gave the best fit to the observed budgetary data. And in all of the remaining 22 cases, one of the two simple equations described above in combination with one more complex question provided the best fit. In no case was the best fit provided by a pair of the more complex equations.

The Davis-Dempster-Wildavsky formulation would appear to have devastating implications for the models of fiscal choice described in Chapter Three. The Davis-Dempster-Wildavsky model explains budgetary choice without reference to such notions as median preference voter and marginal tax prices. Instead, a purely mechanical linear decision rule is able to explain much budgetary behavior.

While the mechanical, incremental formulation of the budgetary process seems to predict budgetary policies reasonably well, especially over short intervals of time, the incremental formulation contains some obvious weaknesses, which become especially glaring as the time interval lengthens beyond a few years. Davis, Dempster, and Wildavsky found that the values

[4] Davis, Dempster, and Wildavsky, "On the Process of Budgeting," 82.

of α and β varied both among bureaus and for any single bureau over time. The estimate of β for the Bureau of Indian Affairs during 1948–54 was 0.832, but it increased to 1.037 for the period 1956–63. Similarly, the estimate of α was 1.321 during 1947–53, but it fell to 1.081 during 1954–63.[5] As the authors noted, "shifts" occurred in the underlying functions during the mid-1950s. Moreover, the value of β for the Bureau of Mines during 1948–54 was 0.915, a significantly higher figure than the 0.832 estimated for the Bureau of Indian Affairs. Likewise, the estimated value of α for the Bureau of Mines during 1947–55 was 1.116, which was significantly less than the value of 1.321 estimated for the Bureau of Indian Affairs. And while the estimated value of α and β for the Bureau of Mines also shifted after the mid-1950s, the amount of shift was quite small in comparison with the shift that occurred for the Bureau of Indian Affairs. The incremental explanation of budgetary choice is unable to explain either why the coefficient of any single Bureau varies over time or why the coefficient varies among bureaus at a single point in time.

In an important contribution to this discussion, Oliver Williamson showed that the incremental theory of budgetary choice is but a short-run approximation to a phenomenon that is explained more fully by such a rational theory of budgeting as that explored in Chapter Three.[6] The reasons why α and β are higher for some bureaus than for others, that is, why budgets increase faster for some bureaus than for others, can be explained by introducing some concept of demand for the services supplied by the various bureaus: α and β are higher for those bureaus that face relatively strong demands for their services than do those bureaus that do not. Similarly, some concept of demand must be introduced to explain why the values of α and β change over time: α and β increase more rapidly for those bureaus that are experiencing the more rapidly increasing demand for their services. Williamson clearly showed that an important determinant of the pattern of budgetary equilibrium is the relative demands for the services of various bureaus. The fact that the incremental formulation gives good results over short periods of time indicates merely that the demand for most services changes at a fairly slow rate. But as the time interval lengthens, these changes can become substantial, in which event this "shift" in parameters must be incorporated into an incremental formulation of the budgetary process.

Consider just one of the two primary decision rules formulated by

[5] *Ibid.*, 166.

[6] Oliver E. Williamson, "A Rational Theory of the Federal Budgetary Process," *Public choice*, 2 (1967), 71–89.

For a related effort showing that budgetary policies reflect citizen demands, see John E. Jackson, "Politics and the Budgetary Process," *Social Science Research*, 1 (April 1972), 35–60.

Davis, Dempster, and Wildavsky—$X_{it} = \beta Y_{it-1} + \epsilon_{it}$, where X_{it} is the President's budgetary request for bureau i during year t, and where Y_{it-1} is congressional appropriation for bureau i during the preceding year, $t–1$. The parameter β is considered a constant, markup term, although its value may shift both over time and among bureaus at any point in time. If average cost equals marginal cost over the relevant range of output, a simple rule of markup pricing is equivalent to profit maximizing behavior by the firm.[7] A simple model of markup pricing is one where $P_i = b_i(AC_i)$, where p_i is the price of commodity i, AC_i, is the average cost of i, and b_i is the appropriate coefficient of markup, a coefficient that differs between commodities in accordance with the elasticity of demand for the various commodities. As the elasticity of demand increases, the markup coefficient falls. A commodity with a more elastic demand would then carry a lower markup than would a commodity with a less elastic demand.

A political model of markup pricing can be developed by extending the standard model of markup pricing, as Williamson showed. Politicians support various public expenditures because they yield political value in the form of increased political support. If we let V_{it} denote the political value from the service provided by bureau i during period t, we have $V_{it} = V_{it}(X_{it})$. If the President's budgetary problem is construed as one of maximizing the political value of his budget subject to a given total budget constraint, we find the relation $X_{it} = \beta_i^n Y_{it-n}$ holds, which reduces to $X_{it} = \beta_i Y_{it-1}$ when $n = 1$. This latter relation is precisely the relation estimated by Davis, Dempster, and Wildavsky. The estimate of the shift parameter that is implied by Williamson's formulation is $V_{it}^* = 1/(\beta_i^\beta)^n$, which says that the shift parameter depends upon political value, i.e., demand conditions. Thus, the incremental phenomenon described by Davis, Dempster, and Wildavsky is but a special case of a rational theory of budgetary choice in which demand and supply elements enter explicitly into the model. The parameters shift over time because demand does not grow uniformly over time for all bureaus, and these shifts in budgetary parameters are a response of politicians to this change in the demand for alternative public expenditures.

SOME EMPIRICAL EVIDENCE RELATING TO BUDGETARY CHOICE

Williamson developed a rational model of budgetary choice that could describe the empirical results described by Davis, Dempster, and Wildavsky. Such evidence suggests that the development of rational models of bud-

[7] *Ibid.*, 73–76.

getary choice might be fruitful. In recent years, there have been numerous examinations of the differences among the expenditure patterns of various government units. Most of these works have been purely empirical and were not formulated as an attempt to probe the potential explanatory power of rational models of budgetary choice. One set of works developed directly with the intention of shedding evidence on the usefulness of rational models of budgetary choice was prepared by Otto Davis, James Barr, and George Haines.[8]

The analytical framework adopted in these two studies is one in which budgetary choices are made by the person whose preferences are median for the collectivity. In choosing a candidate, voters vote for that candidate whose platform represents the least loss in utility from their own most desired platform. Each voter will have some preference pattern for various patterns of taxing and spending. The chance that a politician will adopt a platform that exactly duplicates a person's most preferred platform is remote. In most instances, a voter will have to choose among candidates none of whom offers a platform that corresponds precisely to his most preferred platform. When confronted with this type of choice, a voter will choose that platform and candidate that offers the least reduction in utility from his own most preferred platform.

In a two-party system, the candidates will tend to cluster about the position most preferred by the median voter. If one candidate does this precisely, he will offer the platform that is most preferred by the median voter. In a system of party competition, politicians that succeed in offering platforms that express the preferences of the median voter will tend to survive. To the extent that political competition works along these lines, differences in budgetery policies among government units will reflect differences in the preferences of median voters. But do observed differences in budgetary patterns actually correspond to differences in the preferences of median voters? If the empirical evidence is consistent with such an interpretation, the potential fruitfulness of a rational theory of budgetary choice would be further enhanced.

We shall report only the Davis and Haines findings, as they are more detailed than are the Barr and Davis findings. Davis and Haines explored the proposition that variations in public expenditures among localities can be related to variation in the price of public services to median voters on the one hand and to variation in the incomes of median voters on the other. Davis and Haines examined the per capita expenditures on six public ser-

---

[8] Otto A. Davis and George H. Haines, Jr., "A Political Approach to a Theory of Public Expenditure: The Case of Municipalities," *National Tax Journal,* 19 (September 1966), 259–75; James L. Barr and Otto A. Davis, "An Elementary Political and Economic Theory of the Expenditures of Local Governments," *Southern Economic Journal,* 33 (October 1966), 149–65.

vices by municipalities in the Pittsburgh area in 1959.[9] These six dependent variables were:

E_1: general government;
E_2: public safety;
E_3: health and sanitation;
E_4: streets and highways;
E_5: interest;

and

E_6: operation and maintenance.

Each dependent variable was related to the following five independent variables:

X_1: population density;
X_2: percent of electorate that owns property;
X_3: market value of personal property;
X_4: market value of industrial property,

and

X_5: median family income.

The variable, X_5, median family income, is intended to capture the effects of increases in demand for the public service attributable to increases in income. Assuming a positive income elasticity of demand for the service, we would thus expect the sign of the coefficient of X_5 to be positive. Each of the variables X_2, X_3, and X_4 give information about the price of the service to the median voter. If we assume that revenues are raised primarily by property taxation and that property taxes are paid by owners of property, an increase in X_2—the percentage of the electorate owning property—would subject a greater fraction of the electorate to taxation, which leads us to expect a negative coefficient for X_2. An increase in X_3—the market value of personal property—would produce an increase in property tax liability for voters. This rise in tax price associated with a rise in personal property values leads us to expect a negative coefficient for X_3. An increase in X_4—the market value of industrial property—would increase the locality's tax base, which would reduce the rate of tax on personal property. As a result, we should expect a positive coefficient for X_4.

Because Davis and Haines also included population density, X_1, in their empirical model, we shall report their results below. Yet X_1, does not have the same direct bearing upon a rational theory of budgetary choice as have the other four independent variables. The variables X_2 through X_5 are clearly demand-side variables, reflecting the impact of price and income on the demand for a public service. The variable X_1, however, represents

[9] "Political Approach to a Theory of Public Expenditure," 264–65.

TABLE 5-2
Signs and Significance of Coefficients in Davis-Haines
Model of Budgetary Choice

	E_1	E_2	E_3	E_4	E_5	E_6
X_1	+ - -	(+) + (+)	(+)(+)(+)	- - -	+ - -	(+) + -
X_2	(-) - (-)	(-)(-)(-)	- - -	- + -	- - -	(-) - -
X_3	- (-)(-)	+ - (+)	+ - (-)	- - (-)	+ - -	- - (-)
X_4	(+) + (+)	(+)(+) -	+ (+) +	(+) + +	(+)(+)(+)	(+)(+)(+)
X_5	(+)(+)(+)	(+)(+)(+)	+ + +	(+) + -	(+) + +	(+) + +

a mixture of demand-side and supply-side influences. On the supply side, it might reasonably be expected that an increase in X_1 would reduce the number of policemen needed to patrol a given population, thus tending to reduce expenditures for public safety. On the demand side, it might reasonably be expected that an increase in X_1 would increase the demand for police services in response to a rise in the expected loss from criminal activity and traffic accidents associated with an increase in population density.

Table 5-2 summarizes the results attained by Davis and Haines. Note that for each dependent variable, three estimated signs of coefficients are included. In an order from left to right, these are the estimates for boroughs and first- and second-class townships. Coefficients that are significantly different from zero at the .05 level have been placed in parentheses. In only one instance did a significant coefficient possess a sign opposite from what was expected: the sign for the market value of personal property, X_3, was positive instead of negative when related to per capita public safety expenditures, E_2. The Davis-Haines study clearly suggests that budgetary choices will tend to reflect the demands of median voters for public services.

Of course, the current state-of-the-art in the econometric testing of fiscal choice models is still quite crude in contrast to the testing of models of market choice. Empirical relations often are developed without specifying clearly the underlying theoretical framework that is being tested. This makes interpretation of some results difficult and others impossible. Consider Booms' finding that among Ohio and Michigan cities of populations between 25,000 and 100,000, annual per capita expenditures on common functions were $16.49 less in city manager cities than in mayor-council cities.[10] There are two antipodal explanations of this result. One is that city manager cities are more efficient than are mayor-council cities.

[10] Bernard H. Booms, "City Governmental Form and Public Expenditure Levels," *National Tax Journal*, 19 (June 1966), 187–99. The common functions were police, fire, interest on local debt, noncapital outlays for highways, sanitation, and public health.

Hence, the supply curve of city manager cities lies below that of mayor-council cities, and, additionally, the demand for public services is inelastic over the range of the price reduction. The other explanation is that mayor-council cities more sensitively reflect demand for public services by the citizenry than do city manager cities. Hence, the demand curve for public services in mayor-council cities would lie above the demand curve for city manager cities. While Booms gives an ad hoc defense of the first explanation, a rigorous interpretation of the result is impossible unless a theoretical model is first specified, for only then will a framework be created in terms of which the empirical result can be interpreted.[11]

In spite of the currently crude state of fiscal econometrics, it seems quite reasonable to conclude that differences in preferences for public services by voters is an important factor in explaining budgetary decisions, and that models of budgetary choice based on median voters have real world applicability.[12]

THE CHOICE AMONG BUDGETARY CONCEPTS

When speaking of the government's budget, we should realize that there is no unique entity called the budget. Rather, a budget is something that must be chosen; definitions that exclude some transactions from the budget and include others are formulated. In January 1968, President Johnson presented his budget in a new format and labeled it the unified budget. In previous years, the government made use of three alternative budgetary concepts in varying degrees: the administrative budget, the consolidated cash budget, and the national income accounts budget. The unified budget replaced these three alternative budgetary concepts.

Before fiscal 1969, the administrative budget formed the basis for appropriations legislation. This budget excluded expenditures and receipts

[11] In addition to the frequent failure to specify carefully the theoretical model being tested, inappropriate econometric techniques are sometimes used. Multicolinearity among some of the independent variables sometimes has existed, and in some instances, single equation estimation may be inferior to simultaneous equation estimation. On the latter point, see Ann R. Horowitz, "A Simultaneous-Equation Approach to the Problem of Explaining Interstate Differences in State and Local Government Expenditures," *Southern Economic Journal,* 34 (April 1968), 459–76. Horowitz, however, did not specify a theoretical model of fiscal choice, so her analysis was also limited to an exercise in empiricism.

[12] There are many other possible ways of testing the explanatory power of median voter models of political competition. For instance, the primary implication of the median voter model is that politicians who survive political competition will tend to reflect median preferences more closely than do those who fail. This implication suggests that a median voter model will have less explanatory value in states where competition among political parties is weak than in states where it is strong.

of such trust funds as Social Security and highways because these expenditures were not subject to annual legislative choice. As the magnitudes of the trust funds increased, so did the belief that the administrative budget did not adequately reflect the impact of governmental fiscal activities on the economy. The consolidated cash budget, a comprehensive statement on a cash basis of all government payments and receipts, was developed in response to this concern. Unlike the administrative budget, the consolidated cash budget included the transactions of the trust funds. The third budgetary concept, the national income accounts budget, differed very little from the consolidated cash budget, and the amounts of neither of these two budgets differed greatly from those of the unified budget. The national income accounts budget differed from the consolidated cash budget in two ways. On the one hand, taxes and expenditures were based on an accrual basis rather than on a cash basis. Taxes enter the national income accounts budget when the liability is incurred, not when the payment is made. Similarly, expenditures enter the budget when the goods are delivered rather than when payment is made. On the other hand, such purely financial transactions as the purchase of a used typewriter by a bureau are excluded from the national income accounts budget.

Prior to fiscal 1969, the President's budget reflected all three budget concepts: the administrative budget, the consolidated cash budget, and the national income accounts budget. With the submission of the 1969 budget, however, these three budgets were replaced by the unified budget. Whether the unified budget is the most desirable format for the budget and whether one budget is preferable to three depends on the objectives of budgeting. One format might be preferable for one objective, but not for another. A budgetary concept is a rule for processing information, and budgetary information can be presented in a variety of formats. Which budgetary format is most appropriate depends on the type of information that is desired.

The unified budget has as its primary objective the use of the budget as an instrument for measuring the impact of the national government on such aggregative economic variables as national income and total employment. Implicit in this budgetary concept, then, is the view that the primary objective of the government's fiscal activities should be to promote stability in these macroeconomic variables. To promote this objective, it is necessary that the budget be designed to make it possible to assess the macroeconomic impact of the government's fiscal activities.

Alternative objectives would require alternative budgetary formats. Largely, trust fund transactions are not controllable by Congress, especially in the short run, for they represent fixed obligations determined by past legislation. Social Security benefit payments, for instance, represent fixed future obligations, which make them an uncontrollable element in the government's fiscal activity. While many items that were included in older administrative budgets were also uncontrollable, some distinction such as that between the administrative budget and the consolidated cash budget would be desirable if the ability to distinguish elements of the budget that are noncontrollable and those that are partially controllable in the short run are considered to be important.[13]

Another possible objective toward which budgets could be directed is efficiency in the allocation of public resources. The unified budget, which sheds light on the aggregative impact of government but not on allocative issues could be replaced by several smaller budgets, each based on some appropriately defined program. If emphasis is placed on the efficient use of scarce public resources, budgetary information should be presented along program lines. The number of programs is itself open to definition, of course, for programs can be defined with varying degrees of narrowness or broadness. A narrow definition might distinguish several hundred programs. Thus, there could be programs for general and for vocational education. In addition separate general education programs for children with above-average, average, and below-average intellectual endowments could be maintained. A broader definition of a program might have only one program for education and similarly broad programs for health and community development. On the other hand, "life, liberty, and the pursuit of happiness" could be defined as a program, in which case the entire budget would be reduced to a single meaningless program.

There is no uniquely best way of defining the elements of the government's budget. Any particular method of displaying the budget will emphasize certain types of information and conceal others. The replacement of the earlier budget concepts with the unified budget represents a strengthening of the view that the budget should be considered primarily as a macroeconomic instrument. If it is felt that other types of information are also valuable, other budgetary formats would be required. This would produce a simultaneous existence of alternative budgetary formats. If generally we desire several types of information concerning the fiscal activities of the government, several types of budgets will be necessary; each one will emphasize certain types of information and conceal others.[14]

---

[13] See Murray L. Weidenbaum, "On the Effectiveness of Congressional Control of the Public Purse," *National Tax Journal,* 18 (December 1965), 370–74.

[14] Within this perspective, a report of the Tax Foundation noted that "in recent years there has been a growing tendency to focus emphasis upon a concept of the Federal budget which has as its primary purpose the measuring of the impact of Federal finances on national income, employment, and the economy in general. . . . Only time will tell whether the trend to modify the budget concept for this purpose will eventually strengthen or weaken the effectiveness of the budget

The state of mind that inspires the search for a uniquely best way of presenting the budget is but a reflection of the state of mind that laments the excessive fragmentation and specialization that characterize the budgetary process. For instance, each appropriations subcommittee is responsible for only one class of public expenditure. At no time during the budgetary process does some single committee consider the budget in its entirety. Many commentators suggest that it would be desirable to achieve greater coordination through a more unified approach to the budget process. Congress once attempted a unified budgetary review by considering an omnibus appropriations bill for fiscal 1952. This attempt failed miserably, as the amount of information required to make decisions was too voluminous and complex to be digested by any single congressman. As a result, Congress reverted to the system of fragmented appropriations bills.

Fragmented budgetary review, however, should not be equated with inefficient budgetary review. On the contrary, given the impossibility of a truly effective, comprehensive review of the budget, a system of fragmented review may be an efficient process of budgetary choice. Our decentralized, fragmented budgetary process has many attributes of a market system in securing an efficient allocation of resources; a fragmented budgetary process has merit as an economizer of scarce information.[15] Bureaus compete among themselves for resources that are granted them by politicians, and politicians compete among themselves for political office. This system of competition is a coordinating device that has some of the features of ordinary market processes.[16] While there are substantial differences in the performance of market competition and political competition, as we shall see in Chapter Seven, there are also similarities.

---

for another highly important purpose—its . . . role as a management tool [for attaining] efficiency in spending." *The New Federal Budget Concept: An Explanation and Evaluation,* Government Finance Brief No. 14, (New York: Tax Foundation, 1968), p. 12.

[15] For a careful examination of knowledge and market processes, see the seminal papers by Friedrich A. Hayek: "Economics and Knowledge," *Economica,* 4 (February 1937), 33–54; and "The Use of Knowledge in Society," *American Economic Review,* 35 (September 1945), 519–30; both of which are reprinted in Frederick A. Hayek, *Individualism and Economic Order* (Chicago: University of Chicago press, 1948), pp. 33–58 and 77–91, respectively.

[16] See Ronald N. McKean, *Public Spending* (New York: McGraw-Hill, 1968), pp. 10–30; and Wildavsky, *Politics of the Budgetary Process* for explorations of this theme.

6. Economic Analysis to Promote Efficiency in Public Output

To what extent can economic analysis be employed to secure greater efficiency in public spending? "Efficiency" is the critical word in this question. Is it possible to specify criteria by which we can distinguish efficient from inefficient choices concerning public spending? While the Wicksellian notion of efficiency has much analytical merit, it is not one that can be measured empirically by some external observer. Whether a budgetary choice is Wicksellian-efficient depends, among other things, on the subjective preferences of those participating in the choice. Because a marginal valuation is known only to the individual chooser, it is impossible for an external observer to compute the optimal size and composition of the public budget.[1] Nevertheless, economic analysis can be used to increase understanding of the consequences of alternative budgetary choices. A careful analysis of the alternatives subject to choice may reveal consequences of certain alternatives that previously had been unseen, seen only dimly, or seen in a different perspective. By systematically explaining the consequences of alternative budgetary choices, economic analysis can be used to increase the knowledge that informs budgetary choice. Analysis itself, however, cannot be used to determine efficient choices; rather, analysis can improve the knowledge that informs fiscal choice, and this increased understanding may in turn promote greater efficiency.

Economic analysis to promote efficiency in public output has been applied most strenuously to military choices, but it has also been applied to such nonmilitary areas as health, education, water-related projects, and

[1] For an examination of how an external observer relates to judgments about efficiency, see James M. Buchanan, "Positive Economics, Welfare Economics, and Political Economy," *Journal of Law and Economics,* 2 (October 1959), 124–38.

transportations systems.[2] When we employ economic analysis as a technique for suboptimization, our task typically falls into four stages. First, we must specify the objective to be attained by public expenditure. An illustrative objective would be to achieve a ten percent reduction in the loss from crime. Second, we must describe the alternative ways of attaining the objective. Illustrative ways of reducing the loss from crime include increasing the size of the investigative force of the police department, increasing the size of the patrol force, and inducing people to install more secure locks on their doors and windows. Third, we must assess the cost and benefit of each alternative way of attaining the objective. Fourth, we must select a criteria by which alternative ways of attaining the objective can be compared. Because the first two of these stages are pre-analytical, the bulk of the ensuing discussion will focus on the last two stages.

TIME AND THE DISCOUNT RATE

In assessing the cost and benefit of alternative public expenditures, a special set of issues arises when cost or benefit extends into the future rather than being confined to the present. Suppose Project A costs $6.5 million initially and $3 million annually for five years, while Project B costs $15 million initially and $1 million annually for five years. Which project is less costly? If we simply compute total outlays over the five-year period, we see that Project A sums to $21.5 million while Project B sums to $20 million. But simply adding total outlays regardless of when they occur is inappropriate, for the timing of the payments will affect the judgment as to which stream is most costly.

We can see this impact of time by considering a simpler illustration. Suppose Stream a requires a payment of $2 now and $1 in one year, while Stream b requires a payment of $1 now and $2 in one year. While both require a total payment of $3, they are not equally costly. Since both streams require a common outlay of $1 each year, the difference between them is that the third dollar is paid now with Stream a and is paid in one year with Stream b. Something that costs $1 one year from today is cheaper than something that costs $1 now, given a positive rate of interest. If the $1 payment is deferred one year, that $1 can be invested and earn interest over the year. If the prevailing rate of interest is 6 percent, the

[2] On the use of economic analysis in military choices, see Charles J. Hitch and Roland N. McKean, *The Economics of Defense in the Nuclear Age* (Cambridge: Harvard University Press, 1960). For a general survey of nonmilitary applications, see A. R. Prest and R. Turvey, "Cost-Benefit Analysis: A Survey," *Surveys of Economic Theory*, Vol. III, "Resource Allocation," (New York: St. Martin's Press, 1966), pp. 155–207.

$1 can be paid in one year and $0.06 still will remain. With an interest rate of 6 percent, then, a cost of $1 now is equivalent to a cost of $1.06 in one year, $1.12 in two years, and $1.19 in three years.

Alternatively, we can ask what current cost is equivalent to a cost of $1 in one year—that is, what amount must be invested now at the prevailing rate of interest if we are to receive $1 in one year? This unknown amount, which is the present value of the future receipt of $1, is determined from the formula,

$$PV = \sum_{i=1}^{n} [A_i/(1 + r)^i],$$

where r is the discount rate and A_i is the amount of cost outlay or benefit receipt in year i. With a discount rate of 6 percent, the present value of $1 paid or received in one, two or three years is $0.94, $0.89, and $0.84 respectively. With a discount rate of 10 percent by contrast, the present value of $1 paid or received in one, two, or three years is $0.91, $0.83, and $0.75 respectively. Thus, both the time stream of cost and benefit and the rate at which they are discounted significantly affect their assessment.

We may now return to our initial question concerning the relative costliness of Projects A and B. Table 6-1 shows the present value of these projects for six alternative assumptions about the rate of discount. Project A has a lower initial cost but a higher future cost than does Project B. The lower the discount rate, the more equally weighted are present and future costs. Thus, as the discount rate falls, the cost of Project A in relation to Project B will rise. Table 6-1 shows that Project A is least costly with discount rates of 6, 8, and 10 percent, while Project B is least costly with discount rates of 4, 2, and 0 percent. Clearly, the choice of a discount rate can exert considerable influence on the assessment of alternative projects for public expenditure. If we assume that Table 6-1 shows the

TABLE 6–1
Alternative Discount Rates and the
Choice Among Projects

| | Present Value of Cost | |
Discount Rate	Project A	Project B
10%	$17,880,400	$18,793,467
8	18,530,605	19,010,202
6	19,149,526	19,216,509
4	19,864,083	19,454,694
2	20,661,031	19,720,343
0	21,500,000	20,000,000

expected net benefit (benefit less cost) of Projects *A* and *B*, the choice between a 4 percent rate and a 6 percent rate of discount is, in effect, a choice of which project to undertake.

What is the appropriate rate of interest by which to discount future streams of benefit and cost? The rate of interest in the capital market, the marginal productivity of investment, has been suggested by some as the appropriate rate of discount. The cost of an investment is the return that could have been received from the best alternative investment. The rate of return on private investment—the market rate of interest—measures what could have been produced had the public project not been undertaken, so it indicates the opportunity cost of public spending.[3] By contrast, others have suggested that the rate of interest at which the government can borrow is a more appropriate rate of discount. Because an investment in the private capital market carries some risk of failure, market rates of interest will reflect some risk premium. The market rate of interest, then, is a composite of the return on capital and a premium for bearing risk. However, because investment in securities of the national government is relatively riskless, the government's borrowing rate would more accurately reflect the productivity of capital than would the market rate of interest, or so the agreement goes.

The argument that public investment is less risky than is private investment is based on the law of large numbers. Because the large number of projects in which the government invests results in a greater pooling of risk, the consequences of any particular project failure will not endanger the returns to investors. No private enterprise has such a diversified portfolio, so the risk faced by an investor is greater. Pauly has shown, however, that by investing in a variety of firms, individuals secure a personal portfolio that is diversified by some multiple of any single firm's investments.[4] As both private and public investment permit a substantial pooling of risk, the degree of risk will tend not to differ substantially among the two types of investment. The government borrowing rate is lower than the private borrowing rate not because government investment is less risky than private investment is, but because the risk associated with public investment is borne by taxpayers. If government investment is less productive than expected, tax revenues will be less than what they would otherwise have been. Consequently, an additional burden will be placed on taxpayers in order to prevent default on the bonds. If the risk were borne by bond-

---

[3] See, for instance, Arnold C. Harberger, "The Interest Rate in Cost-Benefit Analysis," Joint Economic Committee, 85th Congress, 1st Session, *Federal Expenditure Policy for Economic Growth and Stability* (Washington, D.C.: U.S. Government Printing Office, 1957), pp. 239–41.

[4] Mark V. Pauly, "Risk and the Social Rate of Discount," *American Economic Review*, 60 (March 1970), 195–98.

holders, the government borrowing rate would rise to reflect the risk premium paid to bondholders. Once we realize that borrowing rates differ not because of differences in risk, but because of differences in the locus of risk, the market rate of interest appears to be the appropriate rate of discount.

However, Baumol has shown that the appropriate social rate of discount is approximately twice the market rate of interest.[5] Suppose the rate of tax on corporation income is 50 percent and that resources for public investment are extracted from the corporate sector. If the interest rate in the corporate sector is 8 percent, the gross rate of return on corporate investment is 16 percent. Under such circumstances, the opportunity cost of public investment will be 16 percent, for corporate investment not only returns 8 percent to stockholders but also 8 percent to the taxpaying citizenry via the tax on corporate income. In practice, of course, not all public investment replaces corporate investment and the tax on corporation income is a little less than 50 percent, so the appropriate social rate of discount is somewhat less than twice the market rate of interest.[6]

THE MEASUREMENT OF COST AND BENEFIT

Suppose that somewhere, there is a benevolent despot. Presumably, he is benevolent because he is interested only in maximizing the net benefit from the expenditure of public resources. The claims on the despots' resources, however, will exceed his available resources, so he must choose how to allocate his limited resources among the competing uses so as to maximize the net benefit from his expenditures. A wealth of economic analysis on efficient forms of public expenditure is at his disposal. The benefits of any expenditure program will be the products of the program, while the costs will be the value of the other activities that are forgone by undertaking the program in question. Once we apply economic analysis to a particular program in order to ascertain its costs and benefits, we can compare the result with a criterion that will tell us if the program is an efficient use of resources.

Consider some government unit that has decided to replace its dilapidated prison facility with a new one and must decide what type of facility to construct. One possible type is purely incarcerative, containing no facilities for rehabilitation. Another type of facility is one in which prisoners

[5] William J. Baumol, "On the Social Rate of Discount," *American Economic Review*, 58 (September 1968), 788–802.

[6] There are, of course, numerous market rates of interest rather than a single rate. Yet the principle involved in selecting a social rate of discount is undisturbed by this complicating factor.

are trained for one among a narrow range of vocational skills. Still another type of facility is one in which prisoners are trained for one among a broad range of occupations. How would we go about choosing among these various types of facilities? How would we go about assessing the benefit and cost of the prison facility that provides its inmates with the opportunity to choose among the narrow range of vocational skills? How would we go about trying to judge whether investment in this rehabilitative facility is more efficient than investment in the purely incarcerative facility? How might we try to measure the benefit and the cost of investing in prisoner rehabilitation?

The Measurement of Cost

The measurement of cost is usually considered a simpler task than is the measurement of benefit. While cost is usually assigned a clear monetary dimension, many elements of benefit are not so easily assigned a monetary measure. We find it easy to say that it costs $5 to go to a movie, but we find it considerably more difficult to assess the benefit. Yet cost is a benefit forgone; the cost of going to a movie is the benefit that was sacrificed by, say, not going to a football game instead. Under conditions of competitive equilibrium, we may measure this forgone benefit at $5.[7] While the ease of assigning a measure may differ between the cost and benefit sides of the account, cost and benefit are not separate, distinct features of a choice situation. Rather, one is an image of the other.

In enumerating the various types of cost associated with some proposed project, it is customary to distinguish those that are attributable directly to constructing and maintaining the project and those that accrue indirectly as a consequence of the project's existence and operation. An investment in prisoner rehabilitation will require some initial capital outlay for equipment necessary to provide the desired training. If the prisoners are trained as automobile mechanics, the training program will require a capital investment in such items as garage facilities, tools and equipment, and a supply of automobiles on which to practice. Besides these capital outlays, operating expenses will be incurred for training personnel and for material and equipment used to train them. Suppose the program entails an initial capital cost of $2 million and annual expenditures of $1 million for the following ten years. If the rate of discount is 10 percent, the present value of this ten-year program is $8,144,565, assuming the capital equipment will have zero salvage value at the conclusion of the program.[8]

---

[7] James M. Buchanan, *Cost and Choice* (Chicago: Markham, 1969).

[8] $\$8,144,565 = \$2,000,000 + \dfrac{\$1,000,000}{(1.1)^1} + \dfrac{\$1,000,000}{(1.1)^2} + \cdots + \dfrac{\$1,000,000}{(1.1)^{10}}.$

Forms of indirect cost associated with prisoner rehabilitation do not seem as evident as they do for many other programs. One indirect cost might stem from an increase in traffic congestion around the prison, especially if part of the training program contains a garage offering repair service to the public. Increased congestion slows down the rate of traffic flow, and a measure would have to be assigned to this effect. Given specific information about traffic patterns, primarily the volume, speed, and destination of the traffic, an estimate can be made of the loss of time associated with the increased congestion. Moreover, if the prison garage should compete with a private garage, creating private unemployment in the process, the cost of this unemployment would also be an indirect cost of the rehabilitation program.

The Measurement of Benefit

In examining the benefit from some proposed public expenditure, it is customary to distinguish benefits that can be attributed directly to the expenditure and benefits that can be attributed only indirectly to the expenditure. One direct benefit of investment in prisoner rehabilitation might be a reduction in the rate of recidivism. Another direct benefit might be an increase in tax payments and reduction in welfare costs resulting from an increase in the earnings of released prisoners. An indirect benefit of investment in rehabilitation might be a reduction in future police, prison, and crime costs that would follow from the reduction in recidivism.

Consider the benefit from the reduction in recidivism. The first step in measuring this benefit might entail construction of a model of the prison population. At any point in time, a prison contains prisoners; some are first offenders and others are recidivists. Each year, some prisoners are released and replaced by new entrants. Some of the new entrants are first offenders and some are recidivists. Among those who have been released, some will never be imprisoned again while others will be imprisoned again. Based on this information, a model of the steady-state equilibrium of the prison population can be developed. To illustrate, suppose that the equilibrium prison population is 2,000 inmates and that each prisoner serves a five-year term. Each year, then, 400 prisoners are released and 400 are incarcerated in their place. If recidivism takes place only once, and at a rate of 50 percent, 200 of the 400 prisoners that are released each year will be incarcerated again. Moreover if all the recidivists are returned to prison in the year following their release, 200 of the 400 entering prisoners will be recidivists. Under these conditions, the prison will contain 1,000 inmates who are first offenders and 1,000 who are recidivists.

If the investment in prisoner rehabilitation is expected to reduce the rate of recidivism to 25 percent, only 100, not 200, of the 400 prisoners who are released probably will be incarcerated again.[9] If we continue to assume that 200 first offenders are incarcerated each year, the equilibrium prison population will fall from 2,000 inmates to 1,335 inmates. Once this new equilibrium is attained, 267 prisoners will be incarcerated each year, and as that group is released, only 67 will be incarcerated again. Thus, the reduction in the rate of recidivism from 50 to 25 percent eventually produces a 33 percent reduction in the prison population.

Within the context of our ten-year horizon for the rehabilitation program, how would we assess the benefit from this reduction in recidivism? We must first estimate the prison population for each of the ten years. This task is simple as long as we continue to assume a uniform 25 percent rate of recidivism and a five-year sentence for all prisoners. The prison population still will be 2,000 during the first year of the program, but the population will fall by 100 inmates per year during the second through sixth years of the program. This reduction results because each year's class of 400 is now replaced by a class of only 300. In turn in the seventh through tenth years of the program, the prison population will fall by 25 per year, thus producing an inmate population of 1,400 the tenth year. In this case, the annual reduction occurs because a class of 300 is replaced by a class of 200 new entrants plus 75 (25 percent of 300) for a total of 275 recidivists. If the annual per prisoner operating cost is $4,000 and the discount rate is 10 percent, the present value of this reduction in future cost is $7,878,340.[10]

Once we allow for growth in the prison population over time, the rehabilitation program will also permit a reduction in capital cost. Suppose the prison's capacity is 2,200 inmates and that prison population rises by 100 inmates each year. Without the rehabilitation program, the prison's capacity will be reached in two years, at which time new facilities must be constructed. With the rehabilitation program, however, the capacity will not be reached until the seventh year. Under these postulated conditions,

[9] The development of this estimate would itself require the construction of an economic model. This would be a model of labor supply, for we would need to estimate the impact of an increase in a released prisoner's expected earnings in a legitimate occupation relative to his expected earnings in criminal activity. For a treatment of criminal activity within the framework of a theory of occupational choice, see Gary S. Becker, "Crime and Punishment: An Economic Approach," *Journal of Political Economy,* 76 (no. 2, 1968), 169–217.

$$[10] \ \$7,878,340 = \frac{\$400,000}{(1.1)^2} + \cdots + \frac{\$2,000,000}{(1.1)^6} + \frac{\$2,100,000}{(1.1)^7} + \cdots$$
$$+ \frac{\$2,400,000}{(1.1)^{10}}.$$

the rehabilitation program permits postponement of construction for five years. This benefit may be measured by the reduction in the present value of the future cost of construction.

The reduction in recidivism, moreover, will ultimately expand the labor force by 665 members. By becoming gainfully employed, these former prisoners will contribute to the government's tax base. The present value of these future tax payments is also a benefit of the investment in rehabilitation for, in effect, the rehabilitated prisoners partially will repay the cost of their training.

While these problems of valuation are often difficult to implement empirically, they possess the simplifying feature that they are amenable to a monetary measure. Not all elements of benefit, however, are similarly amenable. A new prison, for instance, may reduce episodes of homosexual rape and improve on generally subhuman living conditions. Even if recidivism is not reduced, some value might be placed on the improvement in living conditions. But what value is appropriate, and how can the appropriate value be determined? Conceptually, we can answer our question by asking: "how much would you be willing to pay for a new prison, assuming it will produce no reduction in recidivism?" Because such conceptual questioning cannot be implemented properly, we are left with noncommensurable forms of benefit, which itself indicates that economic analysis can elucidate the consequences of alternative choices, but it cannot eliminate choice by making it wholly computational.

THE CRITERIA FOR CHOICE

Once we have assessed the cost and benefit of alternative spending programs, we must specify a criterion in terms of which we may choose among the alternatives. The appropriate criterion will depend on the circumstances within which the choice is to be made. This dependence may be illustrated with reference to the three projects illustrated in Table 6-2, where we assume a 10 percent rate of discount. Project *A* costs $200 now and in one year yields a benefit valued at $500, which entails a present value of $455. Similar explanations hold for Projects *B* and *C*. If projects

TABLE 6-2
Cost-Benefit Analysis of Three Projects

Project	Cost	Benefit	Benefit (Present Value)
A	$200	$500	$455
B	400	750	682
C	600	950	864

are not mutually exclusive, a budget constraint must be absent, for the choice of one project does not entail the sacrifice of another. An efficient rule will be one that chooses all projects for which the present value of benefits exceeds the present value of costs. Application of such a rule ensures that projects that are undertaken will be valued more highly than will the private projects that are sacrificed as a consequence.

Because budget constraints rarely are absent, projects are generally mutually exclusive. The construction of a reservoir to impound one million acre feet of water precludes the construction of a larger or a smaller reservoir on that site. While the selection of all projects for which the ratio, in present value terms, of benefits to costs is appropriate when projects are not mutually exclusive, it does not follow that selection of the project for which the ratio, again in present value terms, of benefits to costs is highest is appropriate when projects are mutually exclusive. In Table 6-2, the ratio of the present value of benefits to the present value of costs is 2.275:1 for Project *A*, 1.705:1 for Project *B*, and 1.44:1 for Project *C*. If choice is based on the benefit-cost ratio, Project *A* would be the selection. Note, however, that Project *B* offers additional benefits of $227 in present-value terms for an additional cost of $200. Because the discount rate of 10 percent indicates that the $200 would yield only $220 in alternative uses, Project *B* will be the most efficient allocation of resources. Thus, in choosing among projects, the project with the highest ratio of benefits to costs will not necessarily be the most efficient choice. Instead, the appropriate criterion is to choose projects so as to maximize the present value of net benefits, where net benefits for any year *t* are defined as $B_t - C_t / (1 + r)^t$, where *B* and *C* refer to benefit and cost respectively and where *r* is the rate of discount.[11]

The preceding example also illustrates a problem that can arise because benefit and cost are often measured in total rather than in marginal terms, for analysis is often performed in terms of discrete alternatives. The benefit and cost of a specified rehabilitation program may be analyzed, and the rehabilitative facility may be compared with a purely incarcerative facility. It is possible that a rehabilitative facility may be judged to be more efficient than is an incarcerative facility, yet the marginal cost of the rehabilitative facility could exceed the marginal benefit, which indicates that a smaller project would be even more efficient. It may be estimated, for instance, that the cost of the program will be $3 million and the benefit will be $4.5 million, thus giving a benefit-cost ratio of 1.5:1. But suppose

[11] For a careful discussion of this criterion problem, see Roland N. McKean, *Efficiency in Government Through Systems Analysis* (New York: Wiley, 1958), pp. 25–49 and 74–95; and Roland N. McKean, *Public Spending* (New York: McGraw-Hill, 1968), pp. 135–45.

it is also estimated that a smaller-scale rehabilitative program will yield a benefit of $3.6 million at a cost of $2 million. The marginal cost of the larger program is $1 million, but the marginal benefit is only $0.9 million, so the smaller-scale rehabilitative program would be more efficient than the larger-scale program would be.

LIMITATIONS OF SUBOPTIMIZATION TECHNIQUES

Suboptimization is subject to many limitations. The estimation of cost and benefit is subject to many uncertainties: estimates must be based on incomplete data; arbitrary choices of estimates and models are often necessary; and various types of noncommensurable elements are usually present. Moreover, there is no unambiguously appropriate means of choosing a rate at which to discount over time. But let us ignore these limitations for now. Assume that our benefit-cost analysis unambiguously reveals one project as the most efficient. Suboptimization is still open to the danger that the suboptimized project is not worth suboptimizing; it tells us the best way of doing something, but it does not tell us if that something is worth doing in the first place.

Suppose benefit-cost analysis suggests that one particular size of prison facility is the most efficient alternative. Are we justified in concluding that the investment ought to be made? Our analysis merely says that *given* the necessity to choose among alternative prison facilities, the facility that is chosen is probably the most efficient choice. But why restrict our choice to this set of alternatives in the first place?

Because a prison facility is but one part of a judicial system, an alternative such as judicial reform may be preferable to building a new prison. Most local prisons contain a mixture of sentenced and unsentenced prisoners. A prominent feature of American justice is the long delay between a person's time of arrest and his time of trial. It is not uncommon to find that about one-half of the inmates of a local prison are unsentenced prisoners awaiting trial. A delay of several months' between arrest and trial also is common. If the time between arrest and trial could be reduced by 50 percent, say from 8 months to 4 months, the prison population could be reduced by 25 percent. Thus, a judicial reform that would double the number of prisoners handled by the courts would produce the same effect as would a 25 percent increase in the capacity of the prison. Thus, an increase in the speed with which justice is given is a substitute for the provision of additional prison facilities.

On one level, we may look on our problem as choosing the optimal size of prison. But on another level, a prison is but one part of a larger judicial system, and at that level, our problem is to choose whether to build a new prison, to provide more judges, to speed up trial procedures, or to combine some or all of the three. The benefit-cost frame of reference is also appropriate for this choice, but the alternatives are more difficult to define, which reduces the force of an empirical comparison.

Moreover, the level of choice among alternatives could be advanced still farther. The burden placed on prisons and courts, for instance, is dictated by provisions of the applicable criminal code, and this burden could be reduced by revising our criminal codes. Prostitution could be legalized, for instance, thereby reducing the burden placed on our judicial facilities. There are similar possibilities for other classes of crime. Certain narcotics offenses, for instance, may very well be erased from our criminal code in the near future. At least conceptually, we are discussing a benefit-cost analysis of varying degrees of inclusiveness in our criminal code. For instance, we can compare, the benefit and cost of treating prostitution as a crime or not as a crime.[12] We can thus attempt to determine whether the benefit of treating prostitution as a crime exceeds the cost, or whether some modification in the law might be socially profitable. But it is obvious that the uncertainties involved in this kind of analysis vastly exceed those involved in estimating the return from prisons of different sizes. The choice among prison sizes is dominated by monetary considerations, and data relating to market prices are useful indicators of relative social value. But the choice concerning the criminal treatment of prostitution is rife with noncommensurable considerations in which market prices are either absent or unacceptable as indicators of social value.

A primary danger associated with the application of suboptimization techniques is that the technique itself induces a mind-set within which consideration of radically different ways of achieving the desired objective is almost automatically precluded.[13] The critical choice of any analyst is his choice concerning the form in which the question is posed. Once the question has been posed, it is a matter of applying some suboptimization technique to generate an answer. The posing of the question by itself restricts the analyst's view to a subset of the possible alternatives. Once we have asked "should we expand our prison facilities by 25 percent?" we have almost automatically excluded from consideration such alternatives as judicial reform and changes in the definition of criminal activity.

Suboptimization is a technique that is useful in supplying information

---

[12] For a suggestive development along these lines, see Edward Erickson, "The Social Costs of the Discovery and Suppression of the Clandestine Distribution of Heroin," *Journal of Political Economy,* 77 (no. 4, 1969), 484–86.

[13] For interesting observations on this phenomena, see Edward deBono, "Thinking Sideways," *Bell Telephone Magazine,* 44 (no. 4, 1969), 26–32.

relating to the choice among answers to some well-defined question. While the technique will not make the choice for us, as the existence of noncommensurable and immeasurable elements of cost and benefit will leave an element of subjective evaluation, it may produce a more informed choice among answers to the question that has been posed. But suboptimization as a technique can be applied only after a question has been posed; the technique itself does not pose the appropriate question. The choice of question to pose is a matter of intelligent action: it is pre-analytical.

7. Bureaucracy and Efficiency in Public Output

Public services can be provided through a variety of institutional forms. Governments often contract with private, profit-seeking firms for the provision of public services. In other instances, governments supply public services themselves through bureaus, financing the services either by user charges or by taxation. In this chapter, we shall examine the insight economic analysis provides concerning the supply of services by bureaus, for public bureaus have considerably different characteristics than private firms have. Obviously, bureaus are nonprofit institutions; more important, they provide their total output in exchange for a total budget. This sale of a total output for a total budget contrasts sharply with such nonprofit institutions as hospitals and museums that sell units of output at a per unit price.[1] Moreover, bureaus, are institutions for which the rights of ownership are nontransferable among owners. While a bureau is owned by the citizenry, individual citizens can neither sell their shares of ownership nor buy the ownership shares of others. Instead, ownership is bought automatically by virtue of residence and can be sold only by moving to a different political jurisdiction.[2] Both the sale of output for a lump-sum grant and the nontransferability of ownership are institutions that operate to produce output choices that are different for bureaus than for firms.

INSTITUTIONAL FRAMEWORK AND ORGANIZATIONAL PERFORMANCE

In the previous chapter, we examined how a more systematic presentation of information about alternative proposals for public spending may in-

[1] The treatment of public bureaus in this chapter draws heavily on William A. Niskanen, *Bureaucracy and Representative Government* (Chicago: Aldine, 1971).

[2] Some implications of nontransferable ownership rights are explored in Armen A. Alchian, "Some Economics of Property Rights," *Il Politico,* 30 (December 1965), 816–29.

crease the efficiency of budgetary choices. Because public officials are utility maximizers, not selfless automatons, however, it follows that the choices made by public officials will be influenced by the cost-reward structure within which they operate.[3] It was within this perspective that Adam Smith enunciated the general principal that "public services are never better performed than when their [public officials] reward comes only in consequence of their being performed, and is proportioned to the diligence employed in performing them."[4] To continue with our illustration from the preceeding chapter, we should expect that the operation of a penal system will depend on the cost-reward structure faced by penal administrators. Consider two penal systems, one in which administrators are given a fixed budget and a fixed salary and one in which administrators are given some type of proprietary interest in the facility's output of released prisoners, perhaps by having administrative salaries vary inversely with the rate of recidivism. We should surely expect that these differences in cost-reward structure would yield differences in the performance of these penal systems. In this chapter, we shall examine some of the ways in which the institutional framework within which public output choices are made can affect the efficiency with which these choices are made.

It is well recognized that the performance of a market economy will depend on the underlying institutional framework. The comparative analysis of competition and monopoly is but one illustration of the importance of the institutional framework. Although we say that a competitive market will yield a more efficient output choice than will a monopolistic market, the analytical framework developed to reach this conclusion does not enable an external observer to compute efficient price and output policies. Rather, the analysis focuses upon explaining the process by which resources tend to become allocated to more efficient uses when an industry is competitive than when it is monopolistic. True, the theory specifies that the optimal rate of output for a firm occurs when marginal cost equals marginal revenue and that the optimal combination of resource input occurs when the marginal product per dollar's worth of one equals the marginal product per dollar's worth of the other. But the analysis is not concerned with techniques of computing the various marginal magnitudes. Rather, it says that firms that survive such competition will be those that are successful in making such computations and that a competitive market

---

[3] Roland N. McKean, "Divergence Between Individual and Total Costs Within Government," *American Economic Review,* Proceedings, 54 (May 1964), 243–49.

[4] *Wealth of Nations* (New York: Modern Library Edition, 1937), p. 678. On this general topic, see Nathan Rosenberg, "Some Institutional Aspects of the Wealth of Nations," *Journal of Political Economy,* 68 (December 1960), 557–70.

will place a stronger penalty on unsuccessful computation than on a monopolistic market.[5]

It could even be argued that the same division of labor between institutional analysis and computational techniques should be applied to the public economy. The central focus of fiscal analysis would then be to show how different political and fiscal institutions affect the performance of the public economy. The development of such computational techniques as cost-benefit analysis would be relegated to the domain of public administration and operations research. While such a division of labor has merit, it seems likely that the very publicness of public spending choices makes computational techniques an appropriate subject for fiscal analysis. The public concern in the private economy is focused on the choice of institutional framework; the public chooses the institutional framework of the market economy, but it does not choose the price and output policies of individual firms. With the public economy, however, the public ultimately chooses both the institutional framework and the price and output policies of its bureaus.

Yet the study of institutions would seem to command primacy over the study of computational techniques. Better institutional frameworks will induce better computations by public administrators. But the design of better computational techniques will not ensure that public administrators will make use of those techniques. Benefit-cost types of computations are irrelevant if the institutional framework within which bureaus operate is such that it permits decision-makers to ignore such computations.[6]

Following our examination of the output of a single bureau in the next two sections, the output choice of an entire bureaucracy will be discussed. Because a government is a collection of bureaus, let us consider the behavior of a single bureau—the public counterpart of a private firm—before we then turn to a discussion of the behavior of the entire collection of bureaus, the bureaucracy—the public counterpart of a private industry.

[5] Armen A. Alchian, "Uncertainty, Evolution, and Economic Theory," *Journal of Political Economy*, 58 (June 1950), 211–21.

[6] A striking illustration of how the institutional framework influences public output choices is found in Charles R. Plott, "Some Organizational Influences on Urban Renewal Decisions," *American Economic Review*, Proceedings, 58 (May 1968), 306–21. Whether or not the establishment of a local public agency to implement urban renewal requires approval by referendum will significantly affect the outcome. Plott found that when a referendum was required, the local share of the cost was more likely to be the provision of such public utilities as sidewalks, sewers, streets, and playgrounds than a cash contribution. Moreover, urban renewal is the responsibility of the House Banking and Currency Committee. In 1964, this committee comprised 7 percent of the total House membership, but 25 percent of expenditures for urban renewal took place in the metropolitan areas represented by those 7 percent.

LUMP-SUM GRANTS AND A
BUREAU'S OUTPUT CHOICE

While there are some cases in which a bureau faces competition from suppliers of close substitutes, it is generally more appropriate to treat a government bureau as a monopoly. However, unlike monopoly firms, monopoly bureaus can show no profit. Thus, a bureau is a nonprofit monopoly. Moreover, unlike monopoly firms and nonprofit institutions that sell units of output at a per unit price, public bureaus sell their entire output for a lump-sum budget. Thus, because public bureaus operate under a different cost-reward structure than do private firms, we should expect the output choices for bureaus and for firms to be different even when both institutions face identical demand and cost conditions.[7]

Figure 7-1 illustrates the output choice of a public bureau and compares that choice with the choices of both a profit-seeking monopoly and a nonprofit institution. We assume that all three institutions face identical demand and cost conditions for their outputs and that, in the long run, marginal cost and average cost are constant. This latter assumption facilitates geometrical exposition, but it does not alter the essential implication of the analysis. All this assumption does is ensure that production takes place with both the optimum scale of plant and at the optimum rate of output. This feature of our analysis, in turn, allows us to focus on the essential difference between monopoly bureaus and monopoly firms, a difference that exists even though a monopoly firm produces the optimum rate of output at the optimum scale of plant.

Given the conditions depicted in Figure 7-1, the monopoly will produce the output rate X_1 and earn a profit of *ab* per unit of output. However, if the owners are unable to appropriate the excess of revenue over cost because it is a nonprofit institution, the nonprofit firm will produce the output rate of X_2. At this output rate, the value to consumers of the marginal unit of X is equal to the marginal cost of X. At the output rate X_1, by contrast, the value to consumers of the marginal unit of X exceeds the marginal cost of X by *ab*.

[7] For an exploration of the output choice of a public bureau, see Niskanen, *Bureaucracy and Representative Government;* and William A. Niskanen, "The Peculiar Economics of Bureaucracy," *American Economic Review,* Proceedings, 58 (May 1968), 293–305. For one examination of a nonprofit private institution, see Joseph P. Newhouse, "Toward A Theory of Nonprofit Institutions: An Economic Model of a Hospital," *American Economic Review,* 60 (March 1970), 64–74. For a more general statement of the influence of the cost-reward structure on the choices that an organization makes, see Roland N. McKean, "The Unseen Hand in Government," *American Economic Review,* 55 (June 1965), 496–505; and Roland N. McKean, *Public Spending* (New York: McGraw-Hill, 1968), pp. 10–30.

FIGURE 7-1
Equilibrium Output and Organizational Form: Profit-Seeking
Monopoly, Nonprofit Firm, and Public Bureau

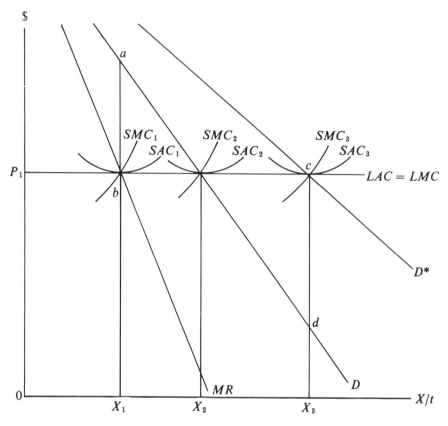

Public bureaus, however, usually sell their entire output for a single sum. For instance, a public school does not price its output to each child, but rather charges the community a lump sum for its package of services. Under such conditions, the seller acts as if it were a discriminating monpoly. Thus, the monopoly bureau acts as if it faced the all-or-nothing demand curve, D^*. The bureau's rate of output will be X_3, at which point the value to customers of the marginal unit of X falls short of the marginal cost by Cd. Although the implicit per unit price of the bureau's output is P_1, the bureau sells the entire output, X_3, for the lump-sum budget OX_3cP_1, and this budget is fully exhausted in supplying X_3.

This analysis suggests that the problem with the supply of public services through bureaus is allocative inefficiency rather than technical inefficiency. Bureaus produce their output in the least-cost manner, but their rate of output is such that, at the margin, the bureau's output is valued less highly than are other outputs that are sacrificed in exchange. It seems reasonable to assume that a bureau is motivated to maximize the output from a given budget and to maximize its total budget. A bureaucrat cannot profit directly from his bureau's operations; unlike the monopolist, the bureaucrat cannot take home the profits. Profit can be captured only indirectly. The bureaucrat's salary, the perquisites of his office, his reputation and power, and his ability to trade on patronage are monotonically increasing functions of the bureau's budget.[8] Thus, a bureaucrat would seem likely to be motivated to expand the output of his bureau as long as his total budget covers the total cost of his output. The output of a bureau will thus be allocatively inefficient in a converse manner to the output of a monopoly: the bureau's output will be excessive while the monopoly's will be deficient. Both the bureau and the monopoly, however, will produce their output in the least-cost manner.[9]

NONTRANSFERABILITY AND A BUREAU'S OUTPUT CHOICE

The conclusion that a bureau will produce an excessive rate of output at the least-cost combination of inputs would seem to be correct under a regime of transferable ownership rights. But once we recognize that ownership rights in a bureau are nontransferable, there is no longer any reason to expect that a bureau will produce its output at the least possible cost. Each resident of a government acquires a proportionate ownership interest in the bureaus of his government, but these ownership shares cannot be bought and sold. When ownership rights are transferable, ownership will tend to gravitate toward those who are most interested in those activities or to those who have the greatest ability for exercising entrepreneurship with respect to those activities. With nontransferability of ownership rights, however, people will not be able to specialize in ownership according to their interests and abilities.

In effect, nontransferability makes ownership rights a common property resource. Gains and losses from both good and bad choices are thus diffused over the entire population. If some innovation will save a bureau $1,000 and the community contains 1,000 resident owners, each person will gain only one dollar. Similarly, losses will be diffused over the entire population. Consequently, the incentive both to search for more effective

[8] Niskanen, "The Peculiar Economics of Bureaucracy," 293–94.

[9] If long-run cost functions are upward sloping, the excess supply of the bureau's output will produce factor rents for specialized inputs. If bureaus were required to sell their output at a per unit rate, these factor rents would be dissipated substantially. Hence, it is not at all surprising to observe the intense hostility of the educational bureaucracy to such programs as vouchers and tuition loans.

modes of operation and to avoid ineffective modes are blunted under a regime of common ownership.

It might be objected that the blunting of incentives is attributable to the multiplicity of ownership, which would create a similar situation for a firm with many owners vis-à-vis a firm with a single owner. Transferability of ownership rights, however, operates to prevent this type of inefficiency in firms in spite of the diffusion of ownership. Suppose a firm in which ownership rights are transferable fails to act as efficiently as it could. The cost of supplying any given rate of output will rise above the least-cost level, reducing the current rate of return on capital invested in the firm. Consequently, the market value of equity ownership in the firm will fall below what it would be if the firm were operated efficiently. This differential in price indicates the amount of capital gain that could be achieved by taking over the inefficiently operated firm and operating it efficiently. If, for instance, the potential price per share is $50 while the actual price is $40 and 100,000 shares are required for effective control, someone could buy the necessary 100,000 shares at $40 per share and capture a capital gain of $1 million. When ownership rights are transferable, inefficient policies will drive the price of shares below their potential value, creating an incentive for a takeover in the hope of capitalizing on the greater efficiency. If a public bureau is operated inefficiently, however, such a market for control cannot exist because of the nontransferability of ownership rights.[10]

Because of the nontransferability of ownership rights in a public bureau, failure to operate with the least-cost combination of inputs will not tend to be eradicated through the operation of market processes. Thus, there will be a tendency for public bureaus to have a higher cost per unit of output than the minimum possible cost for that rate of output. The effect on the bureau's rate of output is shown in Figure 7-2, where the solid lines are carried forward from Figure 7-1. The inefficiency in operation raises the cost curves to LAC', LMC', SAC'_3, and SMC'_3. The bureau's equilibrium rate of output thus falls to X'_3, at which point the loss from inefficiency in the input mix is ef per unit of output. At the same

---

[10] For a careful examination of such markets for corporate control, see Henry G. Manne, "Mergers and the Market for Corporate Control," *Journal of Political Economy,* 73 (April 1965), 110–20.

Nontransferability of ownership rights raises important issues concerning governmental consolidation in metropolitan areas. The cost of transferring ownership in government is the cost of migrating to a different jurisdiction. By reducing the number of alternative jurisdictions, consolidation increases the cost of mobility. In the extreme case of complete consolidation, ownership could be transferred only by migrating to a different metropolitan area. Hence, metropolitan consolidation would seem likely to intensify the separation of ownership and control, thereby increasing the ability of public managers to operate public bureaus according to their personal desires.

FIGURE 7-2
Impact of Nontransferable Ownership Rights upon Bureau Behavior

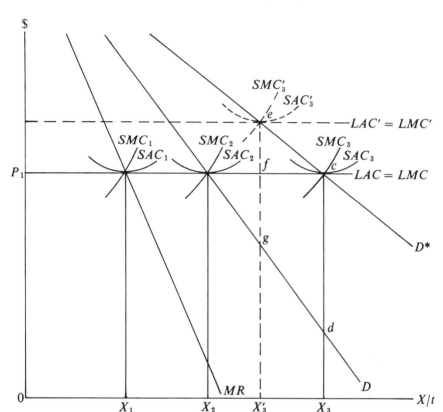

time, of course, the marginal allocative inefficiency has fallen from *cd* to *fg* per unit of output.

Hospitals, certain recreational facilities, and public utilities are examples of instances in which both private firms and government bureaus supply the same services. The existence of such cases of duplicate services makes empirical testing of the propositions described in this chapter possible. Recently, one major test of these propositions concerning nontransferability of ownership rights and the relative efficiency of firms and bureaus was formulated by David Davies.[11] Of the two Australian airlines, one is a private firm with transferable ownership rights and the other is a public firm with nontransferable ownership rights. In an effort to produce equal outcomes from competition, the government has prescribed routes, schedules,

[11] David G. Davies, "The Efficiency of Public versus Private Firms, The Case of Australia's Two Airlines," *Journal of Law and Economics,* 14 (April 1971), 149–65.

prices, and type aircraft that are practically identical. In spite of this strenuous effort to equalize the outcome of competition between the two airlines, productivity of the private firm was considerably higher than productivity of the public bureau over the 1958–59 period examined by Davies. The private firm carried an average of 10.73 tons of freight and mail per employee while the public bureau carried only 4.86 tons. Similarly, the private firm carried an average of 337 passengers per employee and the public bureau carried an average of only 279 passengers. Finally, the private firm earned an average of $9,627 per employee, while the public bureau earned only $8,428.[12] While Davies' data is but one observation and output per employee is an imperfect measure of productivity, Davies' results would seem to be an important beginning in examining the impact of alternative ownership rights on the efficiency with which productive inputs are utilized.

Nontransferability also creates inefficiency in that investment choices will be undertaken from an excessively short-run perspective.[13] When ownership rights are transferable, decisions of varying short-run and long-run impacts will be capitalized into the present value of the firm. With nontransferability of ownership rights, by contrast, no such capitalization can occur. A bureaucrat can neither gain from the long-term benefits of his decisions nor lose from the long-term costs. Instead, his payoff is contingent on his being in office. Thus, public officials will have a higher rate of time preference than private entrepreneurs will have. Consequently, they will desire low discount rates as a means of reallocating investment from the future to the present, thereby increasing the bureau's budget *during their tenures in office.*

When ownership rights are nontransferable, then, profits and losses cannot be internalized to the decision-maker. Instead, they are diffused throughout the entire community. Profits and losses become a common property resource under nontransferable ownership rights, and the standard results are applicable.[14] Transferable ownership rights perform a valuable social function in that the existence of appropriability increases the element of personal responsibility in the use of property, thereby promoting a more effective use of scarce resources. There are numerous instances of primitive tribes that hunt game for a living and have property institutions for assigning individual ownership in the catch, yet the members of the tribe consume the game in common. There are several different rules

---

[12] *Ibid.,* p. 163.

[13] For an explanation of this important insight, see Louis DeAlessi, "Implications of Property Rights for Government Investment Decisions," *American Economic Review,* 59 (March 1969), 13–24.

[14] H. Scott Gordon, "The Economic Theory of a Common-Property Resource: The Fishery," *Journal of Political Economy,* 62 (April 1954), 124–42.

for assigning ownership: to the person who first sights the game, to the hunter whose weapon kills the game, to the person who recovers the game, or to the person who carries the game back to the tribe. Although the game is consumed in common, the legal owner is able to offer the game to the community. By conferring prestige on the assigned owner, the assignment of ownership rights operates to promote a more efficient use of resources than would have resulted under common ownership, so the entire community is better fed.

The use of an administrative rule of thumb, perhaps by applying such techniques as cost accounting and program budgeting, may offset somewhat the inefficiency resulting from nontransferability of ownership shares, although such rules create other sources of inefficiency.[15] The usefulness of such rules is likely to be inhibited by a confounding of inputs and outputs when dealing with public bureaus. Distinction between inputs and outputs is usually clear when the output is a tangible commodity, but the distinction is often impossible to make when the output is some intangible service, for usually it becomes impossible to get clear measures of both inputs and outputs. It is relatively easy to measure the inputs into the provision of police or fire services, but the outputs are not nearly so evident. Because of the inability to specify objectively the output of a public bureau, resource cost rather than product output has become a primary indicator of a bureau's output; the amount spent on inputs is the only objective indicator of the bureau's activity that is easily assessable. Public attention is riveted to the bureau's inputs, and budgetary discussion takes place mostly with respect to inputs and their appropriate amounts.[16] With inputs rather than outputs tending to be equated with the bureau's production, the objective of maximizing the amount of output produced from given inputs tends to be replaced by an objective of maximizing the bureau's inputs, as inputs are more controllable than are outputs.[17]

[15] See William J. Baumol and Richard E. Quandt, "Rules of Thumb and Optimally Imperfect Decisions," *American Economic Review,* 54 (March 1964), 23–46.

[16] Rational decision requires a focus on outputs rather than on inputs, whereas political competition tends to operate so as to focus on inputs rather than on outputs. On this conflict, see James R. Schlesinger, "Systems Analysis and the Political Process," *Journal of Law and Economics,* 11 (October 1968), 281–98.

[17] Another source of inefficiency in the performance of bureaus has been attributed to the loss of control associated with creation of noise in the communication system of a hierarchical organization. See the clear description of this phenomenon in Gordon Tullock, *The Politics of Bureaucracy* (Washington, D.C.: Public Affairs Press, 1965), pp. 137–220. Oliver E. Williamson, "Hierarchical Control and Optimum Firm Size," *Journal of Political Economy,* 75 (April 1967), 123–38, shows that this loss of control exists also for private firms, and it is probably the most significant reason why returns to scale eventually decrease.

OUTPUT CHOICE WITHIN A BUREAUCRACY

One bureau does not operate in isolation from other bureaus. If we assume that the public budget is fixed in size, the flow of resources to one bureau can be increased only at the expense of another bureau, whose flow of resources will be decreased. The interests of the various bureaus that comprise the bureaucracy would thus seem to conflict, at least to some extent. Because one bureau is unlikely to remain passive and allow another bureau to take resources away from it, some form of competition among bureaus will exist. Such competitive processes limit the discretion of bureaucratic decision-makers and force some elements of competition on them. We must examine the properties of such competitive pressures, and ask to what extent the competition among bureaus and the bargaining that results is likely to form a public analogue to the invisible hand.[18]

Competition among public agencies has unappreciated merits. Such fragmentation of functions as exists between the Corps of Engineers and the Bureau of Reclamation is usually condemned. It is almost unanimously suggested that centralization would be superior, for it would enable us to avoid a duplication of functions. It is this spirit that motivated President Nixon's 1971 proposal to rearrange his cabinet offices (aside from Defense, State, Treasury, and Justice) into departments of Natural Resources, Human Resources, Community Development, and Economic Affairs.

But centralization also has costs, which tend to be ignored in the condemnation of fragmentation. The greater the centralization, the fewer the views of the future that go into producing and determining actions to be taken. The whole debate over the relative merits of large and small dams—although predicated on the assumption that dams of some size or other were worthwhile—resulted from competition between the Corps of Engineers and the Bureau of Reclamation, two separate agencies that build dams. Centralization reduces the ability of a bureaucracy to adapt to future exigencies. This cost is especially great in cases where future courses of action are higly uncertain, as in the centralization of education.[19]

Competition among bureaus in a bureaucracy can have effects similar to competition among firms in an industry. If bureaus compete among themselves for the right to supply a sponsor, the demand curve faced by any one bureau becomes more elastic. Hence, the ability of the bureau to

---

[18] These issues are raised in McKean, "The Unseen Hand in Government."

[19] These issues are examined carefully in McKean, *Public Spending*, pp. 147–52.

In addition to reducing the alternatives that are explored, centralization aggravates conflict among individuals. Under centralization, dissidents have no place else to go, so they must fight rather than switch. With the greater variety that exists under decentralization, greater homogeneity results and conflict is lessened.

act as if it were a discriminating monopoly is reduced, thereby retarding the tendency toward excessive supply. Currently, there may be substantial merit in creating a greater number of competing bureaus rather than in trying to consolidate bureaus. Such an action, moreover, will strengthen the adversary system within the bureaucracy. Bureaus that supply services that are weak substitutes for one another are less likely to stimulate effective adversary preceedings than are bureaus that provide close substitutes, for only the latter set of bureaus will contain the technical knowledge necessary to effectuate such proceedings.[20]

The fragmentation of government entailed in a decentralized form of government may also provide competition among bureaus. In some instances, a national bureau may be competitive with its counterpart state and local bureaus. Whatever other functions they may serve, conditional grants-in-aid operate to reduce such competitive pressures among bureaus. Conditional grants establish a cartel-like arrangement between a national bureau and the counterpart state bureaus. Aside from the existence of competing bureaus at the national level, the existence of similar bureaus at the state and local level is usually the only source of competition among bureaus within the bureaucracy. And conditional grants operate to constrict this latter form of competition.

Bureaucrats face a system of costs and rewards that influences the input and output choices of bureaus and the bureaucracy. Competition among bureaus provides an unseen hand in government, although it is presently one that seems to work with considerable imperfection. One of the most promising areas of research in the public economy lies in examining the performance of alternative institutional frameworks for strengthening the operation of this unseen hand.[21]

---

[20] On the contribution of an adversary system and its complementarity to cost-benefit analysis, see Henry S. Rowen, "Assessing the Role of Systematic Decision Making in the Public Sector," in Julius Margolis, ed., *The Analysis of Public Output* (New York: National Bureau of Economic Review, 1970), pp. 219–27.

[21] In this context, see the concluding remark in Jack Hirshleifer and Jerome W. Milliman, "Urban Water Supply: A Second Look," *American Economic Review, Proceedings,* 57 (May 1967), 169–78: "In the private sector, those who regularly commit mistakes lose control . . . over the disposition of resources. In the government sector, this process operates weakly, if at all. If appears that the agenda for economists . . . should place lower priority upon the further refinement of advice for those efficient and selfless administrators who may exist in never-never land. Rather it should center upon the devising of institutions whereby fallible and imperfect administrators may be forced to learn from error. In short, can we construct a 'hidden hand' for the government sector" (p. 178).

II

The Instruments of

Public Financing

8. User Pricing, Tax Earmarking, and Trust Funding

As a means of financing the supply of public services, user pricing is an alternative to taxation, borrowing, and money creation. During fiscal 1970, revenue from user charges exceeded 30 percent of state revenue and comprised nearly 35 percent of local revenue.[1] In its pure form, the supply of a service by government through user pricing operates identical to the supply of a service by a business firm through market pricing. In both cases, people can consume the service only by paying the required price, and the supply of the service is financed by the revenue derived from the sale of the service. For example, the output of both municipally and privately owned water companies is financed by revenue collected from the sale of their service. In cases where user pricing is not feasible for one reason or another, tax earmarking is a substitute means of financing services by charging the consumers of those services. Because financing highways by revenue derived from user pricing currently is not feasible, financing highways from the proceeds of a gasoline tax that is earmarked for a highway trust fund is a substitute means of charging highway users for the supply of highway services.

[1] These figures are computed from Table 1-6, with user charges defined to include revenues from insurance trust funds and with total revenue defined to exclude net debt issue. For careful discussions of the possible scope for user pricing in state and local government, see Alice J. Vandermeulen, "Reform of a State Fee Structure: Principles, Pitfalls, and Proposals for Increasing Revenue," *National Tax Journal,* 17 (December 1964), 394–402; and Jacob Stockfish, "Fees and Service Charges as Source of City Revenue: A Case Study of Los Angeles, *National Tax Journal,* 13 (June 1960), 97–121.

SOME PRINCIPLES OF USER PRICING

If user pricing is to be effective, three conditions usually must be satisfied. First, the service must be divisible among the users. Different people must be able to consume different amounts of the service. The user pricing of divisible services thus stands in contrast to the tax pricing of indivisible services. Because the output from a program of mosquito control is not divisible among the residents of the affected area, individuals cannot choose to purchase their preferred output of the service, and user pricing is not feasible. In contrast, the output from a municipally owned water company is divisible among consumers, and it is feasible to charge each consumer according to his consumption of water.

Second, the cost of administering the user charge must be relatively low; it must not be too costly to exclude those who do not pay the charge. It is relatively inexpensive to monitor a person's consumption of water and to charge him accordingly. It is relatively expensive to monitor a person's consumption of highway services. Although highway services are divisible among users, currently, it is not feasible to finance such services by user pricing.

Third, user pricing of a service becomes relatively more efficient as the elasticity of demand for that service increases. If, by contrast, the demand should be completely inelastic between the market price and a zero price, a user charge would perform no rationing function at all. Under such circumstances, the service could be made available at a zero price without increasing the quantity of the service demanded. In this respect, it is widely recognized that governments cannot efficiently supply at a zero price those divisible services for which the demand is fairly elastic between the market price and a zero price.

The specification of an appropriate principle to follow in setting user prices has been given considerable attention. As long as the service to be supplied is characterized by nondecreasing average cost, the principle of pricing is relatively simple. If average cost is decreasing, however, the choice of a user price becomes more complex.

Figure 8-1 illustrates the selection of a user price when average cost is nondecreasing. The rule for efficient pricing in this case is to set price equal to marginal cost, which gives the equilibrium rate of output, X_0, and price P_0. Any price other than P_0 is inefficient, for at any other price, the marginal value of the service will differ from the marginal cost. If price is set at P_1, for instance, the value of a marginal unit of the service exceeds the value of the marginal unit of the other output that must be sacrificed to get the additional X. This divergence is shown as ab in Figure 8-1. Similarly, if price is set at P_2, the value of the marginal unit of X falls

FIGURE 8-1
User Pricing with Nondecreasing Average Cost

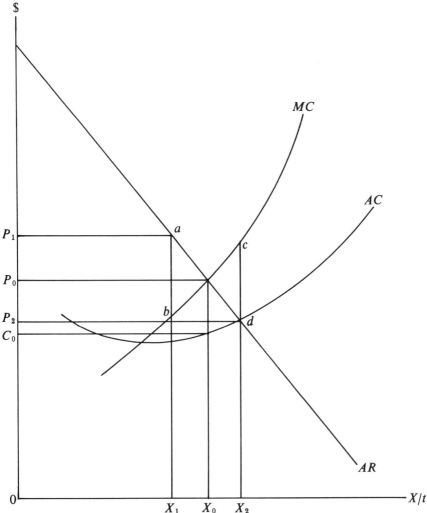

short of the value of the marginal unit of the other output that must be
sacrificed to produce X. This divergence is shown as cd in Figure 8-1.
Only when price is set at P_0 will the value of the marginal unit of X equal
the value of the marginal unit of whatever must be sacrificed in exchange.

Because the average cost of the output rate X_0 is C_0, a profit of
$P_0 - C_0$ per unit is being earned. The existence of profit attracts new investment in a competitive industry. Because the selection of an efficient

user price is regarded as one of simulating a competitive industry, the existence of profit would elicit additional investment in the supply of X. If a park is the service being financed, the profitability criterion would indicate that the size and/or quality of the park should be increased. Conversely, the earning of a loss on the supply of some service would call for a contraction in investment, which, again, is what would transpire in a competitive industry.[2]

When average cost is decreasing, however, a rule of marginal cost pricing is no longer so applicable. With decreasing cost, marginal cost pricing will not generate sufficient revenue to cover cost. As depicted in Figure 8-2, marginal cost pricing entails a price of P_0 and an output rate of X_0. When output is X_0, however, average cost is C_0. In this instance, a loss of $C_0 - P_0$ per unit of output thus results from marginal cost pricing. With average cost pricing, by contrast, price will be P_1 and the rate of output will be X_1. Losses will no longer be incurred, but the value placed on X_1 will exceed the marginal cost of that rate of output by *ab*, which indicates inefficiency in the allocation of resources.

When average cost is decreasing, apparently, a conflict emerges among alternative rules for setting the price and supplying the service. We should note, however, that this conflict is largely self-imposed by the conventional requirement that average price should equal marginal price. Without the convention that price should be uniform over quantity, the dilemma presented by user pricing would lose much of its force.[3] Consider the situation at the output rate, X_2, in Figure 8-2. With uniform pricing, *cd* indicates the amount per unit by which average cost will exceed average revenue. But now consider the choice of consumers of X when faced with a choice between X_2 and X_0. The average revenue curve shows the maximum amount that consumers would be willing to pay for an expansion in output beyond X_2, which is X_2d. The cost to consumers of an expansion in output is given by the marginal cost curve, X_2e. When output is X_2, then, consumers of X value additional X at more than the cost of additional X. Gains from the trade between buyers and sellers thus remain unexploited as long as the rate of output is less than X_0. If the transaction cost were relatively low, consumers would themselves agree to some scheme of nonuniform pricing to permit the attainment of X_0. At X_0, the price paid for the marginal unit of X would be P_0, which would be equal

[2] A government may practice monopoly pricing and use the monopoly profit to finance the general budget. Such pricing is practiced, for instance, by state-owned liquor stores where private competition is illegal.

[3] For an examination of the need to distinguish between the average price paid for an entire bundle and the price paid for the marginal addition to that bundle, see James M. Buchanan, "A Public Choice Approach to Public Utility Pricing," *Public Choice*, 5 (Fall 1968), 1–17.

FIGURE 8-2
User Pricing with Decreasing Average Cost

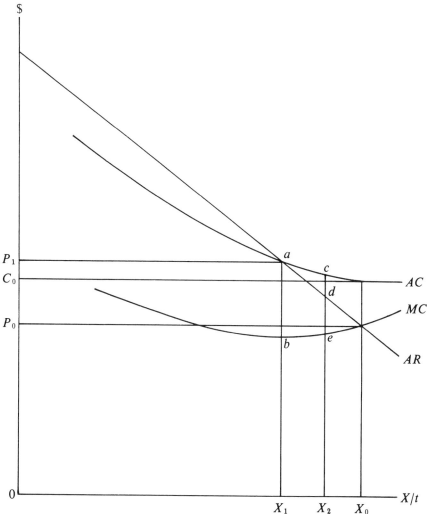

to marginal cost. In this trading equilibrium, the marginal price of X thus differs from the average price.

For average price to differ from marginal price, at least two forms of charging for X must be used. Such pricing formulas are institutionalized in a multi-part pricing tariff, in which two or more charges are levied. A service may be financed by levying both a charge that varies directly with amount consumed and a charge that is independent of consumption. A golf club, for instance, may levy both a flat annual fee and a per unit fee for each round of golf. Similarly, telephone services are financed by using a fixed installation charge and a price that varies directly with the amount of service consumed. Although their specific features may differ from case to case, a multi-part pricing scheme is an institutional means of creating a divergence between the average price of a service and the marginal price.[4] Thus, not only can a multi-part tariff reconcile the conflict between average cost and marginal cost pricing, but it may be preferred by all consumers of X to the results that would transpire under uniform pricing.[5]

User pricing has considerable merit as a means of securing efficiency in public output. When user pricing is used in place of general fund financing, consumer responses to the price and output choices of suppliers transmit stronger signals concerning desired rates of supply. Consumer purchases convey information about relative preferences, and this information is an ingredient in the process by which resources become allocated to more highly valued uses. If a single service is sold via user pricing, the information generated by consumer purchases is clear: the earning of a profit, which indicates that the service is valued more highly than other services, signals for an expansion in the output of the activity. But if several services are sold jointly via a general budget, information concerning profit or loss tells little about which services to expand or to contract. Thus, price is less sensitive as a conveyor of information when several services are jointly supplied by a general budget than when a single service is supplied by user pricing.[6]

There is considerable scope for vigorous implementation of user pricing; areas in which some user pricing is now feasible include highway and

[4] A classical treatment of multi-part pricing is Roland H. Coase, "The Marginal Cost Controversy," *Economica,* 13 (August 1946), 169–82.

[5] The feasibility of user pricing, of course, varies inversely with the transaction cost of the pricing scheme. A multi-part tariff may in some instances entail transaction costs that are sufficiently high to make them infeasible. In such circumstances, we would still confront the conflict between average cost and marginal cost pricing. Uniform pricing at marginal cost would then entail a loss, and this deficit would have to be covered in some manner. The use of taxation to cover this deficit will also entail inefficiency, and the amount of this inefficiency would have to be compared with the transaction cost of the multi-part tariff before a judgment could be reached about which means of financing is more efficient.

[6] See Richard E. Wagner, *The Fiscal Organization of American Federalism* (Chicago: Markham, 1971), pp. 52–54.

Moreover, user pricing raises questions concerning the alleged exploitation of city residents by suburban residents. Many facilities such as parks, museums, and shopping facilities that are used by suburban residents are amenable to user pricing. Admission can be charged for parks and museums. Shopping facilities can be priced indirectly by charging for parking in the downtown area. Similarly, charges could be levied for many other services currently provided without charge. Thus the city could eliminate much of the alleged exploitation by undertaking more extensive user pricing.

parking services, education, library and recreational facilities, museums, health services, and refuse collection.[7] Nevertheless, finding that user pricing is preferable to taxation in some particular instance does not end our analytical task. A particular pricing scheme must be specified, and the choice of a particular scheme is by no means inconsequential. For instance, James A. Johnson examined ten reasonable formulas currently used for setting user charges for sewers and found an enormous variation in the percentage of the total charge placed on various users.[8] The percentage of the burden placed on residential users ranged from 33.1 percent to 94.2 percent. On commercial users, the burden ranged from 5.3 percent to 25.7 percent, while the burden on industrial users ranged from 0.4 percent to 51.2 percent. Johnson estimated that residential users would pay 94.2 percent of all charges if charges were uniform per user. With a uniform charge per user, commercial and industrial users would pay only 5.3 and 0.4 percent respectively. Residential users would pay only 33.1 percent if charges were a constant rate per pound of sewage discharged, while industrial users would pay 51.2 percent. The highest relative payment for commercial users, 25.7 percent, would result when charges were levied proportionate to assessed property value.

TAX EARMARKING AND TRUST FUNDING

Tax earmarking is a substitute for user pricing as a means of financing the supply of a public service. As an alternative to the direct charge on consumers for their use of a service, a tax can be levied on the consumption of a closely related product, with the proceeds earmarked for expenditure on a designated service. For example, highways are financed to a considerable extent from the proceeds of taxes on gasoline and related products. Because the consumption of gasoline, which determines tax liability, corresponds closely to the consumption of highway services, an earmarked gasoline tax is a close substitute for user pricing of highway services.[9]

---

[7] For discussions of user pricing in terms of potential applicability, see Werner Z. Hirsch, *The Economics of State and Local Government* (New York: McGraw-Hill, 1970), pp. 43–47; William S. Vickrey, "General and Specific Financing of Urban Services," in Howard G. Schaller, ed., *Public Expenditure Decisions in the Urban Community* (Washington, D.C.: Resources for the Future, 1963), pp. 62–90; and Milton Z. Kafoglis, "Local Service Charges," in Harry L. Johnson, ed., *State and Local Tax Problems* (Knoxville: University of Tennessee Press, 1969), pp. 164–86.

[8] James A. Johnson, "The Distribution of the Burden of Sewer User Charges Under Various Charge Formulas," *National Tax Journal*, 22 (December 1969), 472–85.

[9] This assumes that the gasoline tax is paid by consumers of gasoline rather than by producers. Such an issue of incidence exists for any earmarked tax, and we shall examine these issues in Chapter 11.

Earmarking is an alternative to general fund financing as a means of financing public services. Rather than financing the supply of highway services from a trust fund maintained by the revenue from an earmarked gasoline tax, the tax revenue could be placed directly in the general fund, in which case decisions concerning highway finance would emerge from the general budgetary process. When several public services are financed simultaneously through a general fund rather than individually through an earmarked tax, a form of tie-in sale is created. The services supplied from the general fund are offered as a package, and the package must be purchased as a unit. The services supplied through the general fund will have varying elasticities of demand, and both the consumers and the supplying bureaus of services with elastic demands will secure a larger expenditure if they can tie in the sale of their service to the sale of a service with an inelastic demand. Conversely, both the consumers and the supplying bureaus of services with inelastic demand will secure a larger expenditure for their service if they can have it financed by earmarked taxation.[10]

When several services are sold as a package, the effective elasticity of demand is a weighted average of the demand elasticities of the individual services. Suppose the elasticity of demand is -1.4 for one service and -0.6 for the other. If the budget is distributed equally between the two services, the effective demand elasticity becomes -1.0 for each service. Thus, the effective demand elasticity is lowered for the service with the elastic demand and raised for the service with the inelastic demand. The tie-in sale that results from general-fund financing increases expenditure on the demand elastic service relative to the demand inelastic service. Under such circumstances, a conflict of interest will arise between the consumers and producers of service with elastic demands and those with inelastic demands.

An earmarked tax, of course, is not a charge, but only a proxy for a price. Moreover, no competitive market exists to keep this pseudo-price at its appropriate level. For these reasons, there may be a disequilibrium between the amount of the service demanded and the amount of revenue collected.[11] As income grows over time, equilibrium automatically will persist only if the income elasticity of demand is equal to the revenue elasticity of the earmarked tax, which, in turn, approximately is equal to the income elasticity of demand for the item subject to the earmarked tax.

If the income elasticity of demand for highway services is unity, a

[10] On tax earmarking, see James M. Buchanan, "The Economics of Earmarked Taxes," *Journal of Political Economy,* 71 (October 1963), 457–69; and Charles J. Goetz, "Earmarked Taxes and Majority Rule Budgetary Processes," *American Economic Review,* 58 (March 1968), 128–36.

[11] Walter W. McMahon and Case M. Sprenkle, "A Theory of Earmarking," *National Tax Journal,* 23 (September 1970), 255–61.

ten percent rise in income will generate a 10 percent rise in demand for highway services. The revenue to finance the supply of highway service, however, is determined in the market for gasoline, as there is no market for highway services. If the income elasticity of demand for gasoline is unity and the amount of highway service consumed per gallon of gasoline remains unchanged, a 10 percent rise in income will also generate a 10 percent rise in revenue from the gasoline tax. If, however, the income elasticity of demand for gasoline is less than unity, earmarked revenue will fall short of the demand for highway services unless the rate of tax is increased. Or, if the income elasticity of demand for gasoline exceeds unity, earmarked revenues will exceed the demand for highway services unless the tax rate is reduced. While we might expect some tendency for political competition to rectify any disequilibrium, the less perfectly such competition operates, the longer a disequilibrium can persist.

Clearly, tax earmarking is an imperfect substitute for user pricing. Financing highways from the revenue generated by an earmarked gasoline tax places the cost of highway facilities on the consumers of gaoline, which gives tax earmarking some characteristics similar to user pricing. But earmarking is a crude form of pricing, for the charge varies with gasoline consumption, not with highway consumption. Moreover, a consumer's payment depends on neither the time nor the place of consumption. Thus, tax earmarking, unlike user pricing, can do nothing to alleviate the peak load congestion that plagues our highway facilities. Only by user pricing, where price would vary according to the time and place of consumption, could highway facilities be effectively rationed.[12]

Some people contend that the highway trust fund encourages excessive investment in highway facilities. They propose that some of the earmarked revenues should be diverted to the financing of mass transit systems. This line of criticism, however, is not so much an argument against tax earmarking as it is an argument maintaining that the service being financed by earmarked revenues has been specified improperly. Instead of financing *highway services,* for instance, the earmarked revenues could be used to finance *transit services,* which would include both highways and

---

[12] For a discussion of the feasibility of metering and monitoring street usage, see William S. Vickrey, "Pricing in Urban and Suburban Transport," *American Economic Review,* Proceedings, 53 (May 1963), 452–65.

Imagine telephone service financed in the same manner as is highway service. A user would be charged a flat fee per minute, regardless of the time at which he places his calls. Because rates would remain the same regardless of time, peak-load congestion would be exacerbated. Similarly, one could imagine highway services priced in the same manner as telephone services. With price being varied according to the time of use, peak-load congestion would be diminished, as some people would be induced to travel at different times and others would be induced to adopt alternative modes of transit.

mass transit. If private transit and public transit entail reciprocal externalities, user pricing of one service, let alone tax earmarking, need not promote an efficient allocation of resources.[13]

THE SOCIAL SECURITY TRUST FUND

The dominant form of tax earmarking and trust funding in the United States is the Social Security program, which had revenues exceeding $50 billion in fiscal 1971. In contrast, revenues of the highway trust fund were less than $6 billion. The Social Security program actually consists of three separate trust funds: the old-age and survivors insurance trust fund, the disability insurance trust fund, and the health insurance trust fund. For 1974, the Social Security program will be financed by a tax of 11 percent for employees and 8.25 percent for the self-employed levied on the first $12,000 of earnings. Moreover, an unemployment insurance trust fund is financed by a 3.1 percent tax on earnings. While the unemployment tax and half of the social security tax are assessed against the employer rather than the employee, practically the entire 14.1 percent is paid by the employee.

Figure 8-3 illustrates the impact of the payroll tax on the level of wages. In the absence of tax, the wage rate is W_1 and the quantity of labor is l_1. The tax increases the cost of labor, which reduces the demand for labor from D to $D - t$. If the supply of labor is completely inelastic, which is indicated by S_1, the tax will be paid wholly by employees. If the supply of labor is given by S_1, the posttax return to labor falls from w_1 to w'_1 which is the amount of tax paid by the employer. To the extent that there is some elasticity in the supply of labor, which is indicated by S_2, the tax will reduce the quantity of labor supplied. This will generate some increase in gross-wages, thus shifting a small part of the tax to the buyers of labor—employers. If the labor supply curve is S_2, the tax will reduce the quantity of labor supplied to l_2, which increases the level of wages to w'_2. In this case, wages are lowered by only $w_1 - w'_2/w_2 - w'_2$ percent of the

[13] See James M. Buchanan and Gordon Tullock, "Public and Private Interaction Under Reciprocal Externality," pp. 52–73 in Julius Margolis, ed., *The Public Economy of Urban Communities* (Washington, D.C.: Resources for the Future, 1965); and Otto A. Davis and Andrew B. Whinston, "Externalities, Welfare, and the Theory of Games," *Journal of Political Economy,* 70 (June 1962), 241–62.

At the same time, however, the mere fact of automobile ownership carries a substantial commitment to automobile travel because average cost falls with use. This implies that without substantial change in the institutions of ownership, the scope for inducing changes in the mode of transit is quite limited. See Roger Sherman, "A Private Ownership Bias in Transit Choice," *American Economic Review,* 57 (December 1967), 1211–17.

FIGURE 8-3
Incidence of Payroll Taxation

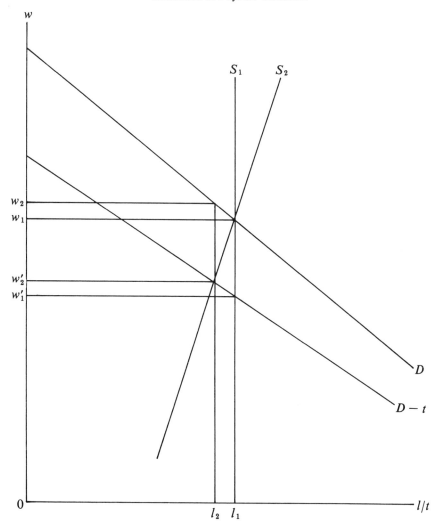

tax. Because the elasticity of the aggregate supply of labor is fairly low, the preponderance of the tax will be paid by employees. Distinguishing portions of the tax paid by employee and employer, then, merely serves to make taxpayers less aware of their real tax liability.[14]

[14] John A. Brittain, "The Incidence of Social Security Payroll Taxes," *American Economic Review*, 61 (March 1971), 110–25, found it impossible to reject the hypothesis that payroll taxes are paid by labor.

The Social Security system was initiated as a program for retirement insurance. As with any insurance program, the Social Security program would have to accumulate reserves in an actuarially sound manner. If Social Security were operated according to insurance principles, a person would contribute funds during his working years and consume the principal and interest during his retirement years. The Social Security system has never been operated in an actuarially sound manner, however, and it now possesses an unfunded liability of about $400 billion. The system has actually been operated as a means of transferring income from those who are working to those who are retired. Retirees receive payments considerably higher than their contributions justify, and this subsidy is paid by employed workers.

Nevertheless, recognition that Social Security may be viewed more fruitfully as an intergenerational compact for the transfer of income than as an insurance program is increasing.[15] It is possible to look on a worker as transferring part of his income to government to finance retirees in exchange for the agreement of government to finance their own retirement in a similar manner.[16] Such an intergenerational compact produces a rate of return on retirement contributions equal to the sum of the real rate of growth in per capita income and the rate of growth in the labor force. If real per capita income grows at an annual rate of 2 percent and if the labor force grows at 2 percent, a worker will receive a 4 percent real rate of return on his contributions.

Such an integenerational compact, however, is somewhat fragile. As long as per capita income and the labor force grow at constant rates, such an implicit contract might seem relatively secure. But continuous exponential growth is not a reasonable long-term expectation, and, in the absence of such steady exponential growth, this intergenerational compact will become increasingly fragile. We may illustrate these issues with a simple example. Suppose people work one period and are retired the next, and let real income and population both increase by 10 percent per period. Assume that average income per worker is initially $10,000, and is taxed at 10 percent to finance contributions to retirees. In the following period average income per worker will have risen to $11,000, and the labor force will have increased by 10 percent. Under such circumstances, a payroll tax of 10 percent would transfer $1,210 to each retiree, producing a 21 percent rate of return on contributions made during one's working period.

[15] For a discussion of different conceptions of Social Security, see Colin D. Campbell, "Social Insurance in the United States: A Program in Search of an Explanation," *Journal of Law and Economics,* 12 (October 1969), 249–65.
[16] The seminal statement of this perspective is Paul A. Samuelson, "An Exact Consumption-Loan Model of Interest With or Without the Social Contrivance of Money," *Journal of Political Economy,* 66 (December 1958), 467–82.

Suppose, however, that the rate of growth in the labor force falls to zero the next period. Average income per worker would have risen to $12,100, and this set of workers would have responsibility for financing the retirement of the previous set of workers. These retirees had contributed $1,100 during their working period, and to finance a transfer to these retirees that would reflect a 21 percent rate of return would require a payroll tax of 11 percent on present workers—an increase of 10 percent in the tax burden. A decline in the rate of growth of real per capita income, moreover, would exacerbate the intergenerational tax rate differential that would be required to maintain the intergenerational compact. A lengthening of life beyond retirement would have the same impact as a reduction in the rate of growth, as would a shortening of life spent working. In several respects, then, such an implicit intergenerational compact would seem relatively fragile.[17]

[17] James M. Buchanan, "Social Insurance in a Growing Economy: A Proposal for Radical Reform," *National Tax Journal,* 21 (December 1968), 386–95, in recognition of this inherent fragility, proposed that the present insurance scheme be retained, but that a person's contributions be accumulated at the larger of the rate of growth in nominal GNP or the interest rate on Treasury bonds. A contributor would receive Social Insurance Bonds that would accumulate at the appropriate rate and, upon retirement, he would redeem his bonds for a retirement annuity.

9. The Taxation of Personal Income

Liability for personal income tax, as for any tax, is determined by the product of a tax rate and a tax base. Essentially, the tax base is personal income, although various deductions and exemptions shrink the tax base to about one-half of personal income. The tax rate applied to this base is steeply progressive, with marginal rates for a married couple filing a joint return ranging from 14 percent on the first $1,000 of taxable income to 70 percent on taxable income in excess of $200,000. Taxation of personal income is the primary source of revenue for the national government, producing nearly half of all national revenues. Because it applies to everyone and especially because its rates are steeply progressive, the personal income tax has been the focus of considerable attention and the subject of extensive analysis. In this chapter, we shall examine the impact of the personal income tax on such variables as the distribution of income, the supply of labor, the supply of risk-taking, and the size of the public budget.

THE DEFINITION AND MEASUREMENT OF INCOME

The definition and measurement of income forms both the primary conceptual and the primary administrative problem associated with personal income taxation. It is notable that Henry Simons' still timely treatise on the taxation of personal income was subtitled, "The Definition of Income as a Problem of Fiscal Policy."[1] The fiscal literature contains two primary

[1] Henry C. Simons, *Personal Income Taxation* (Chicago: University of Chicago Press, 1938). For evidence on the timeliness of Simons' work, see Kenneth LeM. Carter, "Canadian Tax Reform and Henry Simons," *Journal of Law and Economics,* 11 (October 1968), 231–42; and John Bossons, "The Value of a Comprehensive Tax Base as a Tax Reform Goal," *Journal of Law and Economics,* 13 (October 1970), 327–63.

definitions of income, income as a flow and income as an accretion. Under the accretion definition, income is the sum of consumption and changes in net wealth over some period of time.[2] Under the flow definition, income is the net value of payments received by an individual over some period of time. While these two definitions usually produce identical measures of income, instances in which they differ are notable. Moreover, it seems reasonable to say that the accretion definition of income is considered conceptually superior while the flow definition is considered administratively more convenient.

Under either definition, a person who receives wages of $10,000 per year and has no assets would be considered to have an income of $10,000. When an individual owns assets or saves part of his income, however, the two definitions of income may produce different measures of income. Assume that a person owns stock that was valued at $5,000 at the beginning of the year and appreciated to $6,000 during the year. Under the accretion definition, the appreciation would be defined as income because the person could consume this $1,000 and still maintain his initial capital value. In contrast, the appreciation would not be income under the flow definition, for the mere appreciation of the asset does not represent a flow of payments to the individual. Whether the value of the stock rises, falls, or remains unchanged does not affect the flow of payments to a taxpayer. Gains or losses are realized when the asset is sold and it is at this time that they are counted as income. Thus, unrealized capital gains are income under the accretion definition of income, but not under the flow definition. With respect to unrealized capital gains, the flow definition seems administratively more convenient. For example, effective administration of the accretion definition would require estimates of annual changes in the value of assets. It seems much simpler for administrative purposes to ignore annual changes in the value of assets and to count the sum of annual changes as income when the assets are sold, which is appropriate for the flow definition.

Another difference between the two definitions arises in connection with the contention that the taxation of interest income is double taxation of saving. This claim is correct under the flow definition of income, but not under the accretion definition. Consider a person who earns $10,000 in each of two years. In each year he saves $1,000, and in the second year, he receives $100 interest on his savings from the first year. Under the accretion definition, his income is $10,000 for the first year and $10,100 for the second. In the first year, he consumes $9,000 and in-

[2] For a thorough examination of the conceptual basis of alternative definitions of income, see Simons, *Personal Income Taxation,* pp. 41–102.

creases his wealth by $1,000, while in the second year he consumes $9,000 and increases his wealth by $1,100. In contrast, under the flow definition, his income is $10,000 in each year. In the first year, he receives a payment flow valued at $10,000, of which he chooses to consume $9,000 and to save $1,000. In the second year, he again receives a payment flow valued at $10,000. The $100 receipt of interest is not a new flow to him, but merely represents a consequence of the use of last year's flow.

Additional problems arise once it is recognized that not all income is received in a monetary form. Nonmonetary forms of income usually present extremely difficult issues of measurement. A familiar illustration of income accruing in nonmonetary form is the case of the farmer who feeds his family from food grown on his farm. His monetary income is the revenue from the sale of his crop. The value of the crops consumed by the farmer's family is also income, but it is not assigned a monetary measure through a market transaction. The value of a housewife's services is similar to the farmer's own consumption. The housewife produces something of value for the family, something that otherwise would have been purchased on the market. The income of an Army private is another example; this income is understated significantly, for in addition to a monthly salary of $288, the private receives his meals, his housing, and his medical care free of charge. Such durable goods as owner-occupied housing also produce nonmonetary sources of income for the family. Expense accounts and company cars are another source of nonmonetary income.[3] Sources of nonmonetary intangible income could be expanded indefinitely. Nonpecuniary advantages associated with working conditions or geographical location are a form of nonmonetary income. A person who works under pleasant conditions or lives in a desired location will not switch to a less pleasant working arrangement or location if additional compensation is not offered. If he is being paid $10,000 for doing pleasant work in pleasant surroundings and a salary of $11,000 were the minimum that could induce him to switch jobs, the value of the pleasantness is worth $1,000 to him.[4]

Once income has been defined and measured, the problems of selecting the unit to whom the income is attributed and the time period over which the measurement is made remains. There is a difference in whether the taxable unit is defined as an individual recipient or a family unit. A

---

[3] The general rule is that such nonmonetary income is taxable if it is received as a part of salary, but not if it is received as a part of employment.

[4] While there is a problem of including certain nonmonetary elements in the definition of income, there is also a problem of excluding certain monetary elements from the definition of income. Not all receipts are necessarily income, for some receipts may reflect the cost of earning income. If a particular job, for instance, should require its practitioners to purchase special clothing or equipment, the resulting payments would be a cost of earning income.

single person with a taxable income of $10,000 will pay a tax of $2,090. A married couple in which one member earns the entire $10,000 will pay only $1,820. Similarly, a person whose taxable income is $8,000 one year and $16,000 another will pay total taxes of $5,420 over a two-year period, but a person with an annual taxable income of $12,000 for two years will pay only $5,260. If income were to be measured over a two-year period, however, both individuals would have equal incomes and hence would pay equal amounts of tax.[5]

INCOME TAXATION AND THE ALLOCATION OF EFFORT

Income taxation may influence both the amount of time a person devotes to earning income and the form in which income is earned. Four possible consequences of income taxation for the allocation of effort will be distinguished. First, income taxation may affect the proportion of a person's time spent earning income through market transactions, for income taxation reduces the net return per unit of such effort. Second, by altering the relative returns to different occupations, income taxation may influence the relative supply of labor among occupations. Third, because only monetary forms of income are taxed, income taxation may increase the relative share of income taken in nonmonetary forms. Fourth, income taxation increases the profitability of effort devoted to tax avoidance and evasion and to seeking special tax concessions.

Income Taxation and the Aggregate Supply of Effort

A perennial topic of fiscal analysis is the effect of income taxation on the absolute supply of effort.[6] On the one hand, increases in the rate of tax reduce the net return per hour of effort, thus discouraging effort. On the

[5] We should note that the selection of the taxable unit and the time period create such variability in tax liability only when tax rates are progressive. Under proportional taxation, by contrast, tax liability is unaffected by arbitrary selection of the taxable unit or the period of observation.

[6] For a sample of a voluminous field of literature, see Richard A. Musgrave, *The Theory of Public Finance* (New York: McGraw-Hill, 1959), pp. 232–46; Malcolm Levitt, "Comparison of the Equilibrium Labor Supply Under Proportional and Progressive Taxation," *Journal of Political Economy,* 72 (October 1964), 496–97; Henry J. Cassidy, "Work Effort Under Proportional and Progressive Taxation," *Journal of Political Economy,* 78 (No. 5, 1970), 1163–67; Robin Barlow and Gordon R. Sparks, "A Note on Progression and Leisure," *American Economic Review,* 54 (June 1964), 372–77; and John G. Head, "A Note on Progression and Leisure: Comment," *American Economic Review,* 56 (March 1966), 172–79. For an earlier work, see Richard Goode, "The Income Tax and the Supply of Labor," *Journal of Political Economy,* 57 (October 1949), 428–37.

FIGURE 9-1
Allocation of Time Between Leisure and Earning Income: No Taxation

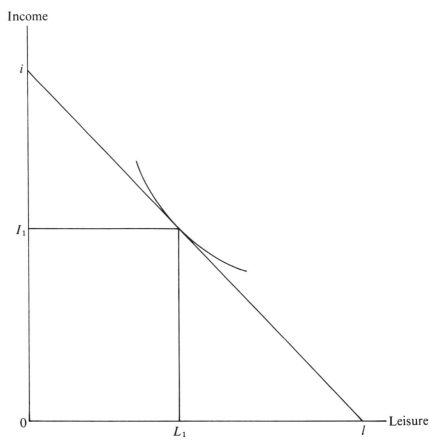

other hand, increases in the rate of tax reduce a person's net income, which may stimulate him to greater effort to recoup part of the loss.

In the 24 hours that comprise each day, an individual is free to allocate his time between earning income and taking leisure. Leisure is command over one's own time; by earning money income, one gains command over the time of others. When the individual gives up leisure by choosing to work, he relinquishes command over some of his own time in exchange for command over the time of others. Clearly, the distribution of a person's time between these two uses will depend on his preferences for use of his own time on the one hand and his preference for use of the time of others on the other. It also will depend on the rate at which he can gain command over the time of others by relinquishing command over his own time. These considerations are illustrated in Figure 9-1. On the Y-axis, we measure a person's income, and on the X-axis we measure a person's leisure. The slope of the budget constraint, *il,* is the negative of the hourly wage rate. If the hourly wage rate is $3, for instance, the budget constraint intersects the income axis at $72, and it intersects the leisure axis at 24 hours. The persons' preference for own time vis-à-vis other's time is indicated by the indifference curve. The most preferred position is indicated by the point of tangency of the highest indifference curve to the given budget constraint. The person depicted in Figure 9-1 would take L_1 hours of leisure per day and earn I_1 of income.[7]

Now suppose a 40 percent proportional income tax is imposed. What will happen to the individual's allocation of time betwen effort and leisure? The tax reduces the posttax return on effort to $1.80 per hour. The budget constraint, which is the negative of the net wage, pivots downward to *i'l* in Figure 9-2. The effect of the tax on the choice between effort and leisure would appear to be ambiguous. As is illustrated by the three different indifferent curves tangent to *i'l,* the person may take more leisure, less leisure, or the same amount of leisure, depending on the shape of his indifference map.

Yet the situation described by Figure 9-2 is inconsistent in a general equilibrium setting. It is impossible to impose a general tax without some type of offsetting effect taking place. If the government freezes the tax proceeds, the price level will fall and, ignoring real balance effects, the $1.80 wage will be equivalent in real terms to the initial $3 wage, which means that the tax will have no effect on the supply of effort. Other possibilities are that the income tax will replace another tax or that the revenue will be used to finance the supply of some public service. In either event, there will be no reduction in real income for the community as a whole. The case in which the tax proceeds are spent to finance the supply of a public service that confers general benefits on the entire populace is illustrated in Figure 9-3. Because there has been no loss of real income, the posttax budget constraint becomes *i*l*.*[8] The price of leisure has fallen relative to the price of earning income, but real income has remained unchanged.

---

[7] Working habits are largely institutionalized, of course, so a person is not usually able to select his most preferred combination of work and leisure. Yet an equilibrium workday comes to be established, and market competition will tend to produce a workday equal to the workday generally preferred by the labor force.

[8] The impact on the amount of leisure demanded will vary depending on whether the public service is primarily complementary to the consumption of leisure or to the consumption of private goods and services. The construction of Figure 9-3 assumes neutrality, which seems the appropriate assumption in the absence of special evidence to the contrary. On this issue, see Gordon Winston, "Taxes, Leisure and Public Goods," *Economica,* 32 (February 1965), 65–69.

FIGURE 9-2
Allocation of Time Between Leisure and Earning Income: Proportional Taxation

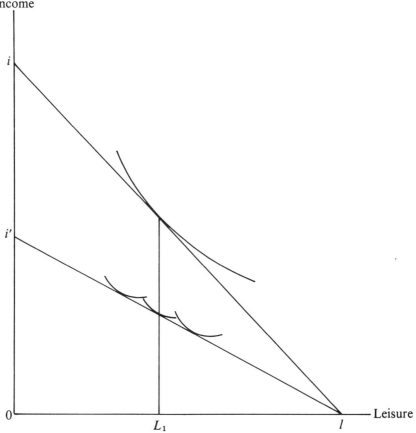

Under these circumstances, the proportional income tax increases the amount of leisure demanded from L_1 to L_2, thus reducing the supply of effort. Furthermore, the higher the rate of tax, the stronger the reduction in the supply of effort.

It is impossible to generalize the analysis to progressive taxation, however, for income effects are an inherent part of progressive taxation. It can be shown that the replacement of a proportional income tax with a progressive income tax of equal yield *as applied to a single person* will reduce that person's supply of effort still further. And the more progressive the tax, the greater the reduction in the supply of effort. But the choice between proportional and progressive income taxation cannot be conducted and examined within a context in which each person pays the same

FIGURE 9-3
Allocation of Time Between Leisure and Earning Income: Proportional
Taxation and Public Expenditure

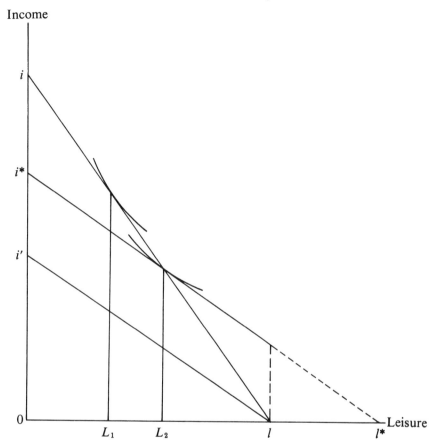

tax bill. The whole idea of progressive income taxation is that some persons will pay more while others will pay less. Thus, income effects are
an integral part of the analysis: once income effects are introduced, we
encounter the problem that income effects and substitution effects may operate in opposing directions.[9]

The substitution effect is determined by the marginal rate of tax; the
income effect is determined by the average rate of tax. An increase in the
marginal rate of tax reduces the price of leisure, which increases the

[9] On this distinction between analysis applicable to an individual and analysis
applicable to an entire community, see Musgrave, *Theory of Public Finance* pp.
241–46; and Head, "Progression and Leisure."

amount of leisure demanded. An increase in the average tax rate reduces net income, which decreases the demand for leisure. Changes in the same direction in marginal and average rates of tax thus have opposing effects on the demand for leisure and the supply of effort. The effect on average and marginal rates of tax of replacing a proportional income tax with a progressive tax of equal yield is illustrated in Figure 9-4. Under proportional income taxation, the average rate of tax equals the marginal rate of tax. With progressive income taxation, the marginal rate of tax exceeds the average rate of tax.

The replacement of proportional taxation with progressive taxation of equal yield creates three distinct sets of citizens, indicated by *A, B,* and *C* in Figure 9-4. Only for the middle income group, *B,* is the effect

FIGURE 9-4
Income and Substitution Effects Under Progressive Taxation

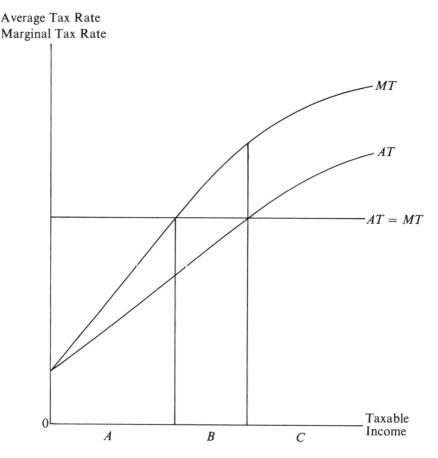

of progression unambiguous. As the marginal rate of tax is increased, the amount of leisure demanded is increased and the average rate of tax is reduced, also increasing the demand for leisure. For the lower income group, *A*, the substitution effect, given by the marginal rate of tax, operates to reduce leisure. But the income effect, given by the average rate of tax, operates to increase leisure. For the upper income group, *C*, the increased marginal rate of tax tends to increase leisure and the increased average rate of tax tends to reduce it.

Since we are caught in a theoretical impasse concerning the impact of income taxation on aggregate supply of effort, empirical analysis is appropriate. Yet changes in the supply of labor in response to changes in taxation can manifest themselves in subtle ways, which magnifies the difficulties of empirical testing. Harberger, for instance, conjectured that tax-induced reductions in the supply of labor primarily have taken the form of: (1) longer vacations; (2) earlier retirement; (3) less labor force participation by women; and (4) less supplemental income.[10]

Perhaps the best known empirical study of the effect of taxation on the supply of effort is Break's study of British accountants and lawyers, a study that recently has been replicated by Fields and Stanbury.[11] Ten percent of Break's sample stated that high tax rates created an incentive to supply additional effort, while 13 percent stated that high tax rates created a disincentive. In their follow-up survey, Fields and Stanbury found that 11 percent stated that high tax rates induced them to supply more labor, an increase of 1 percent from that reported by Break. They also found that 19 percent of their sample stated that high tax rates induced them to supply less labor, an increase of 6 percent from that reported by Break.[12]

Obviously, the impact of a tax depends on what taxpayers perceive as taking place, not what is taking place in some underlying real sense. Wagstaff, for instance, found that the withholding of income reduced a taxpayer's awareness of his tax liability. Wagstaff found that high-income groups actually paid significantly higher rates of tax than they thought they

[10] Arnold C. Harberger, "Taxation, Resource Allocation, and Welfare." in National Bureau of Economic Research-Brookings Institution, *The Role of Direct and Indirect Taxes in the Federal Revenue System* (Princeton, N.J.: Princeton University Press, 1964), p. 50.
[11] George F. Break, "Income Taxes and Incentives to Work: An Empirical Study," *American Economic Review*, 47 (September 1957), 529–49; Donald B. Fields and W. T. Stanbury, "Incentives, Disincentives, and the Income Tax," *Public Finance*, 25 (No. 3, 1970), 381–415.
[12] In another recent study, Holland found that 15 percent of those sampled stated that high tax rates induced them to supply less labor. Daniel M. Holland, "The Effect of Taxation on Effort: Some Results for Business Executives," *1969 Proceedings of the National Tax Association* (Columbus, Ohio: National Tax Association, 1970), pp. 428–516.

paid.[13] Similarly, Gensemer, Lean, and Neenan found that 27 percent of their sample of high-income taxpayers were unaware of the marginal rate of tax they paid.[14] To the extent that taxpayers are only partially aware of real rates at which they pay tax, the disincentive effect of high rates of tax will be softened. Our theoretical analysis of the effect of taxation on the supply of effort is based on the assumption that taxpayers are aware of the act on their real rate of tax. But empirical analysis captures actual behavior, which is based on perceived rates of tax. For this reason, empirical examination of the effect of income taxation on the supply of effort is perhaps as much a test of taxpayer awareness of real rates of tax as it is of the effect of taxation on the supply of effort.

Income Taxation and the Relative Supply of Effort

Income taxation will alter the relative returns among occupations. Hence, it will influence the relative supply of labor among occupations even if there is no impact on the aggregate supply of labor. This impact will occur under proportional taxation, and it will be even stronger under progressive taxation. The return to labor has both monetary and nonmonetary elements, and under proportional taxation, occupations with relatively large nonmonetary returns will be taxed less heavily than occupations with relatively small nonmonetary returns will be. While proportional taxation discriminates among individuals with different nonmonetary returns, progressive taxation discriminates among individuals by the size of their monetary returns.

Consider a simple model in which there are two occupations, *A* and *B*, and assume that *A* is a hazardous occupation. For the sake of illustration, let us suppose that the equilibrium annual returns to *A* and *B* are $10,000 and $8,000 respectively. At the margin, the $2,000 higher income in *A* represents the nonmonetary return in avoiding the hazardous occupation. Now introduce a proportional income tax of 20 percent. The posttax returns fall to $8,000 in *A* and $6,400 in *B*. The tax favors occupation *B* because nonmonetary elements are not included in the tax base. With the posttax differential reduced to $1,600, the labor market will be in disequilibrium. Labor will shift from *A* to *B* until the $2,000 differential is attained once again. A new equilibrium might be attained when, say, the pretax return in *A* rises to $10,250 while the pretax return in *B* falls to

[13] Joseph Van Wagstaff, "Income Tax Consciousness Under Withholding," *Southern Economic Journal*, 32 (July 1965), 73–80.
[14] Bruce L. Gensemer, James A. Lean, and William B. Neenan, "Awareness of Marginal Income Tax Rates Among High-Income Taxpayers," *National Tax Journal*, 19 (September 1965), 258–67.

$7,750. In this event, posttax returns in *A* and *B* will be $8,200 and $6,200 respectively, which maintains the $2,000 differential. The impact of the proportional income tax, then, is to increase the supply of labor in *B* relative to that in *A*.

Progressive income taxation will have an even stronger impact on the relative supply of labor, for the tax also discriminates against occupations on the basis of their monetary returns. If progressive taxation now replaces proportional taxation in the above illustration, the rate of tax paid by labor in *A* will exceed that paid by labor in *B*. The progressive tax thus narrows the differential between the two occupations to something less than $2,000. Once again, at the posttax structure of returns, there will be an excess demand for labor in *A* and an excess supply of labor in *B*. When equilibrium in the labor market has been restored, the labor force in *B* will have increased relative to *A* and the gross income in *A* will have increased relative to *B*. The relative supply of labor among occupations is governed by the net return among occupations, and taxation is one factor that influences the returns to different employments of labor. One of the implications of this analysis, of course, is that increases in progressivity will increase pretax differentials in income, thereby offsetting to some extent the redistributive impact of progressive taxation. The more that net income differences are due to equalizing differentials rather than to the existence of noncompeting groups, the less powerful will be the net redistributive impact of progressive income taxation.

Income Taxation and the Choice Between Monetary and Nonmonetary Forms of Income

By taxing only monetary forms of income, the personal income tax encourages the substitution of nonmonetary for monetary forms of income. The proliferation of such forms of nonmonetary income as pension plans, insurance plans, and expense accounts is at least partly a consequence of high rates of tax on personal monetary income.

Consider an employer who wants to increase an employee's net income by $1,000 per year. If the marginal rate of tax is 20 percent, the employer must increase his employee's gross income by $1,250. Thus, it costs the employer $1,250 to pay the employee an additional $1,000. Similarly, if the marginal rate of tax is 40 percent, it will cost the employer $1,667 to give the employee a net raise of $1,000.

As an alternative to increasing the employee's money income, the employer may give his employee some fringe benefit—for instance, a hospitalization insurance policy valued at $1,000. The employee will receive an increase in income, but not in the form of a direct monetary payment. Instead, the employee receives hospitalization insurance, which enables him to reduce his personal spending on medical care. Such fringe benefits, whether they take the form of subsidized medical or dental care, entertainment on expense accounts, or the use of company cars, are a source of nontaxable income to the employee.

It is widely recognized that a specific payment of a $1,000 hospitalization policy is generally not equivalent to a payment of $1,000 in money income. Only if the employee was previously spending at least $1,000 on hospitalization insurance would the fringe benefit be equivalent to an increase in monetary income. Generally, however, the employee will prefer a monetary payment to an equivalent fringe benefit. Conversely, a fringe benefit will have to cost something more than $1,000 to be valued as equivalent to cash payment of $1,000. As long as the amount of insurance necessary to provide equivalence with $1,000 in money income costs less than $1,250, however, it is potentially profitable for both employer and employee to substitute the fringe benefit for the monetary payment.

Whether it is actually profitable depends on the transaction cost borne by the employer in administering the fringe benefit. To operate a program of hospitalization insurance for employees will entail an administrative cost to the employer beyond what it would cost to increase the gross wage of employees. If an employee requires an insurance policy valued at $1,200 to equal a cash payment of $1,000 and it costs $100 per employee to operate the program, it will cost the employer $1,300 to give the employee a cash-equivalent raise of $1,000. As long as the employee's marginal rate of tax does not exceed 23 percent, it will be less costly to give the additional income in monetary form.

The rate of tax to which a particular employee is subject plays a role in determining the extent to which monetary and nonmonetary forms of compensation are used. If, in the above illustration, the marginal tax rate were 40 percent rather than 20 percent, it would cost the employer $1,667 to give the employee a cash raise of $1,000. Although it was not profitable to give the raise in a nonmonetary form when the marginal tax rate was 20 percent, it is profitable when the marginal tax rate is 40 percent. We should thus expect an increased use of fringe benefits of all sorts to be a response to increased average levels of income taxation. Additionally, the higher the rate of tax to which a particular group of employees is subjected, the higher the cost to the employer of increasing his employees' incomes through monetary payments. It is relatively cheaper for a company to give a monetary raise to a person in the 20 percent rate bracket than to one in the 50 percent bracket. Progressive rates of income taxation, then, especially encourage the use of nonmonetary forms of payment in the higher income brackets.[15]

Income Taxation and Investment in Tax Avoidance

In addition to earning monetary and nonmonetary forms of income through market activities, an individual may also earn income through nonmarket activities. He may try to increase his net income by reducing his tax liability through tax evasion or tax avoidance. He also may support programs and politicians that promise special tax concessions or expenditure benefits. These activities are all means of increasing posttax real income, and the profitability of investing in such activity will vary indirectly with the prevailing rate of taxation.

Tax avoidance is a legal means of reducing one's tax liability, whereas tax evasion is an illegal means of acomplishing the same objective. People may evade tax by failing to report all of their income, which is facilitated if at least part of income is received in cash payments, or by overstating their exemptions or deductible expenses. The temptation to evade tax intensifies as tax rates rise; a person is less likely to attempt evasion if his marginal tax rate is 20 percent than he would be if the rate were 40 percent. It is widely acknowledged that our form of personal income taxation requires a high degree of taxpayer morality for its successful operation. But morality, like everything else, has its price. High rates of tax tend to corrode taxpayer honesty, as it becomes relatively easier to increase net income through tax evasion than it is through earning additional income.

In addition to evasion, a person may try legally to avoid tax liability by rearranging his affairs. By carefully timing sales of assets or donations to charity, for instance, some tax liability may be avoided. A considerable part of the demand for accounting and legal services is derived from the demand by taxpayers for tax avoidance, and increases in tax rates increase the demand for these services. Similarly, people may try to secure tax concessions as a means of reducing their tax liability. Some may support a politician who proposes to increase the annual exemption for dependents; others may support a politician who proposes to retain the current level of depletion allowances. The firms in an extractive industry, for instance, have two sources of income: the sale of their products and the receipt

---

[15] For empirical documentation, see Wilbur G. Lewellen, *Executive Compensation in Large Industrial Corporations,* National Bureau of Economic Research, Fiscal Studies No. 11, (New York: Columbia University Press, 1968).

of subsidies through depletion allowances. Given the production function and prices of these two activities, there will be some optimal allocation of a firm's inputs between producing and selling additional output on the one hand and attempting to maintain or increase favorable tax concessions on the other. The higher the rate of tax, the less profitable it becomes to employ resources in expanding output relative to employing resources in seeking or maintaining fiscal favors.

If the marginal rate of tax is 20 percent, a person earning $20,000 per year must earn an additional $1,250 of taxable income in order to increase his net income by $1,000. If the marginal rate of tax is increased to 40 percent, however, the person must increase his pretax income by $1,667 in order to increase his net income by $1,000. This increase in marginal tax rates increases by $413 the cost of earning an additional $1,000. Approaching the matter from a different direction, a person earning $20,000 subject to a marginal tax rate of 20 percent can reduce his tax liability by $1,000 only if he can reduce his taxable income by $5,000. But if the marginal tax rate is 40 percent, he can reduce his tax liability by $1,000 if he can reduce his taxable income by $2,500. Thus, when the marginal rate of tax is increased, it becomes relatively more profitable to increase net income by tax concession and tax avoidance than by earning additional money income. As the rate of tax increases, the likelihood increases that people will seek to increase their incomes through special tax concessions and tax evasion and avoidance rather than by seeking additional income through market production.

Persons in the higher rate brackets will find it especially profitable to obtain the advice of a tax expert in order to avoid tax. It will also be relatively more profitable for persons in the higher rate brackets to seek special tax privileges. High tax rates increase the demand for both tax avoidance counseling and special tax favors. Market competition will tend to supply the former demand; political competition will tend to supply the latter.[16] Tax base erosion is a predictable outcome of political competition, and the base of the personal income tax includes only about 50 percent of total personal income. Because the demand for tax concessions is stronger in the upper income ranges, we should expect political competition to produce a tax structure in which tax concessions increase with rates of tax. Table 9-1 indicates the extent to which the tax base has eroded at various income levels. The nominal tax rate indicates what would apply if all income were taxed at the rate indicated by the tax schedule. The effective rate of tax is actual tax payment divided by income. The percentage erosion, the rate of reduction in the effective tax rate from the nominal

---

[16] For interesting documentation on political competition, see Philip M. Stern, *The Great Treasury Raid* (New York: Random House, 1962).

TABLE 9-1
Tax Base Erosion By Income Class

Adjusted Gross Income	Average Tax Rate		
	Nominal	Effective	Percentage Erosion
$5,000 and under	15.3%	15.0%	2.0%
$5,000 to $10,000	16.4	16.2	1.2
$10,000 to $20,000	18.1	17.8	1.7
$20,000 to $50,000	24.0	22.8	5.0
$50,000 to $100,000	35.8	32.6	8.9
$100,000 to $200,000	45.6	37.8	17.1
$200,000 to $500,000	52.3	37.9	27.5
$500,000 to $1,000,000	55.3	35.8	35.3
$1,000,000 and over	55.5	32.7	41.1

Source: Bernard P. Herber, *Modern Public Finance,* rev. ed. (Homewood, Ill.: Irwin, 1971), p. 147.

tax rate, increases sharply with the level of income, rising from 2 percent in the lowest income bracket to 41.1 percent in the highest.

INCOME TAXATION, RISK-TAKING, AND INCOME MOBILITY

In choosing among alternatives whose consequences extend into the future, whether those alternatives are different investments, different occupations, or just different places for a vacation, the outcomes of those choices are not certain. In such choice situations, people will confront both an expected value and a variance about the expected value, with increases in the variance denoting increases in the riskiness of the choice. A considerable body of literature has arisen in an attempt to specify the consequences of alternative tax institutions on the supply of risk-taking. An increase in the rate of tax on income will reduce the return from a given pattern of investment; the question is whether individual adjustments in response to the tax will result in a shift toward more risky or less risky investments. While the results are strongly dependent on assumptions concerning individual utility functions and the underlying motivation concerning investment behavior, we shall examine the topic within the standard perspective.[17]

[17] For standard examinations of these issues, see Evsey D. Domar and Richard A. Musgrave, "Proportional Income Taxation and Risk Taking," *Quarterly Journal of Economics,* 58 (May 1944), 388–422; and James E. Tobin, "Liquidity Preference

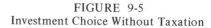

FIGURE 9-5
Investment Choice Without Taxation

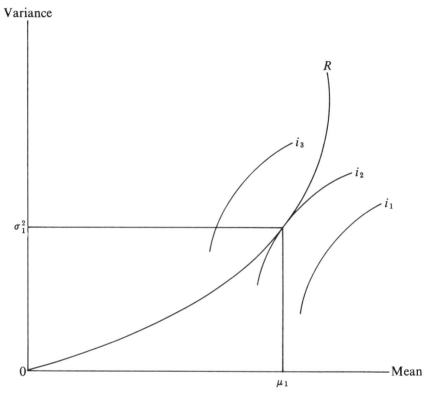

Consider an individual who faces a variety of opportunities for investment with various combinations of mean returns and variances. The alternative combinations of investments available to the individual are bounded
by *OR* in Figure 9-5, which indicates that higher expected yields can be
earned only by accepting greater risk. The individual also has a preference
map that depends on the expected return and the variance, as indicated
by the indifference curves in Figure 9-5. The individual described by Figure 9-5 will choose an investment strategy yielding a mean return μ_1 and
a variance σ_1^2.

---

as Behavior Toward Risk," *Review of Economic Studies,* 25 (February 1958),
65–86. For recent work qualifying the standard analyses, see Martin S. Feldstein,
"The Effects of Taxation on Risk Taking," *Journal of Political Economy,* 77 (No.
5, 1969), 755–64; and J. E. Stiglitz, "The Effect of Income, Wealth, and Capital
Gains Taxation on Risk Taking," *Quarterly Journal of Economics,* 83 (May 1969),
263–83.

The impact of income taxation on investment choice may be introduced in several ways. We can examine proportional income taxation, or we can consider progressive taxation. We can assume that gains are taxed without being offset by losses or that full loss offsets are allowed. Of course, the particular conclusions reached will depend on the particular combinations chosen for analysis. First, we shall consider proportional income taxation with full loss offsets, after which we shall modify our analysis to encompass progressive taxation and the absence of loss offsets.

Figure 9-6 shows the standard analysis of proportional income taxation with full loss offsets. The pretax equilibrium is (μ_1, σ_1^2). The tax with full loss offsets collapses the opportunity locus to OR_t, where:

$$(\mu_{R_t}, \sigma_{R_t}^2) = (1 - t)(\mu_R, \sigma_R^2)$$

with t the rate of tax. That is, any combination of μ and σ^2 on R is reduced by the tax to a corresponding point on R_t. If a person does not change his investment choice in response to the tax, his posttax position is on indifference curve i_3, with mean return μ_3 and variance σ_3^2. This is a posi-

FIGURE 9-6
Investment Choice Under Proportional Taxation with Full Loss Offsets

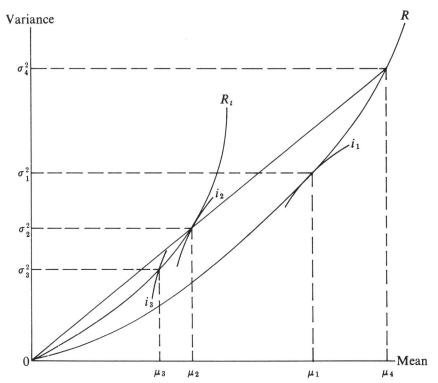

tion of disequilibrium, however, for the individual is now willing to increase his expected return by accepting greater risk. A new equilibrium will be attained at $(\mu_2, \sigma_2{}^2)$ where the indifference curve i_2 is tangent to the posttax opportunity locus, R_t. The relation between the pretax and posttax level of risk is ambiguous. As Figure 9-6 is constructed, $\sigma_2{}^2$ is less than $\sigma_1{}^2$, indicating that the posttax level of risk is less than the pretax level. With full loss offsets, however, the state shares both the risk and the return, and in Figure 9-6 the sum of private and collective risk has risen to $\sigma_4{}^2$.

This analysis of risk-taking has much in common with the preceeding analysis of labor supply; it is subject to similar difficulties in a general equilibrium setting. In Figure 9-6, tax collections are equal to $\mu_4 - \mu_2$. The analysis described by Figure 9-6 assumes that the tax takes resources away from the economy rather than merely transferring them to alternative uses. But the tax revenue will be spent to supply public services, which may be viewed as a component of the return from the investment. The tax will almost surely create differential income effects among individuals, of course, but on the average, income effects will sum to zero. The tax thus reduces the individual's private income from the investment, but the concomitant expenditure creates a form of public return.

The incorporation of public expenditure into the analysis is shown in Figure 9-7, where R_t, R, and the respective indifference curves are replicated from Figure 9-6. The public expenditure is equal to the tax revenue, and appears as a certain return, O_c. Beginning at O_c, the individual then faces the pretax opportunity locus, R^*, which becomes the posttax locus, $R_t{}^*$. Equilibrium is now attained where indifference curve i_0 is tangent to $R_t{}^*$. In this general equilibrium setting, the combination tax-expenditure reduces private risk-taking from $\sigma_2{}^2$ to $\sigma_2{}^2*$.

As compared with a proportional income tax with full loss offsets, a progressive tax will place an additional tax on gains that exceeds the savings from offsets on losses, thus reducing risk-taking from what it would be under proportional taxation. And when losses cannot be used to offset gains because loss offsets are disallowed, progressive taxation will further depress risk-taking in comparison to proportional income taxation with full loss offsets.

The impact of income taxation on the supply of risk-taking has important implications for the mobility of individuals among various positions within the distribution of income. While extensive discussion surrounds the amount of inequality in the distribution of income and the impact of policies designed to alter the degree of inequity, in many respects, the statistical form of the distribution of income seems less important than the rate of mobility of persons within the distribution. Consider three persons

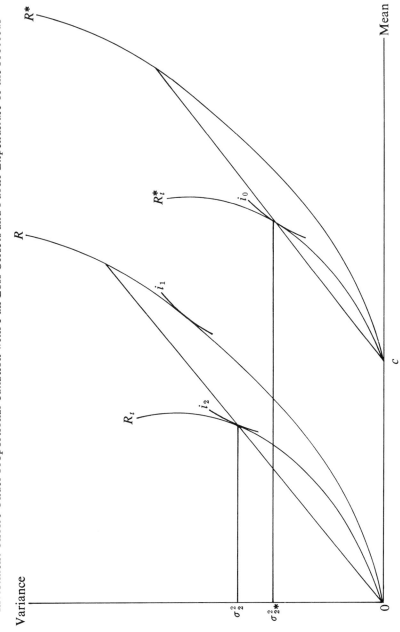

FIGURE 9-7

Investment Choice Under Proportional Taxation with Full Loss Offsets and Public Expenditure of the Proceeds

159

who have incomes of $4,000, $8,000, and $12,000 and assume that the shape of this distribution remains unchanged. One extreme possibility is that a person's income position during the current year is perfectly correlated with his position during the preceeding year. The other extreme possibility is that a person's income position during the current year is uncorrelated with his income position during the preceding year. The distribution of income has an identical degree of inequality in the two extreme cases. Yet it is unlikely that many people would consider these two cases identical, which suggests that the locus of concern is not so much the amount of inequality in the distribution of income as the rate of mobility among persons within the distribution.

While the shape of the distribution of annual income may remain constant, with each decile receiving the same share of income each year, the composition of the deciles will change from year to year. Considerable mobility seems to exist within the distribution of income. For instance, Lowell Gallaway estimated that 77 percent of the difference between the average income and the median income of the lowest income class was eradicated within one generation.[18] The median income in 1960 of the occupational classification with the lowest income was $1,066. But the median income of sons whose fathers belonged to this occupational class was $4,021, which closes 77 percent of the gap between their father's income and the average income of $4,907. The opposite effect took place in the upper income ranges. While the median incomes of fathers in the highest income class was $6,664, the median income of sons was $5,747. Table 9-2 clearly shows that sons of fathers with above-average incomes also tend to earn above-average incomes while sons of fathers with below-average incomes tend to earn below-average income. But Table 9-2 also shows that the incomes of sons of the former classification tend to fall relative to the income of the latter classification.

An examination of income across generations reveals a tendency for personal income to regress toward the mean, in much the same manner that intelligence regresses toward the mean.[19] While children of parents with above-average I.Q.'s also tend to have above-average I.Q.'s, their

[18] Lowell E. Gallaway, "On the Importance of 'Picking One's Parents,'" *Quarterly Review of Economics and Business,* 6 (Summer 1966), 7–15. See, also, Martin David, "Lifetime Income Variability and Income Profiles," 1971 *Proceedings of the Social Statistics Section of the American Statistical Association,* (Washington, D.C.: American Statistical Association, 1972), pp. 285–92.

[19] For additional evidence that poverty cannot be explained primarily as a result of intergenerational transmission, see James N. Morgan, Martin H. David, Wilbur J. Cohen, and Harvey E. Brazer, *Income and Welfare in the United States* (New York: McGraw-Hill, 1962), pp. 206–12 and 359–83.

TABLE 9-2
Median Income of Fathers and Sons by Father's
Occupational Class, 1960

Father's Occupation	Father's Median Income	Son's Median Income
Managers, officials, and proprietors	$6,664	$5,747
Professional, technical, and kindred	6,619	5,735
Craftsmen, foremen, and kindred	5,240	5,195
Sales	4,987	5,608
Clerical and kindred	4,785	5,504
Operations and kindred	4,299	4,834
Service, including private household	3,310	4,833
Laborers, except farm and mine	2,948	4,686
Farmers and farm managers	2,169	4,234
Farm laborers and foremen	1,066	4,021

Source: Lowell E. Gallaway, "On the Importance of 'Picking One's Parents,' " *Quarterly Review of Economics and Business,* 6 (Summer 1966), 12.

I.Q.'s will tend to be less than those of their parents. Similarly, children of parents with below-average I.Q.'s will tend to have below-average I.Q.'s, but their I.Q.'s will tend to exceed those of their parents. Table 9-3 illustrates this regression toward the mean for six occupational classes in Great Britain. While the mean I.Q. of parents in the higher professional class was 139.7, the mean I.Q. of their children was only 120.8. And while the mean I.Q. of parents in the unskilled class was 84.9, the mean I.Q. of their children was 92.6. Although the degree of inequality in the distri-

TABLE 9-3
Mean I.Q. of Parent and Child by Parent's
Occupational Class

Parent's Class	Mean I.Q.	
	Parent	Child
Higher Professional	139.7	120.8
Lower Professional	130.6	114.7
Clerical	115.9	107.8
Skilled	108.2	104.8
Semi-Skilled	97.8	98.9
Unskilled	84.9	92.6
Average	100.0	100.0

Source: James E. Meade, *Efficiency, Equality, and the Ownership of Property* (London: Allen & Unwin, 1964), p. 50.

bution of intelligence remains approximately constant, there is considerable mobility within this distribution.

Because random elements pervade economic activities, luck is an important determinant of a person's economic position and, more important, its stability over time. Any decision by an entrepreneur to create a new product or by an individual to train for a certain occupation is partially a gamble. While an expected rate of return may be computed on the basis of present circumstances, future conditions will almost certainly differ from present expectations, and some will gain by this discrepancy while others will lose. People who decided to become aerospace engineers 10 or 20 years ago faced bright income prospects that have since turned bleak. Some people will have a run of good luck in that they will invest in areas in which the demand for their output will increase. Others will have a run of bad luck in that they will invest in areas that will suffer relative decreases in demand. Among other things, a person with a relatively high income is likely to have enjoyed a run of good luck. Similarly, a person with a relatively low income is likely to have suffered a run of bad luck. A considerable, perhaps unappreciated, amount of random variations enters into determination of the distribution of personal income.

Because income seems to regress toward the mean across generations, the common characterization of the American economy as one of cumulative inequality seems inappropriate. Assertions about the cumulative inequality of wealth usually are based on the arithmetic of compound interest, which produces a truly inexorable accumulation of wealth. If a capital sum grows at 5 percent compounded annually for 30 years, the terminal value will be 4.32 times the initial value, and an average rate of tax on estates of 77 percent would be required to prevent the accumulation of wealth among generations. Or, if $1,000 had been invested 200 years ago at 10 percent, which is about the average rate of return on common stock, the present capital value would be $189.67 billion. If wealth had grown under these conditions, any ten families that possessed $1,000 200 years ago would now own the entire stock of privately held wealth. Although reasoning based on compound interest is temptingly simple, not all families seem to accumulate wealth at the average rate of return for the economy. Rather, some birth and death process operates; some families may accumulate wealth for a time, while others will be plagued either by incompetence or bad luck. A highly competent person might have heirs less competent than his own, and a run of bad luck eventually will strike even the person who has been biologically most fortunate in the procreation of competent heirs.

The problem of the gambler's ruin illustrates these issues, especially the case of the infinitely rich adversary.[20] In its simplest form, the problem of the gambler's ruin states that the probability that a gambler will go bankrupt varies inversely with the size of his fortune relative to that of his opposition. As the wealth of the adversary increases relative to that of the gambler, the probability of the gambler's eventual ruin approaches certainty. In an economic system, an individual who tries to amass wealth is playing against an infinitely rich adversary. Although the gambler may encounter lengthy strings of good luck, eventually he will encounter a string of bad luck that will destroy his fortune.

Nevertheless, it is relatively uninteresting by itself to argue that any fortune is doomed, for the process of ruination might take only 50 years, and then again it might take 500. The length of time before we can expect the gambler to go bankrupt is of considerable interest. Table 9-4 shows the probability of ruin and the expected duration of play for several values of p, q, X, and Y. The general outlines of the table are clear. When the gambler has a 50 percent chance of winning and initially possesses 10 percent of the wealth, the probability of his eventual ruin is 90 percent. When the gambler's initial share of the wealth falls to 1 percent, the probability of his eventual ruin rises to 99 percent. The expected duration of play is highly sensitive to the probability that the gambler will win. When the gambler initially has 10 percent of the wealth and faces a 50 percent chance of winning on any trial, the expected duration of play before ruin is 900 trials. When the probability of winning falls to 40 percent, the expected duration falls to 50 trials, and the expected duration falls to 30 trials when the probability of winning falls to 33 percent.

Entrepreneurs invest in alternatives whose future payoffs are uncertain. Sometimes they will win, but sometimes the adversary will win. An increase in the degree of private risk is equivalent to a reduction in the probability that the gambler will win. The individuals' willingness to bear risk will affect the amount of mobility among persons within various positions in the income scale, so the form of taxation, by affecting the supply of risk-taking, can influence the rate of income mobility. Within the limits of the analytical model described above, the more progressive the rate of tax on winnings, the less willing entrepreneurs will be to take risks. A person might be willing to invest when tax rates are proportional and the probability of success is at least, say, 40 percent, but he might require

---

[20] For a tantalizing survey of the problem of the gambler's ruin, see William Feller, *An Introduction to Probability Theory and Its Applications*, Vol. I, 2nd ed. (New York: Wiley, 1957), pp. 311–13. For a discussion of the gambler's ruin in relation to personal mobility within the distribution of income, see George J. Stigler, *The Theory of Price*, 3rd ed. (New York: Macmillan, 1966), pp. 288–312.

TABLE 9-4
Probability of and Expected Duration Before Gambler's Ruin

p	q	X	Y	P_r	D_r
.5	.5	10	90	.9	900
.4	.6	10	90	1.0*	50*
.33	.67	10	90	1.0*	30*
.5	.5	10	990	.99	9900
.4	.6	10	990	1.0*	50*
.33	.67	10	990	1.0*	30*

Note: Let p denote the probability that the gambler wins and q the probability that he loses. If $p = q$, the probability that the gambler will become ruined is $P_r = 1 - X/(X + Y)$, where X is the gambler's fortune and Y is the adversary's. If:

$$p \neq q, \quad P_r = \frac{(q/p)^{(X+Y)} - (q/p)^X}{(q/p)^{(X+Y)} - 1}.$$

If $p = q$, the expected duration before ruin will be $D_r = XY$. If:

$$p \neq q, \quad D_r = \frac{X}{q-p} - \frac{X+Y}{q-p} \cdot \frac{1 - (q/p)^X}{1 - (q/p)^{(X+Y)}}.$$

*These values are very close approximations. The exact entry for P_r in the second row, carried to 9 decimal points, is 0.999999999.
Similarly, the exact value for D_r in the second row, also carried to 9 decimal points, is 49.999999931.

a probability of, say, 45 percent when tax rates are progressive without full loss offsets. And the more favorable the odds to the gambler, the longer the expected duration of play. To the extent that progressive taxation reduces the willingness of persons to take risks, then, it reduces the rate of mobility of individuals within the distribution of income.

In the absence of inflation, government bonds would be a riskless investment for the bondholder. And if investments could truly be riskless, the arithmetic of compound interest would exert itself. The more progressive the rate of tax, the more inclined people will be to settle for lower, more certain returns. Fortunes will be much less likely to erode under such circumstances, and the fortunes that do erode will erode more slowly. Progressive income taxation may thus be viewed within two different perspectives. Within one perspective, progressive income taxation will tend to narrow somewhat the inequality in the distribution of posttax income. Within the other perspective, however, progressive taxation will tend to reduce the rate of mobility within the income structure. Thus, a person's assessment of progressive taxation as an egalitarian instrument will depend, at least in part, on whether he thinks in terms of the inequality in the distribution of income or in terms of the rate of mobility within the distribution of income.[21]

INCOME MAINTENANCE VIA INCOME TAXATION

A policy that promotes greater equality in the distribution of income will not necessarily also promote greater mobility within the distribution of income, and vice versa. Contemporary discussion has focused on the impact of taxation on the degree of inequality within the distribution of income. The facts about the extent of inequality appear to be fairly simple. The lowest 20 percent of families in terms of income earn just over five percent of the income earned by all families, while the second-lowest 20 percent earn just over 12 percent. In contrast, the highest 20 percent of families earn about 41 percent, while the second-highest 20 percent earn nearly 24 percent. The middle 20 percent earn the remaining 18 percent. Because the revenue generated by the personal income tax could be raised from a proportional income tax of less than 25 percent, the use of a progressive rate structure represents an effort to narrow income differences by transferring income from those whose average rate of tax exceeds the proportional rate to those whose average rate of tax is less.

It is, of course, widely recognized that figures on the distribution of income overstate the degree of inequality. Among persons who have the same expected lifetime income profiles, there will be differences in annual income because of age differences in the population. Nonpecuniary differences among occupations will also cause the statistics on the distribution of income to overstate the extent of inequality. If people generally prefer living in warm climates to living in frigid climates at equal wage rates, they would live in the frigid climate only if they received a higher wage. Yet this inequality in the distribution of monetary income is necessary to offset an opposing inequality in the distribution of nonmonetary income. Or, to choose another illustration, the longer the educational requirements for entering an occupation, the higher the annual income of that occupation must be just to offset the higher cost of entering that occupation—both the direct cost of education and the indirect cost of the income that was forgone during the years of schooling. Once again, statistics on the inequality of income exaggerate the actual degree of inequality, for some of the inequality will merely reflect equalizing differences in income.

Income taxation may be used to promote greater equality in the dis-

---

[21] For a similar discussion of many of the issues that have been raised in this section, although within a context of taxing transfers of wealth rather than receipts of income, see Richard E. Wagner, *Inheritance, Inequality, and Progressive Taxation* (Washington, D.C.: American Enterprise Institute, 1973), Ch. 2.

tribution of income both by reducing tax burdens on low-income citizens as well as by increasing tax burdens on high-income citizens. When the personal exemption reaches $750 in 1973, at which time the low-income allowance will be $1,000, a family of four will incur no tax liability until its income exceeds $4,000. This exemption of $4,000 from tax liability clearly increases the progressivity of the personal income tax.

As long as the personal income tax is limited to positive rates of tax, it will be more effective as an instrument for penalizing those who earn large incomes than for assisting those who earn little income. Negative income taxation is a means of using the tax system to assist more directly families with low incomes. This method has received increasing attention over the past decade. Although there is considerable variety among specific proposals for negative income taxation, all the proposals feature some guaranteed minimum income in conjunction with some rate at which the subsidy is decreased as income rises.[22] As an illustration, consider a negative income tax with a guaranteed income of $2,500 and a tax rate of 50 percent. A person with zero income would receive a subsidy of $2,500, and a person with $5,000 income would neither pay tax nor receive subsidy. Beyond an income of $5,000, the normal tax schedule would take effect. People with incomes below $5,000 would receive a subsidy equal to 50 percent of the difference between a person's actual income and the break-even income. A person with an income of $2,000, for instance, would receive 50 percent of the $3,000 by which his income fell short of the break-even income, giving him a net income of $3,500.

Other rate schedules are possible. The break-even level could be maintained at $5,000, but the rate of tax could be reduced to 40 percent. Or the rate of tax could be maintained at 50 percent, and the break-even level could be raised or lowered. A negative income tax clearly is subject to tradeoffs among the guaranteed income, the breakeven income, and the rate of tax.[23] The lower the rate of negative tax, the less the disincentive

[22] For a survey, see Christopher Green, *Negative Taxes and the Poverty Problem* (Washington, D.C.: Brookings, 1967). While the basic concepts of negative income taxation are simple, the implementation of any particular plan will require decisions concerning such sticky issues as the: (1) definition of income, (2) definition of the family unit, (3) rules for membership in the family unit, (4) selection of the allowance schedule for units of various sizes, (5) relation of negative income taxation to prevailing public assistance programs, and (6) treatment of fluctuating income. On these issues, see James Tobin, Joseph A. Pechman, and Peter Mieszkowski, "Is a Negative Income Tax Practical?" *Yale Law Journal,* 77 (November 1967), 1–27.

[23] For empirical examination of some of these issues, see Richard A. Musgrave, Peter Heller, and George E. Peterson, "Cost Effectiveness of Alternative Income Maintenance Schemes," *National Tax Journal,* 23 (June 1970), 140–56; and Martin David and June Luethold, "Formulas for Income Maintenance: Their Distributional Impact," *National Tax Journal,* 21 (March 1968), 70–93.

effect on the supply of labor. With a 50 percent rate of tax, a person loses $50 in subsidy for each additional $100 he earns. But with a 40 percent tax rate, he loses only $40 for each additional $100 earned. But whereas a person would receive a subsidy of $2,500 if he had zero income with the 50 percent rate of tax, he will receive only $2,000 under the 40 percent rate of tax, assuming the break-even level remains at $5,000. Thus, the lower the rate of negative tax, the weaker the disincentive effect, but also the lower the guaranteed level of income. Conversely, the higher the rate of negative tax, the higher the guaranteed level of income, but also the stronger the disincentive effect. A guaranteed income of $3,000 will require a negative rate of tax of 60 percent if the breakeven level is $5,000. If the rate of tax were reduced to 50 percent, the guaranteed income could be maintained at $3,000 only by raising the break-even level to $6,000. This would amount to subsidizing families whose incomes were less than $2,000 below the median level of family income for the nation.

A negative income tax, which is really a guaranteed annual income combined with a special structure of positive tax rates, and a wage subsidy program are programs that transfer income to segments of the population. Such forms of income maintenance as social dividends would transfer income to the entire population.[24] A social dividend combines a lump-sum transfer with a tax program for raising the revenue to finance the program. For instance, transfers could be $1,000 per person, $1,000 per adult and $200 per child, or any of an infinite number of possibilities. Social dividends would be redistributive because the transfers, which would be invariant, would be financed by a tax for which liability increases with income.

To illustrate, consider a proposed social dividend of $1,000 for all citizens 18 years of age or older, with the program to be financed by a proportionate increase in the personal income tax. Approximately 135 million people would receive the social dividends, so the size of the program would be $135 billion. With taxable income of approximately $450 billion, a 30 percent rate of tax would be required to finance the program. If the tax base were broadened to include all personal income, the required rate of tax would fall to 15 percent. For a family with one adult member, the breakeven income would be $3,333. All one-person families would receive $1,000 and pay an income tax of 30 percent to support the program. The net impact of the program would be a transfer of income from individuals with incomes above $3,333 to individuals with incomes below $3,333. For a family with two adult members, the break-even income would be $6,667. For this grouping of families, the program would transfer income

[24] For a brief description of social dividends, see Green, *Negative Taxes and the Poverty Problem*, pp. 52–56.

from those with income above $6,667 to those with income below $6,667.

When compared with a negative income tax, a social dividend would seem to fare poorly. If equal transfers were made to all adults, the amounts transferred to those whose incomes are above that of the median adult will be equal to the amounts transferred to those whose incomes are below the median. A social dividend will be considerably more expensive than a negative income tax will be. A negative income tax rate of 50 percent combined with an income guarantee of $2,500 probably would cost only about 10 percent of what the $1,000 social dividend would cost. We have seen that the higher the rate of tax, the relatively more profitable it becomes to invest resources in such socially unproductive activity as attempting to earn real income through finding ways to evade and to avoid tax and to secure favorable tax treatment through legislation. Schemes for such per capita transfers as social dividends, then, would seem likely to generate substantial excess burden as a consequence of the high rates of tax required to finance the program.

Perhaps we should note, however, that there is no reason why current tax liability must be based on current income. Instead, tax liability could be based on past income, which is equivalent to subjecting current income to future tax. The permanent income hypothesis seems to be consistent with a subjective rate of discount of about 33 percent.[25] A 33 percent rate of discount suggests that decisions are made with a three-year horizon. In turn, a three-year horizon implies that if current income is subjected to tax liability in three years—that is, if current tax liability should be related to income earned three years ago—income taxation would exert income effects without exerting substitution effects. Such a program of future-oriented taxation would relate tax liability to income, but it would perform as if it were a lump-sum tax with respect to its impact on taxpayer behavior. By assigning tax liability prospectively rather than currently, then, some program of per capita transfers might be financed without creating the excess burden that ordinarily would be associated with the high rates of tax that would be required to finance the program.

FISCAL CHOICE AND PROGRESSIVE TAXATION

Because the predominant share of the complexity in our income tax system stems from the use of nominally progressive rates and would largely vanish

---

[25] Milton Friedman, "Windfalls, the 'Horizon,' and Related Concepts in the Permanent-Income Hypothesis," in Carl F. Christ et al., eds., *Measurement in Economics* (Stanford, Calif.: Stanford University Press, 1963), pp. 3–28.

if rates were proportional, it is perhaps useful to ask why income is taxed at progressive rates rather than at proportional rates. The system of progressive taxation frequently has been rationalized in terms of such notions as ability to pay. But rationalization is not explanation. Tax rates become established within the institutions of fiscal choice, and we want to examine progressive taxation within such a context.

Some people have suggested that progressive taxation is a form of collectively supplied charity that may be explained as similar to the explanation of private charity.[26] When utility functions are interdependent in that the utility of one person depends on some other person's level of consumption, private markets will tend to produce some volume of charitable contributions.[27] But if charity has elements of joint consumption combined with nonexclusion, in that person C may benefit from A's transfer to B without A's being able to prevent C's consumption, market institutions will tend to supply a suboptimal amount of charity. Progressive taxation may thus be viewed as a compact among the more wealthy citizens to tax themselves to subsidize the less wealthy, thereby supplying themselves with a collective good and increasing both their own utility and the utility of the less wealthy citizens. Within this frame of analysis, progressivity is essentially initiated by the more wealthy citizens, and they specify how heavily they are going to be taxed to subsidize the less wealthy.

A strongly opposed explanation of progressive taxation is that it represents theft by the majority coalition. Because the income of the median voter is less than the mean income for the entire citizenry, a majority of the voting populace will have below-average incomes. Progressive taxation is thus a device for the less wealthy majority coalition to exploit the more wealthy minority coalition. Under such circumstances progressive income taxation becomes a type of politically sanctioned theft. While this explanation of progressive taxation might seem to contain a considerable amount of plausibility, it fails to explain why taxes are not even more progressive. If progressive taxation is theft, why does the thief stop before he has taken all he can? That is, why don't we observe complete equality as the outcome, for that would maximize the transfer to the majority coalition. Without explaining why the equilibrium amount of theft is less than the maximum amount, the explanation is seriously incomplete.

---

[26] The primary development of this point of view is Harold M. Hochman and James D. Rodgers, "Pareto Optimal Redistribution," *American Economic Review,* 59 (September 1969), 542–57.

[27] For an economic analysis of private charity, see Robert A. Schwartz, "Personal Philanthropic Contributions," *Journal of Political Economy,* 78 (No. 6, 1970), 1264–91.

One possible explanation of the reason that full equalization does not result is that the majority coalition is aware of disincentive effects from extremely progressive taxes. Such disincentive effects create a trade-off between gaining from greater equalization and losing from the reduction in the total amount of income available for redistribution. Progressive taxation thus becomes analogous to taking an increasing share of a shrinking pie. As long as one's share of income increases more rapidly than the total income shrinks, such action is rational. Under such circumstances, a majority coalition will choose a degree of progessivity that will achieve less than complete equalization.

A second, more plausible explanation for the lack of greater equalization is that the less wealthy voters do not *effectively* outnumber the more wealthy. Because political competition is costly, some voters will become more influential than others will.[28] Voters who have a comparative advantage in persuading other voters and those who have the wealth to assist in this persuasion will be relatively more influential than other voters will be. Political campaigning is expensive and, consequently, more attention will be devoted to securing the support of more wealthy citizens than to less wealthy citizens. No longer will coalitions form wholly along income lines. Instead, coalitions will contain a mix of more wealthy and less wealthy voters. One implication of this line of analysis is that financing political campaigns from the public treasury probably would increase progressivity, for such a shift in the means of financing campaigns will erode the value of wealthier citizens to political coalitions.

A third possible explanation as to why full equalization does not result is that those in the lower income ranges do not expect to remain there permanently. We saw earlier that there is mobility of persons within the distribution of income. Some who are in the less wealthy half of the population can expect to be in the more wealthy half at some time in the future. Conversely, some who are in the more wealthy segment of the population can expect to be in the less wealthy segment in the future. By supporting extreme degrees of progression now, some members of the less wealthy group will harm their chances to enjoy greater income in the future. And by acquiescing in some amount of progressivity now, some members of the more wealthy group will protect themselves against a run of bad luck in the future.[29]

Progressive taxation would thus appear to contain features of income

---

[28] Anthony Downs, *An Economic Theory of Democracy* (New York: Harper, 1957).

[29] This explanation suggests that progressive taxation will be supported more strongly among both individual citizens and among societies as the expected rate of mobility within the income distribution decreases.

insurance.[30] Yet we must be careful not to push this insurance analogy too far. Insurance purchases are made before the buyer knows the outcome; insurance is purchased before the accident, not afterwards. What if insurance purchases were made after the outcomes were known? Those without accidents would not want insurance, while those with accidents would want extremely comprehensive coverage. There would be no room for agreement between the two groups, and insurance would be impossible without such agreement. By making choices before outcomes are known, agreement becomes possible because the identities of accident victims are unknown.

Tax institutions are chosen after the outcomes are known. Those who have high incomes will be in the position of those who have had no accidents; they will desire little coverage. Those with low incomes, by contrast, will be in a position analogous to those who have had accidents; they will opt for extensive insurance. Only if fiscal institutions are chosen before the outcomes are known can progressive taxation meaningfully be viewed as a form of income insurance. This would require that the members of each generation choose the degree of progressivity of their tax institutions—the amount of income insurance—while they are young, when their future income prospects are most uncertain.

[30] This view is developed in James M. Buchanan, *Public Finance in Democratic Process* (Chapel Hill: University of North Carolina Press, 1967), pp. 225–40.

10. The Taxation of Corporation Income

The taxation of corporation income is the second largest source of general revenue for the national government. State governments also tax corporation income, and both levels of government together presently collect about $40 billion from the taxation of corporation income. In spite of its importance as a source of revenue, severe criticism of the corporation income tax has increased steadily in recent years. Among the various criticisms of the tax, some of the more strenuous are that it promotes inefficiency in the allocation of capital, that it generates considerable inequity in the distribution of tax liability, and that because not even professional economists can agree on the incidence of the tax, it injects a dose of fiscal anesthesia into the process of budgetary choice.

DEFINITION OF THE TAX BASE

The rate of tax on corporation income falls into two parts: a 22 percent rate of tax is levied on the first $25,000 of taxable income and a surtax of 26 percent is applied to taxable income over $25,000. Because the bulk of corporate income is earned by corporations with incomes that exceed $25,000, the marginal rate of tax on corporation income is effectively 48 percent. This rate of tax is then multiplied by the tax base, a corporation's net income, to determine tax liability.

While definition of the base of the corporation income tax is simple in principle, it is fraught with complexities in practice. In its essentials, the tax base is a corporation's net income, which is the value of sales less the expenses of doing business. The complexities of tax administration primarily revolve around defining and accounting for deductible expenses. Wages and salaries and payments for material, rent, and advertising are expenses of a type that create little problem. Depreciation allowances, contributions to pension funds, and charitable donations are among the expenses that create special problems of tax administration.

If there were no corporation income tax, corporations would be able to choose their most preferred scheme for depreciating assets. Because there is a corporation income tax and because corporate practices regarding depreciation will affect a corporation's reported income, the Internal Revenue Service intervenes in corporate practices concerning depreciation. On the one hand, the IRS issues guidelines concerning asset life for different classes of assets and, on the other, it specifies acceptable formulas for computing depreciation. The double-declining-balance method and the sum-of-the-year's-digits method, for instance, were expressly authorized by the IRS only in 1954. Because the annual amount of depreciation is a deductible business expense, the choice among rules for depreciation can affect a corporation's tax liability substantially. Consider an asset that initially costs $10,000, has a ten-year life, and is assigned no salvage value. Table 10-1 indicates annual depreciation charges computed under three different formulas. Although the total amount of depreciation sums to $10,000 for each method, the present value of the depreciation allowance varies among the three formulas. If future depreciation is discounted at 12 percent, the present values of the schedules shown in Table 10-1 are $5,658 with straight-line, $6,437 with double-declining-balance, and $6,602 with sum-of-the-year's-digits. With a discount rate of 6 percent, the respective present values are $7,370, $7,882, and $8,008. A reduction in the rate of discount diminishes the impact of differences in the timing of depreciation charges, which accounts for the reduced dispersion among the present values with the 6 percent of discount.

TABLE 10-1
Annual Depreciation Charges Under Three Methods

Year	Straight-Line	Double-Declining-Balance	Sum-of-the-Year's-Digits
1	$1,000	$2,000	$1,818
2	1,000	1,600	1,636
3	1,000	1,280	1,455
4	1,000	1,024	1,273
5	1,000	819	1,091
6	1,000	655	909
7	1,000	655	727
8	1,000	655	545
9	1,000	655	364
10	1,000	655	182

In addition to specifying allowable formulas for depreciation and issuing guidelines concerning asset life, another primary regulation of the Internal Revenue Code concerning depreciation is that the total amount of depreciation cannot exceed the original cost of the asset. Although this limitation is inconsequential as long as price levels are stable, when price levels rise over time, this limitation means that corporations are taxed partly on their capital consumption. If the price level is expected to rise by 50 percent over the ten-year period, say by 5 percentage points per year, and if depreciation is computed by the sum-of-the-year's-digits, a real present value of future depreciation of $6,602 requires a nominal present value of $7,704.[1] To attain this higher present value, the sum of annual depreciation charges must be $12,000,[2] which exceeds the original cost of the asset. Unless the total amount of depreciation is permitted to exceed the original cost of the asset, part of a corporation's tax liability will simply be capital consumption. In the above illustration, $5,686 is the real present value of the depreciation allowance,[3] which indicates that $916 is the real present value of capital consumption on which the corporation is taxed.[4]

Corporation income is highly volatile. Consequently, some averaging of corporation income has been introduced through the provisions for carryback and carryover. Corporations may carry back income for three years, which enables them to reduce their present tax liability by offsetting present income against past losses. Corporations may also carry over losses for five years, so a loss suffered in one year can be used to offset income for up to five years in the future. While some such averaging of corporate income is highly desirable, there is some fear that the carryback and carryover provision may create a fiscal inducement for corporations to merge, although a practical distinction between economic and fiscal inducements for merger seems tenuous at best.

[1] $$\$7,704 = \sum_{i-1}^{10} \frac{A_i P_i}{(1+r)^i} = \frac{\$1818(1.05)}{(1.12)^1} + \frac{\$1636(1.10)}{(1.12)^2} + \cdots + \frac{\$182(1.50)}{(1.12)^{10}},$$
where A_i is depreciation in year i, P_i is the price level index for year i, and r is the discount rate.

[2] $$\$12,000 = \sum_{i=1}^{10} A_i P_i = \$1818(1.05) + \$1636(1.10) + \cdots + \$182(1.50).$$

[3] $$\$5686 = \sum_{i=1}^{10} (A_i/P_i)/(1+r)^i = \frac{\$1818/1.05}{(1.12)^1} + \frac{\$1636/1.10}{(1.12)^3} + \cdots + \frac{\$182/1.50}{(1.12)^{10}}.$$

[4] $916 = $6,602 − $5,686, which shows that the inflation would reduce the real present value of the depreciation allowance by 14 percent.

SHORT-RUN INCIDENCE OF THE
CORPORATION INCOME TAX

Who pays the $40 billion per year collected by the corporation income tax? If the corporate tax should be replaced by a proportional income tax of equal yield, for example, who would gain and who would lose? This question of incidence has provoked a substantial volume of both conceptual and empirical analysis over the past decade. In this section, we shall consider the short-run incidence of the tax; in the next section we shall examine the long-run incidence.

Analysis of the short-run incidence of the corporation income tax seems relatively straightforward. The tax on corporation income is a tax on the return to equity capital invested in the corporate sector. If equity capital is employed efficiently before the imposition of the tax (or before an increase in its previous rate), there can be no short-run shifting of the tax. The tax would be paid by owners of corporate equity capital. By the very definition of short-run, equity capital owners cannot leave the corporate sector and seek other employment. Moreover, the tax affects neither the demand nor the cost conditions faced by the firm, so a firm's profit-maximizing combination of price and output will be unaffected by the tax. Conversely, if the corporation income tax is shifted from owners of corporate equity capital to consumers of corporate output via price rises and output contractions, corporations could not have been maximizing their profits before the tax.

Analysis of the corporation income tax depends critically on assumptions concerning the behavior of firms. If the traditional, profit-maximizing theory of the firm is substantially correct, there can be no short-run shifting of the tax. In recent years, however, there has been a growing dissatisfaction with this theory. Moreover, alternative theories may yield different implications concerning the short-run incidence of the corporation income tax. Some economists have suggested that firms should be viewed as maximizing their sales, subject to the constraint that profits must not fall below some minimum acceptable level.[5] An increase in the tax on corporation income may reduce profits below the minimum acceptable level. If this is so, to some extent, an increase in the tax will produce a rise in price rather than a reduction in profit, thereby shifting part of the tax from owners to consumers.

We can compare the responses to the imposition of a tax on corporation income by a profit maximizer and a sales maximizer by reference to

[5] A prominent illustration of this view is William J. Baumol, *Business Behavior, Value and Growth* (New York: Macmillan, 1959).

FIGURE 10-1
Corporate Tax Incidence and Alternative Theories of the Firm

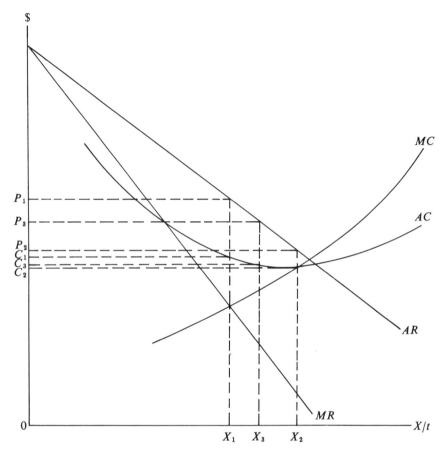

Figure 10-1. The profit-maximizing monopolist described by Figure 10-1 would have the output rate, X_1, price P_1, and profit $(P_1 - C_1)X_1$. Suppose, by contrast, the monopolist wanted to maximize his sales, subject to the constraint that his profit must not fall below some minimum level, say $(P_2 - C_2)X_2$. The sales maximizer would have the output rate X_2 and price P_2. The imposition of a tax of t percent of profit would reduce profit below the minimum acceptable level. In response, the monopolist would raise his price and restrict his output until he regained his minimum level of profit. This new equilibrium occurs at the output rate, X_3, and the price P_3, where $(1 - t)[(P_3 - C_3)X_3] = (P_2 - C_2)X_2$. In this instance, the corporation income tax does not reduce the return to owners of corporate equity capital; rather, it increases the price of the corporation's output.

Clearly, the impact of the corporation income tax depends on assumptions concerning the behavior of firms.

A finding that the corporation income tax is shifted from owners to consumers in the short run would have devastating implications for much of economic analysis, for a finding of short-run shifting would destroy the theory of the firm on which the entire analysis of the functioning of product markets and factor markets is based. For this reason, it is understandable that there has been intense interest in empirical studies designed to estimate the short-run incidence of the corporation income tax. This interest in empirical examination has been especially intense since Krzyzaniak and Musgrave presented their findings that the corporation income tax is more than fully shifted to consumers in the short run.[6]

Krzyzaniak and Musgrave (*K-M*) estimated a model of the gross rate of return on capital in manufacturing for the periods 1935–42 and 1948–59. The essential idea underlying their analysis is that the gross rate of return on corporate capital should not be affected by changes in the tax rate if the tax is paid by owners of corporate equity capital. If, by contrast, the tax is shifted forward to consumers, the gross rate of return on corporate capital should rise in response to a tax increase, thus maintaining the same net rate of return to corporate owners. *K-M* developed a model for testing the hypothesis of forward shifting, then estimated the model and found that forward shifting did take place.

In their model, *K-M* related the gross rate of return on corporate capital to: (1) the corporation income tax as a percentage of the corporate capital stock, (2) the ratio of inventory to sales in manufacturing, which lagged one year, (3) the change in the ratio of consumption to GNP, which also lagged one year, and (4) the current year's ratio of noncorporate tax accruals to GNP less transfer payments. The coefficients of the third and fourth dependent variables were not found to be significantly different from zero, which is perhaps fortunate because the function of such variables in explaining the gross rate of return on corporate capital is puzzling. Nevertheless, the coefficient on the first dependent variable shows the impact of the corporate tax on the gross rate of return to corporate capital. *K-M* found this coefficient to be significant and equal to 1.34, which means that 134 percent of tax increases were shifted away from the owners of corporate equity capital.

Cragg, Harberger, and Mieszkowski (*C-H-M*) showed that the *K-M* conclusion is highly sensitive to the way in which the estimating model is specified and that seemingly innocuous changes in specification can pro-

---

[6] Marion Krzyzaniak and Richard A. Musgrave, *The Shifting of the Corporation Income Tax* (Baltimore: Johns Hopkins Press, 1963).

duce radically different conclusions.[7] A criticism frequently levied against the *K-M* formulation is that their model does not allow adequately either for cyclical changes in economic conditions or for the peculiar circumstances created by the war years. Over the period examined by *K-M*, there was a strong tendency for the simultaneous existence of low rates of return and low rates of tax on the one hand and of high rates of return and high rates of tax on the other. To the extent that such a pattern resulted from cyclical and wartime conditions, the increased rate of return would be attributed incorrectly to the increase in the rate of tax.

Using the *K-M* procedures and data but introducing the employment rate and a dummy variable for the war years, *C-H-M* reestimated the *K-M* model. When the employment rate was added to the original list of *K-M* dependent variables, the value of the tax coefficient fell by one-quarter to 1.024, which indicates a forward shift of 102 percent. But when the wartime variable was added to the list of dependent variables, the value of the tax coefficient fell to .6002.[8] While this coefficient indicates 60 percent forward shifting, it is not significantly different from zero. Thus, by making a few a priori reasonable changes in the specification of the *K-M* model, *C-H-M* were able to reject the hypothesis of short-run shifting of the corporation income tax. The essential rationale of the *C-H-M* analysis was not to present alternative estimates of incidence, but to show that the *K-M* results are highly sensitive to minor changes in the specification of the model.

A major limitation in both the *K-M* and the *C-H-M* analyses is that no alternative theory of the firm is specified from which their results can be derived. In response to this limitation, Gordon examined the short-run shifting of the corporate tax with reference to a model of the firm in which price was set as some percentage markup from cost.[9] He related the rate of return on corporate capital to: (1) gross sales as a percentage of real corporate capital, (2) maximum sales as a percentage of real corporate capital, (3) the rate of change in the price level, (4) the rate of change in real output, and (5) the rate of tax on corporation income. The coefficient of the tax variable, which was .143, was not significantly different from zero. This means that the tax was paid by owners of corporate equity capital. Gordon found that gross sales as a percentage of corporate capital, which is a measure of the productivity of corporate capital, was highly significant, indicating that much of the increase in the rate of return on

---

[7] John G. Cragg, Arnold C. Harberger, and Peter Mieszkowski, "Empirical Evidence on the Incidence of the Corporation Income Tax," *Journal of Political Economy,* 75 (December 1967), 811–21.

[8] *Ibid.,* 817–18.

[9] Robert J. Gordon, "The Incidence of the Corporation Income Tax in Manufacturing, 1925–62," *American Economic Review,* 57 (September 1967), 731–58.

corporate capital was the result of the increased productivity of corporate assets.

The empirical evidence that has been accumulated to date, then, gives little reason for doubting that the American economy may be characterized as essentially competitive and that, as a consequence, firms may be viewed as attempting to maximize the present value of their net wealth. Yet the unsettled state of the theory of the firm and the extraordinary significance that a finding of short-run shifting would have for economic theory suggests that the incidence of corporation income tax will be subject to further examination.

LONG-RUN INCIDENCE OF THE CORPORATION INCOME TAX

The corporation income tax creates short-run disequilibrium in the capital market, which will induce some long-run shifting of the tax.[10] In the short run, the corporation income tax drives the net rate of return on corporate equity capital below the net rate of return on both bonds and noncorporate equity capital. Yet long-run equilibrium will be attained only when the net return on capital is equalized in all directions.[11] Consequently, the corporation income tax will induce a shift of capital from corporate equity capital to bonds and noncorporate equity capital until net rates of return become equalized once again. This shift in the employment of capital will reduce the rate of output in the corporate sector, and prices of corporate products will rise. Simultaneously, this shift in the employment of capital will increase the rate of output in the noncorporate sector, and prices of noncorporate products will fall. Because corporate equity capital is a substantial share of the total stock of capital, the reallocation of corporate capital induced by the increased tax rate will depress the rate of return to all capital. In this manner, some of the tax burden will be shifted from the owners of corporate capital to the owners of noncorporate capital.[12]

---

[10] The classic analysis of long-run shifting of the corporation income tax is Arnold C. Harberger, "The Incidence of the Corporation Income Tax," *Journal of Political Economy,* 70 (June 1962), 215–40.

[11] Equalization of returns should not be confused with *equality* of returns. The return on one investment may exceed the return on another investment, yet an equilibrium may exist, perhaps reflecting that one investment is riskier than is the other.

[12] For a recent documentation of a tendency toward equalization of net rates of return between corporate and noncorporate capital, despite considerable difference in tax treatment and pretax rates of return, see Laurtis R. Christensen, "Entrepreneurial Income: How Does It Measure Up?" *American Economic Review,* 61 (September 1971), 575–85. For instance, in 1969 when the corporate capital stock was $767.7 billion and the noncorporate capital stock was $532.6 billion, pretax rates of return were 18.8 percent and 14.1 percent in the corporate and noncorporate sectors respectively, while posttax rates of return were 9.5 and 9.4 percent.

This proposition about long-run shifting can be illustrated starkly by considering a simple model with two products, X and Y, and two factors of production, K and L. X and Y denote corporate and noncorporate outputs respectively, and K and L denote capital and labor. We assume unitary demand elasticities for X and Y and unitary elasticities of substitution between K and L in the two industries.[13] The industry production functions are $X = L_x^{1/2}K_x^{1/2}$ and $Y = L_y^{1/2}K_y^{1/2}$. In the absence of tax, competitive equilibrium, which results when each factor is paid the value of its marginal product, yields $L_xP_l = 1/2XP_x$; $L_yP_l = 1/2YP_y$; $K_xP_k = 1/2XP_x$; and $K_yP_k = 1/2YP_y$. Assume that the economy's total income is $1,200, with $600 generated in each industry. This requires that labor and capital each earn $300 in each industry. Initially, set $P_l = P_k = 1.00, so there are 300 units of each factor in each industry.

Now suppose a 50 percent tax is levied on income earned by capital in X. Long-run equilibrium in this case requires that twice as much capital be employed in Y as in X—that is, that $K_x = 200$ and $K_y = 400$. In the new equilibrium position, we have $K_xP_{kx} = 300 and $K_yP_{ky} = 300. Inserting the equilibrium values for K_x and K_y and solving gives $P_{kx} = 1.50 and $P_{ky} = 0.75. In long-run equilibrium, the price of capital in X is twice the price of capital in Y, which is necessary to restore an equality of net returns to capital. Although the $150 tax nominally is collected from the corporate sector, the tax is paid by all owners of capital, as the net price of all capital falls to $0.75. The attainment of long-run equilibrium also creates a secondary price effect. Output falls in X and rises in Y and, consequently, the price of X rises and the price of Y falls. But these price changes are offsetting, and consumers as a class are unaffected by the tax. Consumers with relatively strong demands for X will lose, of course, but consumers with relatively strong demands for Y will gain.

Because the corporation income tax is a tax on the return to corporate equity capital, changes in the rate of tax will induce changes in the allocation of resources. Equity capital in the noncorporate sector will be favored relative to equity capital in the corporate sector. Moreover, debt ownership will be favored relative to equity ownership. Additional allocative effects take place because corporate equity capital is taxed at widely varying rates in different industries, which shifts the allocation of capital within the corporate sector.

If there are two sources of equity investment, one corporate and one noncorporate, long-run equilibrium will be attained when the net return on corporate capital equals the net return on noncorporate capital. The

---

[13] This elementary case is described by Harberger, "The Incidence of the Corporation Income Tax," 217–19.

impact of the corporation income tax on the allocation of capital may be illustrated with reference to Figure 10-2.[14] The total capital stock is assumed to be $K_{y1}K_{x1}$, and the equilibrium rate of return is r^*. Of the total capital stock, OK_{y1} is allocated to the noncorporate sector and OK_{x1} is allocated to the corporate sector. If a 50 percent tax is now imposed on the return to corporate capital, capital will leave the corporate sector in the long-run, thereby raising the gross rate of return. Simultaneously, capital will enter the untaxed, noncorporate sector, thereby lowering the rate of return. Equilibrium will be attained only when net rates of return are again equalized between corporate and noncorporate employments of capital. However, this equilibrium position implies that the gross rate of return on corporate capital is twice as high as that on noncorporate capital. In Figure 10-2 the corporate capital stock has shrunk to OK_{x2} while the noncorporate capital stock has expanded to OK_{y2}. The rate of return on noncorporate capital has fallen to r_n, which is also the net rate of return on corporate capital. The gross rate of return on corporate capital, however, is $r_g = 2r_n$.

Although the capital market reaches a new long-run equilibrium, capital will be allocated inefficiently. Returns to owners of capital are equalized between corporate and noncorporate uses. But in turn, this equalization implies that the social return on corporate capital will be twice as high as the social return on noncorporate capital. The social rate of return on corporate capital is r_g, but the private rate of return is r_n. Suppose the gross rates of return on corporate and noncorporate capital are 9 percent and 4.5 percent respectively. Capital invested in the corporate sector will now return 9 percent per year, 4.5 percent to taxpayers and 4.5 percent to owners. Capital invested in the noncorporate sector, however, will return only 4.5 percent per year, all to owners. The total capital stock is thus less productive than it could be, and this reduction in return is an excess burden of the corporation income tax—a dead-weight loss stemming from raising revenues by taxing the income of corporations.

In addition to discouraging equity capital in the corporate sector relative to equity capital in the noncorporate sector, the corporation income tax will discourage equity ownership relative to debt ownership. Because payments on debt claims are a deductible expense for a corporation and a normal rate of return on equity claims is not, the corporate tax will induce a greater amount of debt finance. Of two corporations with equal

---

[14] The diagrammatic representation in Figure 10-2 is based on a fixed total stock of equity capital. This restriction doesn't impinge on the point being illustrated, although a more general formulation would allow the stock of equity capital to be variable. When this possibility is opened, there will be a long-run reduction in equity capital and a long-run increase in such assets as debt claims.

FIGURE 10-2
The Corporation Income Tax and the Allocation of Capital Between Corporate and Noncorporate Sectors

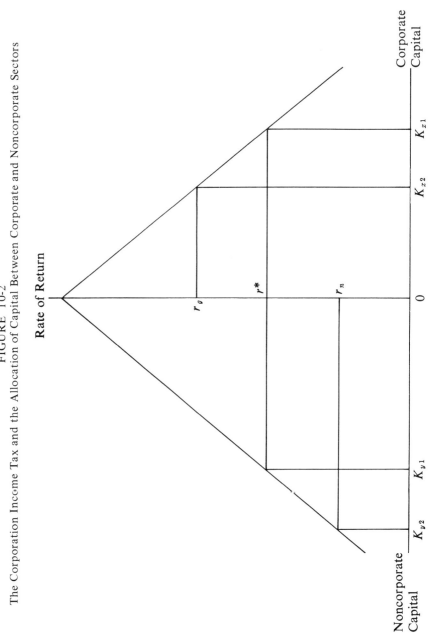

amounts of capital, one in which all capital is equity and one in which capital is evenly split between debt and equity, the latter will be taxed only half as heavily as the former, assuming that the return on debt equals the expected return on equity. Thus, the taxation of corporate income will create an incentive for suppliers of capital to shift from equity to debt. And the higher the rate of tax, the stronger this incentive.

The incentive for equity capital to shift from corporate to non-corporate sectors and for equity to be replaced by debt would exist even if the corporation income tax applied uniformly to all corporations. But uniformity does not prevail, for tax rates vary greatly among industries in the corporate sector. Depletion allowances in the extractive industries are a major source of nonuniformity in the taxation of income from capital.[15] Depletion allowances currently range from 22 percent in such industries as oil and gas, sulfur, and uranium, to 5 percent in such industries as brick, gravel, sand, and shale. Since depletion allowances are taken as a percentage deduction from gross income, a corporation in the oil and gas industry first reduces its gross income by 22 percent and then deducts its ordinary business expenses to determine its taxable income.

If we disallow depletion allowances, capital will become allocated among two industries in the corporate sector such that their net rates of return will be equalized. If percentage depletion is introduced, however, the taxable income of firms in that industry will be lowered, thus raising the net rate of return on investment in that industry. In this way, capital will flow from industries without depletion allowances to industries with depletion allowances until net rates of return are equalized once again. This new equilibrium, however, implies that the gross rate of return in industries without depletion allowances will exceed the gross rate of return in industries with depletion allowances. Because the gross rate of return measures the social rate of return, depletion allowances produce an excess burden that is analogous to the excess burden produced by the corporation income tax.[16]

---

[15] Depletion allowances are not the only source of nonuniformity. Among others, savings and loan associations and life insurance companies are given considerably more favorable tax treatment than are commercial banks. Moreover, the existence of such tax-exempt institutions as foundations, government-owned utilities, schools, and churches is another source of nonuniformity, and capital will generally tend to flow toward employments subject to lower rates of tax.

[16] In the case of the oil and gas industry, it is sometimes argued that the existence of proven oil reserves is a type of collective good, and the depletion allowance is an instrument for promoting the supply of this good. If we accept the argument that oil reserves are partially a collective good, some form of subsidization that is directly related to the size of reserves would seem warranted. The subsidy that is given through depletion allowances, however, varies directly with oil and gas sales, and reserves vary inversely with sales.

WHY CORPORATE TAXATION?

In spite of the considerable inefficiency introduced by the taxation of corporation income, corporate taxation seems to be a permanent fixture in the national tax structure. How is this survival power of corporate taxation explained? What are some possible rationalizations for corporate taxation?

It is sometimes claimed that the personal income tax discriminates against labor income relative to capital income. Of two people who receive equal income, the one who receives it from his labor will be taxed more heavily than the one who earns his income from capital investments will be. The cost of earning income and maintaining capital is deductible in determining the amount of capital income subject to tax. Although a considerable part of labor income is also a cost of maintaining human capital, it is not deductible in determining the amount of labor income subject to tax. If human capital were treated in the same manner as is physical capital, people would be able to deduct certain amounts for expenditures on such items as food, shelter, medicine, and clothing. Because such deductions are not allowed, it is alleged that income from human capital is taxed more heavily than income from physical capital is.

The corporation income tax introduces a double taxation of income from physical capital. The income is taxed once as it is earned by the corporation and once again as the earnings are distributed to stockholders. If it were felt that the personal income tax discriminates against labor income, in some very rough, imperfect sense, this double taxation of income from physical capital would be a means of offsetting the heavier taxation of income from human capital. But double taxation applies only to the earnings from corporate capital. Moreover, it is uncertain whether the resultant impact is to tax both forms of income equally or to tax one more heavily than the other. It would be simpler and more precise to eliminate corporate taxation, or at least to allow corporations to deduct dividends paid in computing their taxable incomes, and to introduce an earned income credit into the personal income tax.[17] With an earned income credit, part of the income generated by human capital would be deductible from gross income in determining taxable income. Furthermore, we shall see in Chapter 12 that prevailing fiscal institutions may not discriminate against labor income and, in fact, may even discriminate in favor of it.

---

[17] There are interdependencies between the elimination of the corporation income tax and reform in the personal income tax, primarily centered on the tax treatment of capital gains. For a few recent analyses, see Martin David, *Alternative Approaches to Capital Gains Taxation* (Washington, D.C.: Brookings, 1968); and Arnold C. Harberger and Martin J. Bailey, eds., *The Taxation of Income from Capital* (Washington, D.C.: Brookings, 1969).

The corporation income tax is often rationalized by claiming that it increases the equity of the tax system by placing an additional tax on owners of corporate equity capital. This judgment is based on the notion that because owners of corporate equity capital come from the higher income classes, the tax increases the overall progressivity of the tax system. This argument based on equity is specious, for the tax violates principles of both vertical and horizontal equity. Although owners of corporate equity tend to have above-average incomes, many persons in middle and lower income classes also own corporate stock. At the same time, many people in the upper income ranges own little or no corporate stock. On the average, the burden of corporate taxation rises in correspondence with increases in personal income levels. Yet corporate ownership is dispersed over the entire income spectrum, so many people with higher incomes will pay less tax than people with lower incomes will pay. A change in the degree of progressivity of the personal income tax could achieve the same relation between average income and average tax liability, but without the capricious reversals found so frequently with the corporation income tax.

The corporation income tax also violates horizontal equity. At any income level, there is wide variation in the share of personal wealth held as corporate stock. The corporation income tax will thus collect different amounts of tax from people at the same income level, depending on variation in relative ownership of corporate stock. Those who hold a relatively larger share of their wealth in corporate stock will be taxed more heavily than their equals who hold relatively less of their wealth in corporate stock will be.

If the corporation income tax performs so poorly, why is it still in use? Why must such a chapter as this one be written? Corporations are inanimate, so they cannot pay tax. Only people can pay tax. Perhaps corporations are popular objects of taxation because they are inanimate. If the corporate tax were replaced by an offsetting increase in the personal income tax, taxpayers would become more aware of the real cost of public services to them. The corporation income tax thus introduces a dose of fiscal anesthesia into the tax system; public services are perceived as less costly when they are financed in part by the corporate tax than they would be if they were financed entirely by personal income taxation.

11. The Taxation of Consumer Expenditure

In Chapters 9 and 10, we examined the assessment of tax liability with reference to the income or factor side of the market. In this chapter, by contrast, we shall examine the assessment of tax liability with reference to the expenditure or product side of the market.[1]

Expenditure may be taxed at any link in the chain of production and distribution. If tax liability is assessed when a product passes from manufacturer to wholesaler, the tax is called a manufacturers sales tax. A sales tax that is assessed when a product passes from wholesaler to retailer is called a wholesalers sales tax. Finally, if tax liability is assessed when a product passes from retailer to consumer, it is called a retail sales tax.[2]

While sales taxes are levied at a single stage in the production-distribution chain, other forms of expenditure taxation may be levied at multiple stages. With a multiple-stage tax, a tax is levied each time a product changes hands in the production-distribution chain. The base of a turnover tax is the gross value of the merchandise sold. If a manufacturer sells merchandise to a wholesaler for $100, who sells it to a retailer for $150, who in turn sells it to a consumer for $200, the tax base will be $450. Such a scheme of taxation clearly creates an artificial incentive for vertical integration. Merely by acquiring the wholesaler, in this instance, the manufacturer could reduce the base of the turnover tax by $100.

The tax base of a value-added tax, by contrast, is the net value of

[1] One of the most frequently advanced rationales for the taxation of expenditure as against the taxation of income is that it is preferable to tax people according to what they take from the stock of wealth than to tax them according to what they contribute. For a recent satement of this position—a position stated by Thomas Hobbes in his *Leviathan*—see Nicholas Kaldor, *An Expenditure Tax* (London: Allen & Unwin, 1955).

[2] A comprehensive treatment of the sales tax is John F. Due, *Sales Taxation* (Urbana: University of Illinois Press, 1957).

the merchandise sold.[3] The tax base of each transaction is the value added by that element of the production-distribution chain. The sale by the manufacturer to the wholesaler would still have a tax base of $100 if we assume that no tax is levied on the assembly of raw materials. When the wholesaler sells the product to the retailer, however, the tax base is only $50. While the product sells for $150, it cost the wholesaler $100, which gives a value added of $50. When the retailer sells the product to the consumer, the value added is again $50. Thus, the total tax base is thus $200, which is also the base of the retail sales tax in this instance. Unlike a turnover tax, however, the base of a value-added tax is unaffected by vertical integration. A merger of manufacturer and wholesaler, would merely make the value added equal to $150 when the product passed from the wholesaler to the retailer.[4]

Sales and excise taxes are the major forms of consumer taxation in the United States. The primary distinction between these two forms of tax is that an excise tax applies to a single product while a sales tax applies to a broad range of products. Because the excise tax applies only to selected products, it is administered by specifying what items are to be taxed and at what rates. However, a sales tax is generally applicable to consumer expenditure, so it is administered primarily by specifying what types of transactions are excluded from tax liability.

SELECTIVE EXCISE TAXATION

An excise tax may be either *specific,* in which case the tax is expressed as a fixed sum per unit of product, or *ad valorem,* in which case the tax is expressed as a percentage of the amount spent on the product. The national government, for instance, levies a specific excise tax of $3 per person on international flights and an *ad valorem* excise tax of 8 percent of the price on domestic flights. The effect of an excise tax on the equilibrium

---

[3] See Clara Sullivan, *The Tax on Value Added* (New York: Columbia University Press, 1965), for an examination of value-added taxation in its alternative forms.

[4] Value-added taxes may be of the *income* or the *consumption* type. Both types begin by subtracting the cost of materials from sales receipts, but they differ in the treatment of investment and depreciation. The income form of the tax subtracts the depreciation of capital assets and adds the purchase of capital assets. The consumption form, by contrast, subtracts the purchase of capital assets and adds the depreciation of capital assets. In an evenly rotating economy where investment is wholly replacement of depreciated capital, the two forms would be identical. In a changing economy, however, the two forms differ. The base of the income type of value-added tax is net national product, while the base of the consumption type is consumption.

price and output of an industry depends on whether the industry is competitive or monopolistic on the one hand, and on the demand and supply conditions facing the industry on the other.

Consider the levy of a specific excise tax on the output of a competitive industry. If the industry is a small part of the economy and resources are fully mobile in the long run, the tax will raise the price of the product by the amount of the tax, as illustrated by Figure 11-1. Before tax, the industry rate of supply is X_1 and the price of its product is P_1. The demand curve D shows the amount that consumers pay for the product. Of this amount, however, the vertical distance $ab = cd$ is the amount of tax payment, which leaves the seller with the amounts indicated by $D - t$. Since resources are fully mobile, the tax will not reduce factor prices, for re-

FIGURE 11-1
Incidence of a Specific Excise Tax on a Competitive
Industry with Unspecialized Inputs

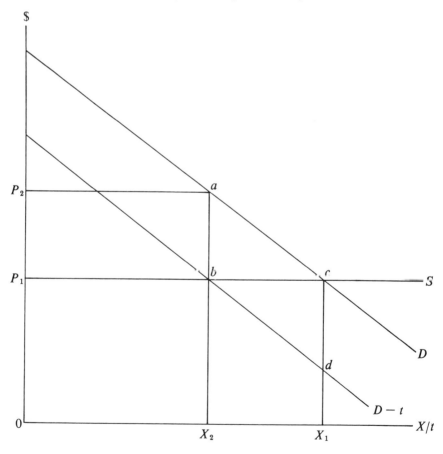

FIGURE 11-2
Incidence of a Specific Excise Tax on a Competitive
Industry with Wholly Specialized Inputs

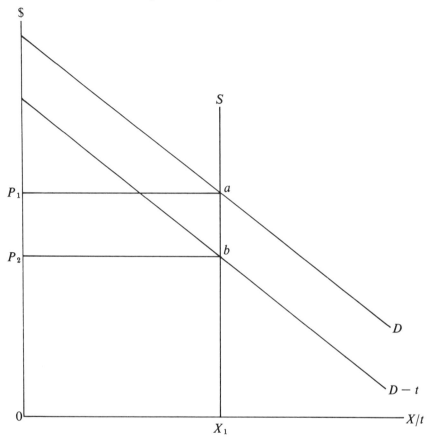

sources must earn the prevailing rate of return or they will shift to alternative employments. Thus, the price of the product will rise by the full amount of the tax. When the posttax equilibrium is attained, the industry price will have increased to P_2 and the industry rate of output will have declined to X_2. The resource inputs that formerly produced the $X_1 - X_2$ of additional X will now be employed in other industries.

Figure 11-2 illustrates the opposing case in which resources are wholly specialized to the industry and, thus, in completely inelastic supply. In this case, a fall in the rate of return will not induce resources to seek other employments. The equilibrium price, P_1, and the rate of output, X_1, are undisturbed by the tax. The amount of tax, *ab*, is wholly paid by factors of production. In this case, the tax is *shifted backward,* in contrast to the preceding case where the tax was *shifted forward.*

If resources are partially, but not fully, mobile, the tax will be split between consumers and factors according to the relative elasticities of supply and demand. This outcome is illustrated by Figure 11-3. The amount of tax is once again $ab = cd,$ and the initial equilibrium position is $P_1X_1.$ In this case, the posttax equilibrium price is P_2 and the rate of output is $X_2.$ The price to consumers rises from P_1 to $P_2,$ which, however, is less than the amount of tax, $P_2P_{2*}.$ Thus, P_2P_1/P_2P_{2*} percent of the tax has been shifted forward to consumers, while P_1P_{2*}/P_2P_{2*} percent has been shifted backward to resource owners.

Slightly different conclusions result if the industry is monopolistic. In

FIGURE 11-3
Incidence of a Specific Excise Tax on a Competitive
Industry with Partially Specialized Inputs

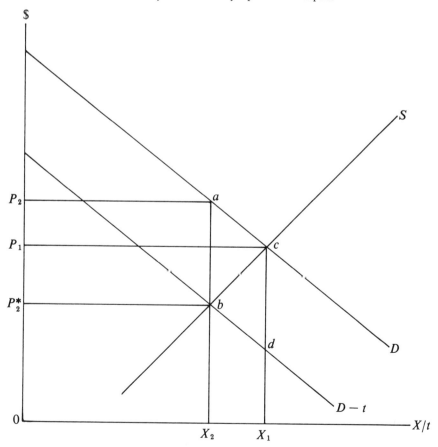

FIGURE 11-4
Incidence of a Specific Excise Tax on a Monopoly
with Partially Specialized Inputs

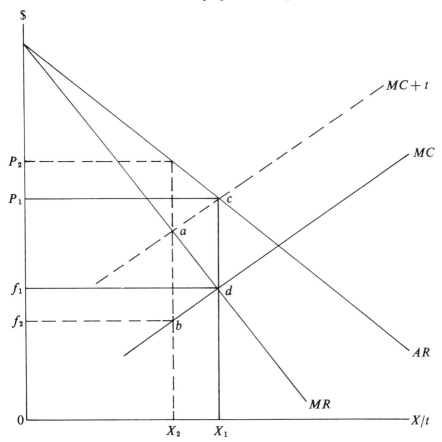

addition to increasing the price paid by consumers and reducing the price paid to factors, the tax may erode part of the monopoly profits. When an industry is monopolistic, then, the tax may be split among three groups rather than two. Figure 11-4 illustrates this possibility. The initial equilibrium price is P_1 and rate of output is X_1. Suppliers of productive factors, however, are paid only f_1, with the difference between the price of the product and the price of inputs, $P_1 - f_1$, accruing to the monopolist. The effect of a tax of $cd = ab$ per unit of output is illustrated by the broken lines. The tax raises the marginal cost curve to $MC + t$, and in the new equilibrium, the price has risen to P_2 and the rate of output has fallen to X_2. The tax has increased the price paid by consumers from P_1 to P_2 and reduced the price received by factors from f_1 to f_2. But the amount of tax per unit, $ab = cd$, exceeds the sum of the increased price paid by consumers, $P_2 - P_1$, and the reduced price received by factors, $f_1 - f_2$, which indicates that part of the tax has also been paid by the monopolist.

CORRECTIVE EXCISE TAXATION

We have seen that an excise tax on an industry's output generally will reduce the equilibrium rate of output. At the same time, it is widely recognized that the production or consumption of some products may entail external costs that are paid by the general community rather than by the producer or consumer of the offending product. Many of the instances of external costs that could be given are examples of pollution in one form or another. In deciding to buy a larger car rather than a smaller car or in deciding to drive to work rather than to travel by mass transit, the individual consumer inflicts costs on other persons by reducing the rate of traffic flow and by increasing the amount of air pollution. Similarly, when pulp and paper firms discharge waste into rivers, they may inflict external costs on downstream users, either by increasing the expense that downstream users must incur before they can use the water or by rendering impossible such downstream activities as fishing and swimming.

Since the output of a product may be inefficiently large if its production or consumption yields external costs, it is often suggested that an excise tax should be levied on such a product to reduce its rate of output toward a more efficient rate. The essential principles of such a corrective tax, as applied to a competitive industry, are illustrated with reference to Figure 11-5. The pretax equilibrium rate of output is X_1, which results in the equilibrium price, P_1. While S represents the marginal cost of resources that must be purchased by the firms in the industry, $S + t$ represents the social marginal cost of the industry's output. At the output rate, X_1, ab represents the marginal cost of those inputs for which the firms in the industry do not pay. If a tax of ab per unit is levied on the industry's output, the industry supply curve will become $S + t$. Such a tax reduces the equilibrium rate of output to X_0, at which point the price of X, P_0, is equal to the social marginal cost of X. The net social gain from this corrective tax is measured by the shaded triangle, abc.[5]

---

[5] This analysis holds for a competitive industry, but not for a monopolist, for two opposing diseconomics exist with monopoly. The tax will reduce the force of the external diseconomy due to the activity in question, but it will exacerbate the diseconomy due to the initial divergence between price and marginal cost. The reduction in output resulting from the tax will produce both a gain and a loss, and the social efficacy of a corrective tax depends on which is larger. On this point, see James M. Buchanan, "External Diseconomics, Corrective Taxes, and Market Structure," *American Economic Review*, 59 (March 1969), 174–77.

FIGURE 11-5
Welfare Gain from a Corrective Excise Tax on a Competitive Industry

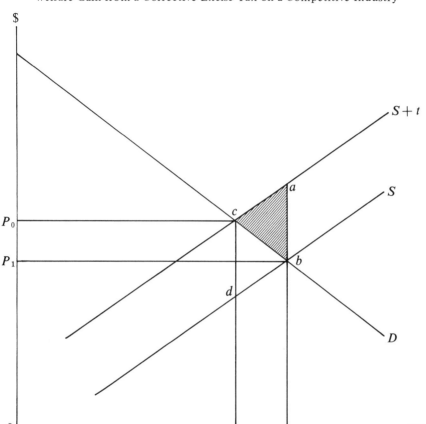

Beginning with papers by Buchanan and Stubblebine and by Coase, the limitations of corrective excise taxation have been carefully explored along several dimensions.[6] Some of these limitations may be examined with the aid of a numerical illustration. Consider some product, X, consumed by A, for whom the marginal valuation function is $V'_{AX} = 30 - X$. The marginal cost of producing X is $C'_X = 20$. We assume individual B is harmed by the production and consumption of X and has the marginal valuation function $V'_{BX} = -X$. An illustration of such a situation might

[6] James M. Buchanan and William Craig Stubblebine, "Externality," *Economica,* 29 (August 1962), 371–84; and Ronald H. Coase, "The Problem of Social Cost," *Journal of Law and Economics,* 3 (October 1960), 1–44.

be for A to denote automobile drivers and for B to denote bicycle drivers, with X denoting a quantity index of automobile services.

When automobile drivers choose their transit mode on the basis of their desire for automobile transit and its cost, equilibrium results when $V'_{AX} = C'_X$ which yields $X = 10$. The Pareto-optimal quantity of X, however, results when $V'_{AX} + V'_{BX} = C'_X$, which gives $X = 5$. When the harm inflicted upon bicycle drivers is taken into account, the index of automobile quantity is reduced from $X = 10$ to $X = 5$. A corrective excise tax of $t = 5$ per unit of X would induce A to choose the optimal quantity of automobile transit. When confronted with the corrective tax, A now chooses a quantity of X such that $V'_{AX} = C'_{AX} + t$, which yields $X = 5$.

Let us now reconsider the pretax equilibrium of $X = 10$. While this outcome is admittedly inefficient, gains from trade between A and B remain unexploited when $X = 10$, which means that $X = 10$ is not truly an equilibrium, unless external constraints are placed upon the development of new institutional arrangements. When $X = 10$, B is willing to pay A to contract the quantity of X at a maximum of $-V'_{BX} = 10$. And B is willing to contract his quantity of X so long as he is paid a minimum of $V'_{AX} - C'_{AX} = 0$. Thus when $X = 10$, it clearly will be possible for B to purchase A's agreement to consume less X, and such trade will be possible until $X = 5$ is attained. The number of individuals involved would typically be large, of course, and in the absence of property rights to street usage, the trades required to attain optimality could not be obtained. If, however, street facilities were priced to users, with automobile and bicycle users comprising a transit club, a set of efficient prices, by maximizing the value of the highway system, would yield the outcome $X = 5$.[7]

Suppose a corrective tax is introduced into a setting in which some mutually profitable trade could be effected, perhaps through institutional modification. Under such circumstances equilibrium results when $-V'_{BX} = V'_{AX} = C'_{AX} - t$, which in more familiar order is $C'_{AX} + t = V'_{AX} + V'_{BX}$, and which is $X = 2.5$. After the posttax equilibrium of $X = 5$, B is willing to pay A to reduce X a maximum of $-V'_{BX}$, which is 5. A is willing to give up X for a minimum of $V'_{AX} - C'_{AX} - t$, which is 0 when $X = 5$. So long as $X > 2.5$, gains from trade exist from a contraction in X. Thus so long as there exist possibilities for trade or for institutional modifications, a corrective tax will bring about an excessive reduction in output.[8]

[7] For a perceptive treatment of related institutional arrangements with respect to urban transit, see Roger Sherman's discussion of Rider's Clubs in "A Private Ownership Bias in Transit Choice," *American Economic Review*, 57 (December 1967), 1211–17.

[8] For similar discussions of corrective taxation when trade does not take place, see William J. Baumol, "On Taxation and the Control of Externalities," *American*

In addition to being used to alter the rate of output, corrective excise taxation also may be used to alter the input mix by which an output is produced, which in some instances may also promote efficiency in the use of resources.[9] In many sections of our major cities, the steady noise level is above 100 decibels, which is louder than a rock band and able to cause permanent loss of hearing. Most items that produce much noise can be produced in a variety of ways, but some are noisier than others are. A fairly quiet jackhammer has been produced, although apparently few have yet been sold. A tax levy that would vary directly with the decibel rating of the product would be one way of inducing the production of quieter motorcycles, trucks, musical instruments, and related sources of noise. Because such products can be produced in a variety of ways, a tax on the decibel rating would induce a shift in the mix of productive inputs such that would result in production of a quieter product.[10]

GENERAL SALES TAXATION

When an excise tax is levied on the output of an industry that is a small part of the total economy and has resources that are mobile, the tax will be paid by consumers of the taxed product. Prices paid to factors cannot fall because factors will shift to alternative employments. With a general sales tax, however, there are no untaxed industries, so factors will have no untaxed alternative employments available. The incidence of a general sales tax, therefore, is equivalent to the result that would obtain from an excise tax if factors were completely immobile. Because resources cannot

---

Economic Review, 62 (June 1972), 307–22; and Hirofumi Shibata, "Pareto-Optimality, Trade and the Pigovian Tax," *Economica,* 39 (May 1972), 190–202. In the absence of trade, corrective taxation may have the aforementioned optimality properties. Yet the pattern of trade itself depends on the prevailing institutional framework, so this pattern will change as the institutional framework changes. Trade among automobile and bicycle drivers may indeed be impossible as long as highway facilities are a common property resource. By converting highway facilities to a private property resource and instituting user pricing, trade would take place implicitly in the effort of the highway owner's attempt to maximize the value of his facility.

[9] This may depend on both the relationship between the production functions of the affected firms and the character of any single firm's production function. On the former point, see Otto A. Davis and Andrew Whinston, "Externalities, Welfare, and the Theory of Games," *Journal of Political Economy,* 70 (June 1962), 241–62. On the latter point, see Charles Plott, "Externalities and Corrective Taxes," *Economica,* 33 (February 1966), 84–87.

[10] Charles J. Goetz and Italo Magnani, in "Automobile Taxation Based on Mechanical Characteristics: Evidence from the Italian Case," *Public Finance,* 24 (No. 3, 1969), 480–94, show that setting tax liability according to mechanical characteristics can induce considerable change in the character of the output.

avoid the tax by shifting to alternative employments, a general sales tax lowers factor prices and is equivalent to a proportional tax on gross income.[11]

If prices and wages are flexible, a general reduction in factor prices will take place. If prices and wages are inflexible, however, the tax burden will be concentrated on those factors that become unemployed. And even if the price level should rise through an expansion in the money supply, the tax will still be borne by factors rather than consumers. While the inflation increases both product prices and factor prices, factor prices will fall relative to product prices, which indicates that the general sales tax is still borne by factors of production. The imposition of a general sales tax is, in effect, a requirement that producers hire a new factor of production—government consent. The pretax equilibrium results when each factor is paid the value of its marginal product and the total product is exhausted. The yield from the tax may be viewed as the payment to the government factor, which must reduce the returns to other factors because the total value of the product is unchanged by the tax.

Actual sales taxes, of course, deviate considerably from full generality. Services, especially those supplied by government, are almost universally exempt from sales taxation. Moreover, food for home consumption, clothing, utilities, and drugs are commonly exempted from the base of the retail sales tax. When exemptions are introduced, it becomes possible for factors to escape part of the tax, which shifts some of the burden to consumers. The availability of untaxed alternatives prevents factor prices from falling by the full amount of the tax. As the availability of untaxed alternatives increases, the share of the tax that will be paid by factors decreases. In spite of the availability of tax exemptions, however, retail sales taxes are substantially general, so the bulk of the tax is probably paid by factors of production.

However, a fully general sales tax levied by only one state will be paid primarily by consumers in that state. Although there are no untaxed alternatives within the state to which resources can flow, here, the option of moving across state boundaries is still open. The rate of return to factors of production is determined largely within the national economy, and the lower the cost of factor mobility, the less the share of the tax borne by

---

[11] The essential analysis is found in Richard A. Musgrave, *The Theory of Public Finance* (New York: McGraw-Hill, 1959), pp. 347–71. While this conclusion is now widely accepted, it was once a point of contention. For a survey of the debate that once raged, see James M. Buchanan, "The Methodology of Incidence Theory," pp. 125–50 in his *Fiscal Theory and Political Economy* (Chapel Hill: University of North Carolina Press, 1960). For a recent comprehensive survey of the theory of tax incidence, see Peter Mieszkowski, "Tax Incidence Theory," *Journal of Economic Literature,* 7 (December 1969), 1103–24.

TABLE 11-1
Illustration of Regressivity of Sales Taxation

Person	Income	Consumption	Tax	Tax/Income
A	$ 5,000	$4,500	$225	4.5%
B	10,000	8,000	400	4.0

factors. If only a relatively few states levied sales taxes, the tax would be paid largely by consumers in those states, even if it were fully general. However, only Alaska, Delaware, Montana, New Hampshire, and Oregon do not levy sales taxes, so there is relatively little opportunity for factors to escape tax liability. Because sales taxes are neither fully general within any one state nor applicable to all states, some forward shifting of the tax takes place. But the tax is substantially general and most states are covered, so probably the bulk of the tax is shifted backwards.

It is commonly claimed that sales taxation is regressive when the tax is restated in terms of an income base. This charge of regressivity is based on such evidence as the figures shown in Table 11-1. Assume that of two individuals, *A* and *B*, *A* has income of $5,000 and *B* has income of $10,000. *A* spends 90 percent of his income and *B* spends 80 percent of his. At a tax rate of 5 percent, *A* thus pays $225 in tax while *B* pays $400. As a percentage of income, *A* is taxed at 4.5 percent while *B* is taxed at 4.0 percent. On the basis of such evidence as this, sales taxation would seem to be regressive. Thus, the argument that sales taxation is regressive when related to an income base rests on two assumptions: (1) that the tax is shifted forward to consumers, and (2) that the average propensity to consume falls as income rises.

The first assumption on which the claim of regressivity is based seems largely erroneous. Sales taxes will tend to be shifted backwards to factors. A truly general sales tax would be identical to a proportional tax on gross income. Obviously, sales taxes are not truly general, for services and savings largely are exempt from most tax bases. Because sales taxes are not perfectly general, there will be some opportunity for factor mobility, which will introduce an element of forward shifting. Yet this opportunity for forward shifting is relatively small, so only a minority share of the tax is likely to be shifted forward to consumers.

Moreover, even if one assumes that the tax is paid by consumers, the charge of regressivity is critically dependent on the assumption about the income-consumption relationship. Is the appropriate relationship the one indicated by annual measured income, or is it the one indicated by normal or permanent income? Although consumption as a percentage of measured income falls as measured income rises, consumption is a constant

percentage of permanent income for all levels of permanent income. Therefore, we must distinguish an income-consumption relationship based on
current income and one based on permanent income.[12] When liability for
sales tax is related to current income, it is clearly regressive when related
to an income base. But when tax liability is related to permanent income,
sales tax liability becomes distributed proportional to income.[13]

[12] Milton Friedman, *A Theory of the Consumption Function,* National Bureau
of Economic Research, General Series No. 63 (Princeton, N.J.: Princeton University
Press, 1957).

[13] David G. Davies, "Progressiveness of a Sales Tax in Relation to Various
Income Bases," *American Economic Review,* 50 (December 1960), 987–95, showed
that the sales tax in Ohio in 1956, the source of his data, was regressive in terms
of current income but was progressive in terms of permanent income. This illustration
is generally typical, so the conclusions are generally applicable to all retail sales
taxes.

Jeffrey M. Schaefer, "Sales Tax Regressivity Under Alternative Tax Bases
and Income Concepts," *National Tax Journal,* 22 (December 1969), 510–27, used
New Jersey data for 1960–61 and reached conclusions quite similar to Davies'.

12. The Taxation of Capital Value

Taxation may be based on either the value of a stock at some point in time or the value of a flow over some interval of time. In the preceding three chapters, we examined alternative tax institutions that were based on the value of income and spending flows. In this chapter, we shall shift our attention to tax institutions based on the value of capital stocks.

INCOME AND CAPITAL AS BASES FOR TAXATION

When income and capital are defined consistently, it makes no difference whether a tax is levied on an income flow or on the capital stock implied by that income flow. Income is the flow that emanates from a capital stock; a capital stock produces a flow of real goods and services. Given a rate of discount, the valuation of either the stock or the flow implies a value for the other. Consider a capital asset that produces a stream of services valued at $10,000 per year. If the rate of return on capital is 10 percent and the stream is a perpetuity, the implied capital value is $100,000, which is the present discounted value of the income stream. An annual tax of 10 percent on the income flow is identical to an annual tax of 1 percent on the capital value. Because capital and income are merely images of one another, there is a conceptual equivalence between taxing the value of an income flow and taxing the value of a capital stock.[1]

[1] In Chapter 9 we distinguished the flow and the accretion concepts of income. In the above description of the equivalence between capital and income, we have defined income as a flow and, accordingly, assigned it a capital value. If we define income as an accretion, however, we must modify our measure of capital if we are to retain our equivalence between capital and income. The equivalent capital value for the accretion definition of income is net wealth, not gross wealth. If the asset cited above carries an annual obligation for debt retirement of $1,000, the net income from the asset will be $9,000, which produces a net capital value

As we noted in Chapter 10, a rationale that frequently is presented for capital taxation is that it is a means of offsetting the discrimination against labor income that characterizes the personal income tax.[2] The argument that the personal income tax discriminates against income from human capital would seem to have considerable intuitive plausibility. Owners of physical capital can deduct the cost of depreciation and maintenance from the gross income produced by the asset, and are then taxed on the net income. Owners of human capital cannot deduct the cost of depreciation and maintenance, even though a considerable part of personal expenditure is for such capital maintenance. Thus, the personal income tax would seem to discriminate against the income received from human capital vis-à-vis physical capital. Capital taxation in general and property taxation in particular discriminate against the ownership of physical capital, for the tax base includes only the value of physical assets. Income taxation and capital taxation would seem to discriminate in offsetting directions against physical and human capital respectively, although such offsetting discrimination does very crudely what could be done more precisely by introducing an earned income credit into the personal income tax.

The argument that existing tax provisions discriminate against human capital would seem ironclad as long as persons acquired human capital through personal investment. Consider two persons who each invest $10,000, one in himself and one in a physical asset. Let the annual gross return be $2,000 in each case, and assume that maintenance costs are $1,000. Thus, the pretax annual return is $1,000. Suppose the rate of tax on income is 25 percent. The income from human capital would be taxed $500, leaving a posttax income of $500. The income from physical capital would be taxed only $250, leaving a posttax income of $750. Consequently, the net rate of return on physical capital would be 7.5 percent, while it would be only 5.0 percent on human capital. This difference in posttax rates of return would seem to indicate discrimination against income from human capital.

The setting we have just described does not illustrate prevailing institutions adequately, however, because the formation of much human capital is subsidized by government through the supply of education free of user pricing. When the formation of human capital is heavily subsidized, it is

---

of $90,000. Property taxation in the United States, however, is based on gross capital value rather than on net capital value, which makes it a nonpersonal (*ad rem*) tax on assets rather than a personal (*in personam*) tax on individual claims to wealth.

[2] See, for instance, Alan A. Tait, *The Taxation of Personal Wealth* (Urbana: University of Illinois Press, 1967).

as if human capital valued at $10,000 can be acquired by investing, say, only $5,000. Under such circumstances, the $500 posttax income from human capital would indicate a net rate of return of 10 percent. If this were the case, prevailing fiscal institutions would discriminate against physical capital, not against human capital. Whether one form of capital or another is discriminated against is clearly an empirical matter. There is no analytical basis for claiming that the personal income tax discriminates against human capital. Hence, there is no analytical basis for arguing that the introduction of an earned income credit into the personal income tax, the taxation of corporation income, or some other form of capital taxation is needed to offset discrimination against human capital. At the present time, it may very well be that physical capital, not human capital, is discriminated against.

Property taxation, which presently accounts for nearly 85 percent of the tax revenue of local governments, is the dominant form of capital taxation in the United States. In addition to property taxation, capital values also are taxed by national and state governments when they are transferred from one person to another. Capital that is transferred when a person dies is taxed either by estate or inheritance taxation, while capital transferred during a donor's lifetime is taxed under gift taxation. Receipts from the taxation of capital transfers account for less than 12 percent of total receipts from the taxation of capital value.[3] As practiced in the United States, then, the taxation of capital value is primarily the taxation of property value, more particularly, the taxation of real property value, so we shall limit our examination in the remainder of this chapter to the taxation of real property.

THE TAXATION OF PROPERTY VALUE

The base of the property tax is classified into two forms of property: real property (realty) and personal property (personalty). A further distinction is often made between land and improvements in the case of realty and between tangibles and intangibles in the case of personalty. Of the revenues collected from property taxation, over 85 percent are collected from taxes on realty.

Intangible assets include such items as corporate stock, bonds, mortgages, and notes receivable. Intangibles are claims against the income from

---

[3] For a recent description and analysis of the taxation of wealth transfers, see Richard E. Wagner, *Inheritance, Inequality, and Progressive Taxation* (Washington, D.C.: American Enterprise Institute), 1973.

assets. As a result, the nonpersonal nature of the property tax suggests that intangibles should be exempt from tax. For instance, a corporation should not be taxed both as the owner of property in some locality and as citizens who own stock in the corporation. This is clearly double taxation, for the assets are taxed once in their form as buildings and once again in their form as individually held claims of ownership. The taxation of mortgages raises the identical issue of double taxation, for a tax may be assessed simultaneously against the realty and against the mortgage held on that realty. Because intangibles can be hidden from the tax assessor with relative ease, they are a relatively unproductive revenue base, which probably explains the relative infrequency of efforts to tax intangibles.

As a method of producing revenue, taxation of tangible personalty is only moderately more successfully than is taxation of intangible personalty. Automobiles are the only element of tangible personalty owned by individuals that are taxed with any degree of success, although the tax conceivably could be extended to such property as household furnishings and durable goods. The tax levied on businesses is somewhat more successful when it is levied on such property as inventories and equipment.

Property taxation is preponderantly the taxation of realty, and it is common to distinguish the taxation of land and the taxation of improvements. The taxation of residential realty and the taxation of nonresidential realty each yield about 45 percent of the total revenue from the taxation of realty, and the remaining 10 percent is produced by the taxation of farm realty.

Obviously, the revenue produced by any tax is the product of a tax rate and a tax base. Defining the tax base is an especially difficult problem in implementing a tax on realty. In principle, the base of the tax is the value of real property. Because a piece of realty usually changes ownership only intermittently, however, market values are not available for most real property. This creates considerable difficulty in implementing property taxation. With income or consumption taxation, by contrast, market valuations are recorded continually, which greatly facilitates the valuation of the base. In the absence of such market valuations for individual real property, a tax base can be established only by estimating a value for real property and using the valuation to determine the tax base.

There are several techniques by which a parcel of real property can be assigned an appraised value. One method is to examine the sales price of similar properties and to use this information as a foundation on which to make a judgment about the value of the property under examination. Another is simply to value the property at its cost of production, perhaps periodically revising it upward to account for inflation. Still another technique is to determine the annual income derived from the property and to capitalize that income flow to derive a capital value.[4] After property has been assigned an appraised value, an assessed value is established. While an appraised value is, in principle, a reasonable approximation to market value, an assessed value is set explicitly at some fraction of appraised value. The tax rate is then specified as some percentage of assessed value, and the product of the tax rate and the assessed value (tax base) determines the tax liability for the property.

As a matter of arithmetic, of course, it is irrelevant whether property is assessed at 100 percent of appraised value or at 25 percent. Tax liability is a product of base and rate, and a tax rate of 1 percent when property is assessed at 100 percent of appraised value is equivalent to a tax rate of 4 percent when property is assessed at 25 percent. Yet assessed value typically ranges between 5 percent and 80 percent of appraised value. As an assessed value can be established only after an appraised value has been assigned, it is reasonable to ask why property taxes are not based on appraised value. Why take the additional step of computing an assessed value? Part of the explanation lies in the competition among localities for state aid. Many programs of state aid to localities distribute aid in inverse proportion to a locality's share of the total assessed property value in the state. By lowering its assessed value, then, a locality can increase its share of state aid. It is because of such competition for aid that states have intervened through boards of equalization to set lower bounds to the ratios of assessed value to appraised value.

Another feature of property taxation that also operates to distinguish assessed value and appraised value is that responsibility for setting assessed value is divorced from responsibility for setting tax rates on these values. While assessed values are established by an assessor, tax rates applicable to those assessed values are established by a legislative council. Tax liability is thus the product of the actions of two separate offices. An assessor is generally motivated to strive for low assessed values and would rather have responsibility for increased taxes lodged with the city council than with himself. The city council is in the opposite position. It sets the rate of tax and would prefer to increase the budget without raising tax rates, which requires an increase in assessed value. Assessors and legislators thus play somewhat different roles in the local budgetary process.

It is tempting to think that this clash between the assessor and the city council is imaginary. Simple arithmetic suggests that it should be irrelevant to all participants whether tax rates are $1 per $100 of assessed

[4] See, for instance, James W. Martin, "New Dimensions of the Capitalization of Earnings in Appraising Public Utility Property," in Harry L. Johnson, ed., *State and Local Tax Problems* (Knoxville: University of Tennessee Press, 1969), pp. 148–63.

TABLE 12-1
Assessment Ratios and Property Tax Rates

Ratio of Assessed to Appraised Value	Tax Rate		Real Rate as Percent of Nominal Rate
	Nominal	Real	
15–19.9	9.33	1.63	17.5
20–24.9	8.85	1.99	22.5
25–29.9	7.86	2.16	27.5
30–34.9	6.23	2.02	32.4
35–39.9	5.37	2.01	37.4
40–49.9	5.24	2.36	45.0
50–59.9	5.23	2.88	55.1

Source: U.S. Department of Commerce, Bureau of the Census, *Taxable Property Values–1967 Census of Governments* (Washington, D.C.: U.S. Government Printing Office, 1968), p. 15.

value under 100 percent assessment or $4 per $100 of assessed value under 25 percent assessment. But the evidence in Table 12-1 clearly shows the contrary, for real rates of property tax rise significantly with increases in the rate of assessed value to appraised value. Real rates of property tax range from 1.63 percent in localities with an assessment ratio between 15 and 19.9 percent to 2.88 percent in localities with an assessment ratio between 50 and 59.9 percent. Among communities with the lowest ratios of assessed to appraised value, the real rate of tax is 17.5 percent of the nominal rate; among communities with the highest ratios of assessed to appraised value, by contrast, the real rate of tax is 55.1 percent of the nominal rate. This evidence suggests that there is less opposition to tax increases that result from increases in assessed values than there is to tax increases that result from increases in nominal tax rates.

Assessed value as a percentage of market value varies considerably among realty within a metropolitan area. For instance, Oldman and Aaron found that the average ratio of assessed value to sales price in Boston for 1962 ranged from 34.1 percent on single family residences to 79 percent on commercial property.[5] In addition to this variation among classes of property, there was also substantial variation among property of the same class within the metropolitan area. The ratio of assessed value to sales price for single-family residences ranged from 28.1 percent to 54.1 percent, and for commercial property, the ratio ranged from 59 percent to 110.9 percent.

Numerous suggestions have been advanced for dealing with the inequity reflected by the variability in ratios of assessed values to sales

[5] Oliver Oldman and Henry Aaron, "Assessment-Sales Ratios Under the Boston Property Tax," *National Tax Journal,* 18 (March 1965), 36–49.

prices.[6] For the most part, these suggestions retain the essential framework of the tax in that assessed values still would have to be assigned for individual pieces of real property. Typical suggestions for assessment reform assert that greater professionalization of the assessment corps and expanded use of electronic data processing will reduce assessment variability. Yet a system in which a tax base is assigned by third parties instead of emerging automatically through market transactions is almost inherently corruptible.[7] A system in which property value is self-assessed is a radically different institutional format that may have potential merit.[8] Under a self-assessing system, the individual property owner would declare his own property value. To ensure against free-riding by underassessment, the assessment would carry an obligation to sell at some percentage (say 120 percent) of that assessed value. Or, as a modification, some penalty could be levied for the privilege of changing one's declared assessment after someone offered to buy at the assessed price. Self-assessment is likely to produce greater horizontal equity in the distribution of tax liability. Self-assessment also would facilitate the assembly of parcels of land in urban areas, thereby quickening the operation of the urban land market and obviating the need for eminent domain.

INCIDENCE OF PROPERTY TAXATION

Property taxation is primarily a tax on the ownership of real property. Human capital is fully exempt from the tax, and personalty is taxed at rates that are considerably lower than those applied to realty. Thus, the property tax is not truly a general tax on capital value, but because its

[6] Without denying the existence of substantial variability, Warner W. Doering, in "The Use of Statistical Techniques in Equity Determination," *1964 Proceedings of the National Tax Association* (Columbus, Ohio: National Tax Association, 1965), pp. 390–400, makes the important point that measures of dispersion exaggerate the amount of real dispersion. Among all properties with the same expected sales price, there will be random variations in actual sales prices. Even if assessment-sales ratios are uniform in terms of expected sales prices, variations in actual sales prices will introduce dispersion into assessment-sales ratios. Thus, some of the variation in assessment-sales ratios that is attributed to assessment practices should be attributed to normal variation in market prices.

[7] For illustrations of assessment fraud in California, see Ronald B. Welch, "Property Taxation: Policy Potentials and Probabilities," in Arthur D. Lynn, Jr., ed., *The Property Tax and its Administration* (Madison: University of Wisconsin Press, 1969), pp. 203–14.

[8] For a brief proposal, see Arnold C. Harberger, "Issues of Tax Reform for Latin America," in *Fiscal Policy for Economic Growth in Latin America* (Baltimore: Johns Hopkins Press, 1965), pp. 119–20. For a careful exploration of self-assessment, see Daniel M. Holland and William A. Vaughn, "An Evaluation of Self-Assessment Under a Property Tax," in Lynn, ed., *The Property Tax and its Administration*, pp. 79–118.

base is quite broad, it cannot be treated as a selective tax on particular capital. In examining the incidence of property taxation, a selective tax on a particular parcel of real property will be considered; next, the analysis will be extended to a general tax on real property; and finally, the fact that real property is but a subset of all capital will be recognized.

If a parcel of real property yields an annual return of $1,000, and the rate of interest is 10 percent, the capital value of the realty would be $10,000. Suppose a perpetual annual tax of $100 is levied against the property. The posttax annual return from the property falls to $900, but because the rate of return on capital remains at 10 percent, the value of the property falls to $9,000. The tax is thus fully capitalized at the time it is announced; the full burden of the tax is borne by the owner of the realty at the time the tax is announced. Immediately after the tax is announced, the market value of the property falls to $9,000. Although a subsequent owner would be liable for annual tax payments of $100, he would not bear any of the tax because he would receive a net return of 10 percent on his capital.

The conclusion that a specific tax on a particular piece of property will be fully capitalized at the time the tax is announced contrasts sharply with the analysis of a general tax on all capital. While a general capital tax reduces the annual yield from capital, it also reduces the appropriate discount rate—which is the net rate of return on capital. A 1 percent annual tax on all capital will reduce the rate of return on capital to 9 percent. The $900 annual yield along with the 9 percent rate of return produce a capital value of $10,000, which is also the pretax capital value. Whereas a specific tax on a particular piece of property is fully capitalized and wholly paid at the time it is announced, a general tax on all capital is not capitalized at all, but rather is paid over time as the nominal tax payments are made.

A tax on real property falls between the two extreme cases of a specific capital tax and a general capital tax, although it is relatively closer to a general capital tax. Realty is only one element of capital, so a tax on real property is not a general tax on capital. To some extent, therefore, real estate taxes will be capitalized into property values at the time the tax is announced. But capitalization should not be overemphasized. Realty comprises a substantial share of total capital; therefore, a tax on real property will reduce the rate of return on capital. A substantial share of real estate taxes will be paid over time as tax payments are made by the owners of the property.

In the short run, an increase in realty taxes will be borne by owners of realty. The tax on residential property will be borne by the owners of residential property, both owner-occupiers and owner-landlords. The supply of realty is fixed in the short run, and because the tax does not affect the demand for realty, the tax increase will reduce the return to owners of residential realty. Similarly, the tax on business property will be borne by the owners of business. The supply of business realty is fixed in the short run, and the tax does not affect consumer demand for business products. Consequently, the tax will be paid by owners rather than being shifted forward to consumers. For all classes of property, then, the short-run burden of an increase in realty tax rests on property owners.

By imposing the tax on real property, the net rate of return to realty falls below the net rate of return to other forms of capital. Hence, the tax creates disequilibrium in the capital market. Equilibrium will be restored only as the net rate of return on realty becomes equal to the net rate of return on nonrealty. Equilibrium will be reattained only as capital is withdrawn from the supply of real property and reemployed in alternative uses. This reduction in the relative supply of real property will result both from disinvestment in existing property and from a slackening of the rate of investment in new property. By this shift in the employment of capital, part of the tax that was originally paid by owners of real property becomes transmitted to owners of nonrealty capital. The long-run incidence of a tax on real property is quite similar to the long-run incidence of the corporation income tax.[9] As the relative supply of real property decreases in the long run, moreover, there will be some rise in the price of real property, thereby placing part of the burden on consumers of real property rather than on owners of capital.

Real property usually is separated into land and improvements, although the separation usually serves no particular function. It is sometimes suggested that the separation between land and improvements should be sharpened and that increased emphasis should be placed on the taxation of land relative to the taxation of improvements. By shifting tax liability from improvements to site value, a more productive use of land might be encouraged. It is argued that basing tax liability on the value of the land rather than on the combined value of the land and the improvements will induce a more intensive use of urban land, thereby dampening tendencies toward urban sprawl. Generally, the price of improvements relative to the price of land rises as the proximity of the property to the center of the city increases. If property taxation is replaced by site value taxation of equal yield, the tax liability assigned to more proximate locations will decline relative to the tax liability assigned to more distant locations. Consequently, land will be developed even more intensively in the relatively

---

[9] We should note that the standard view of the incidence of property taxation, insofar as there is one, says that the residential tax is paid by consumers of housing (owner-occupiers and renters) and that the nonresidential tax is paid by customers of the businesses subject to tax. See, for instance, Dick Netzer, *Economics of the Property Tax* (Washington, D.C.: Brookings, 1966), pp. 36–46.

proximate locations, causing the density gradient to decline from the center of the city at a steeper rate.[10]

Annual taxes on realty are approximately 1.5 percent of the value of real property and approximately 17 percent of the annual rental value of real property. For owner-occupiers, this is an extremely low rate of tax that clearly encourages investment in real property. The rental value of owner-occupied housing is not subject to income tax, so owner-occupiers are taxed on the average at 17 percent on the income they derive from their real property, which is the marginal rate of tax in the fourth-lowest rate bracket of the personal income tax. Once we allow for the deductibility of mortgage interest payments and local property taxes, taxes on realty average about 15 percent of the income received by owner-occupiers, which is the marginal rate of tax in the second-lowest bracket of the personal income tax. Prevailing tax institutions clearly favor individual ownership of real property over other types of capital.[11]

The claim that property taxation is regressive when related to an income base is heard frequently. This claim of regression is based on the observations that: (1) property taxes are paid by consumers, and (2) the percentage of income spent on housing falls as income rises. Neither observation seems correct. We have already seen that the bulk of the property tax is paid by owners of realty in the short run, and by owners of capital in general in the long run. To the extent that owners of capital have above-average incomes, the property tax becomes progressive when related to an income base. Moreover, the observation that the percentage of income spent on housing falls as income rises depends critically on the definition of income. The relation between tax incidence and the definition of income is the same one that confronted us in examining the regressivity of sales taxation in Chapter 11. If we use annual measured income, relative spending on housing falls as income rises. But if we use permanent income, housing expenditures are approximately a constant percentage of permanent income, which suggests that the share of property taxation that is paid by consumers of housing is paid approximately in proportion to permanent income.[12]

---

[10] For a succinct summary of evidence showing the inconclusiveness of efforts to discern the differential impact of site value taxation, see William B. Neenan, *Political Economy of Urban Areas* (Chicago: Markham, 1972), pp. 264–70.

[11] For a recent examination, see Henry Aaron, "Income Taxes and Housing," *American Economic Review*, 60 (December 1970), 789–809.

The same tax advantage does not exist for owner-landlords, for their rental receipts are taxed under the personal income tax. If, as an illustration, an owner-landlord pays personal taxes at a 28 percent marginal rate, the income from his investment in real property is taxed at 45 percent.

[12] On the relation between income and housing expenditure, see Richard F. Muth, "The Demand for Non-Farm Housing," in Arnold C. Harberger, ed., *The*

PROPERTY TAXATION, LOCAL GOVERNMENT, AND FISCAL CHOICE

User pricing aside, local governments rely on property taxation for nearly 85 percent of their revenue. Property taxation plays an interesting role in the fiscal affairs of local governments, for a property tax may perform in much the same manner as does a user price. In Chapter 4, we saw that the fiscal choices that emerge within a system of localities in a metropolitan area possess characteristics similar to the private choices that emerge through ordinary market exchange. In contrast to a unified metropolitan government, a system of localities can accommodate variation in personal preferences for public services. By permitting variation among localities in the provision of public services, a system of localities enables a person to choose from bundles of public services in much the same way that the market enables a person to choose among competing products. This is not to say that a person's choice among competing localities operates identically to a person's choice among competing products on the market, but only that the two settings for choice operate similarly.

In a system of competing localities, a property tax performs approximately as a benefit tax. Indeed, if competition among localities were perfect, the property tax would be a perfect benefit tax in the sense of Wicksell's principle of taxation. As we saw in Chapter 3, the system of marginal benefit taxation that emerges from fiscal choice under Wicksellian institutions assigns tax prices for nonexcludable public services in a fashion analogous to the way in which competitive prices are established for excludable private services. Because property taxation within a system of localities approaches marginal benefit taxation and a marginal benefit tax is an analogue to a competitive price, it follows that property taxation has many of the features of user pricing.[13] Indeed, if localities were perfectly homogenous with respect to preferences for public services, property taxation would function perfectly as a benefit tax.

The property tax actually creates a tie-in sale: the purchase of public services is tied to the purchase of housing. Thus, a person jointly consumes public services and housing, and the total price of this joint package is the sum of the property tax liability and the price of housing. Even though

Demand for Durable Goods (Chicago: University of Chicago Press, 1960), pp. 29–96; and Margaret G. Reid, *Housing and Income* (Chicago: University of Chicago Press, 1962).

[13] For an empirical examination suggesting that property taxation performs much as a price in a system of localities, see Wallace E. Oates, "Effects of Property Taxes and Local Public Spending on Property Values," *Journal of Political Economy,* 77 (No. 6, 1969), 957–71.

nonexclusion may render it impossible to price the various public services supplied within each locality directly, property taxation performs much as a user price. The purchase of housing, which brings with it a liability for property tax, becomes the device for excluding noncontributors and inducing the revelation of marginal preferences.

Once we consider the role of property taxation within the fiscal choice process of a system of localities, we see that property taxation has considerable merit as a means for promoting efficiency in local budgetary choice. Yet property taxation has become the object of increased and vigorous attack from several directions. Property taxation is condemned as violating horizontal equity on the one hand and as being regressive on the other. The attack on property taxation has inspired several proposals for replacing the tax, or at least for reducing its importance. Federal revenue-sharing financed by a tax on value added often has been suggested as a means of reducing local reliance on property taxation.

Perhaps paradoxically, the increasing dissatisfaction with property taxation might be evidence that the tax does operate essentially as a user price. Since the property tax performs much as a price for local public services, local voters would be relatively well informed as to the cost to them of local public services. A tax on value added, by contrast, is indirect and largely hidden, so it would perform less effectively as an instrument for informing taxpayers of the cost of public services. Taxpayers generally will evaluate public services financed by a $100 property tax as being more costly than public services financed by a $100 value-added tax. Perhaps this difference in taxpayer perceptions of cost explains why proposals for property tax relief are so popular.

Yet both the property tax and the sales tax are distributed approximately in proportion to income. Therefore, we should expect that a shift from one tax form to the other would exert relatively little impact on distribution of cost for public services. Rather, the primary impact would be only a reduction in taxpayer sensitivity to the cost of public services. One significant difference that would result is that to the extent that property tax changes are capitalized, replacement of property taxation by value-added taxation would transfer income from future owners of real property to present owners. The reduction in property tax will be partially capitalized into an increase in property value. Those who buy real property in the future would thus have to pay a higher price because of the capitalization of the tax reduction. The shift in the form of taxation, then, transfers income from future owners to present owners.[14]

[14] This point is developed in C. Lowell Harriss, "Property Taxation: Modernization," *Tax Review,* 33 (May 1972), 17–20.

Capitalization, even if it is only partial, also raises interesting issues regarding the treatment of local public expenditures in the national income accounts. Under the standard accounting convention, public services are entered into the national income accounts at the cost outlay upon them.[15] A city that spends $1 million per year for parks would enter the $1 million as a contribution of the park to national output. Yet to the extent that shifts in the market prices of property are capitalized, it would seem as though such public facilities as police protection, fire protection, street cleaning, and park facilities that are made available without direct pricing should be entered at zero in the national income accounts.

To illustrate the issues at stake, consider a simple model containing two communities, *A* and *B*, which are identical in all respects except that *A* develops and maintains a park free of direct charge while *B* does not. The contribution of *B* to national income would be the sum of the private outputs produced in *B* multiplied by their respective prices. Since *A* devotes some resources to the provision of the park rather than to the production of private outputs, the total value of the private output in *A* would be less than that in *B*. By adding the outlays upon the park to the value of private services, however, *A* would seem to be placed on a parity with *B*. Hence, it would seem as though the cost outlays on freely available public services should be added to the market value of private services. If they are not, the national income of communities that provide relatively more public services will be understated relative to communities that provide relatively more private services.

The fallacy in this standard position is the assumption that the provision of the park in *A* will not be reflected in higher prices for private services in *A*. To the extent that the park is desired by residents of *A*, the provision of the park will increase the demand for residency in *A*, thereby increasing the value of property located in *A*. Consequently, the price of housing will be higher in *A* than in *B*, so the market value of private services in *A* will reflect the valuation placed upon the public park.

Many members of the set of present sellers will belong to the set of future buyers, in which case such income transfers cancel one another. Yet there will be younger persons entering the housing market and older persons leaving the housing market. Moreover, other persons will be moving up to higher quality housing as their incomes rise. Thus, the shift in tax form would subsidize older persons at the expense of younger persons, and it would subsidize those with higher property values at the expense of those with lower property values.

[15] For discussions of treating public expenditures in the national income accounts, see Francesco Forte and James M. Buchanan, "The Evaluation of Public Services," *Journal of Political Economy,* 69 (April 1961), 107–21; and Richard A. Musgrave, *The Theory of Public Finance* (New York: McGraw-Hill, 1959), pp. 184–201.

If full capitalization should take place, the value of the park would be fully reflected in the market value of property in A. Under such circumstances, entering public services at their cost outlays, regardless of whether those services are considered investment or consumption, will entail counting the public services twice—once at their cost outlays and once at their implicit valuation through market prices. By entering public services at cost outlays, then, the national incomes of localities that provide relatively more public services will be overstated relative to the national incomes of localities that provide relatively fewer public services.

Of course, capitalization will be only partial, as we have seen above. Therefore, there will be built-in biases in either accounting convention. Between two communities at the same point in time or for the same community at two points in time, the bias will favor the community that provides relatively more public services if public services are entered at their cost outlays. If, however, no direct value is entered for public services, the bias will favor the community that provides relatively fewer public services.

13. Debt Creation and Money Creation

Of the four instruments for financing the supply of public services, debt creation and money creation are the two that remain for discussion. Debt creation and money creation are distinct fiscal instruments; the creation of money involves a creation of new purchasing power, whereas the creation of public debt involves only an exchange of purchasing power. Nevertheless, we shall examine debt creation and money creation together because they are confounded by prevailing institutions: both money creation and debt creation take place through transactions in public debt. Money is created when the Federal Reserve system purchases either existing, privately owned debt or newly issued Treasury debt. If, instead, this new supply of Treasury debt is purchased by the general public, debt is created. Depending on the particular circumstances surrounding a transaction in public debt instruments, then, either debt or money will be created.

Between 1960 and 1970, the gross amount of public debt increased from $290 billion to $389 billion. If we subtract the amount of public debt held by various government agencies and trust funds, public debt increased from $235 billion to $292 billion over this period. The amount of Treasury debt held by private individuals and institutions—the general public—increased from $208 billion in 1960 to $230 billion in 1970. The remainder of the outstanding Treasury debt is held by the Federal Reserve system and this amount increased from $27 billion in 1960 to $62 billion in 1970. While Treasury debt increased by $57 billion during the 1960s, only $22 billion represented genuine debt creation, for the $35 billion acquired by the Federal Reserve system represented a base for money creation.

In this chapter we shall first compare and contrast tax finance and debt finance as instruments for financing the supply of public services.

Then we shall examine money creation as an instrument for public financing, and relate money creation to taxation and borrowing. Finally, we shall conclude this chapter by examining briefly the relations among debt policy, monetary policy, and fiscal policy in promoting economic stability in the short run.

PUBLIC FINANCING THROUGH DEBT CREATION

What difference does it make, and to whom, whether public expenditures are financed by taxation or by loans? Given the amount of public expenditure to be financed, what is the differential incidence of substituting debt finance for tax finance?

With tax finance, the analysis is straightforward. If we assume that tax liability is assessed through a proportional tax on personal income, individual taxpayers pay for the public output in proportion to their respective incomes. Naturally, the use of alternative tax forms will generate alternative distributions of the cost of the public output among the citizenry. Regardless of which tax institution is used, however, the cost of the public expenditure will be borne by taxpayers at the time when the expenditure is financed.

What difference results if the public expenditure is financed by issuing public debt? Suppose the alternative means of financing the expenditure are through a proportional income tax or through the creation of public debt, with interest payments and periodic amortization to be financed by proportional income taxation.[1] Starting from a position in which the expenditure is financed by a proportional income tax, what differences will result if the expenditure is financed by the creation of public debt? Much analysis of debt finance distinguishes internal debt and external debt, holding that the impact of debt finance varies in accordance with the type of debt issued.[2] Because a common belief is that the impact of external debt

[1] Debt finance could be compared with a different tax institution—for example, a corporation income tax. Because we are comparing debt finance and tax finance, what is important is that the same tax institution is used to finance the public expenditure and to amortize the debt. That is, given a particular tax institution, we want to see what difference it makes whether an expenditure is financed currently by taxation or is financed currently by debt issue, with the debt to be amortized by the same tax institution. The particular form of tax that is used in the analysis is less important than is the consistent use of that tax form and, consequently, an assumption of proportional income taxation is used because of its analytical simplicity.

[2] For a statement of this position, see Seymour E. Harris, *The National Debt and the New Economics* (New York: McGraw-Hill, 1949).

Internal debt is created when the debt is purchased by citizens of the issuing government, whereas external debt is created when the debt is purchased by citizens of other governments.

differs from the impact of internal debt, both forms of debt finance will be examined, starting with external debt.

Consider a locality that chooses to finance some public expenditure by borrowing from residents of other localities, with the debt to be amortized periodically according to some specified schedule. In what respect does debt finance differ from tax finance? With tax finance, residents of the locality reduce their disposable incomes to pay for the public service. With debt finance, disposable incomes are unaffected because the public service is financed by borrowing from residents of other localities. Thus, debt finance enables taxpayers to postpone paying for public services until the debt is amortized. Debt finance, then, produces a shift in the intertemporal distribution of disposable income.

Debt finance may enable taxpayers to postpone paying for public services, but this does not mean that debt finance produces an increase in the net wealth of the locality's taxpayers. With tax finance, the net wealth of taxpayers is clearly reduced by the amount of tax payment. Debt finance carries with it a liability for future amortization payments, and if we temporarily discount the possibility of emigration from the locality, the present value of future tax payments to amortize the debt will equal what would have been paid under tax finance. Thus, debt finance does not enable taxpayers to increase their net wealth (at someone else's expense); rather, it enables them to attain a more preferred intertemporal pattern of paying for public services.

Obviously, some migration will take place, and it might seem that debt finance would enable the taxpayer who migrates before the debt is fully amortized to increase his net wealth as he could not have done under tax finance. Nevertheless, such opportunity for gain will not generally exist. It might seem that the future tax liability created by the locality's choice of debt finance would be capitalized into present property values. If so, an emigrating taxpayer would suffer a capital loss on the sale of his property equal to the present value of his remaining liability for debt amortization.[3] But when we consider debt creation in an entire system of localities, capitalization will not generally occur. Nonetheless, a taxpayer will be unable to increase his net wealth through emigration because in the absence of capitalization, he will inherit liability for debt repayment in his new locality.[4]

---

[3] For a discussion of capitalization in such a context, see George C. Daly, "The Burden of the Debt and Future Generations in Local Finance," *Southern Economic Journal,* 36 (July 1969), 44–51.

[4] While the income effects associated with migration cancel on the average, the substitution effect will operate to make debt finance appear less costly than tax finance. On this point and its implications, see Richard E. Wagner, "Optimality in Local Debt Limitation," *National Tax Journal,* 23 (September 1970), 297–305.

While the proposition that financing public services by issuing external debt enables taxpayers to postpone paying for public services is commonly accepted, the idea that internal debt finance also enables taxpayers to postpone paying for public services is not. The standard argument is that regardless of whether a public service is financed by taxation or internal debt creation, the resources that are devoted to the supply of public services are necessarily withdrawn from other uses at the time the service is supplied. Hence, the burden of the expenditure must rest on taxpayers at the time the public expenditure is undertaken. Whether financing takes place through current taxation or through debt issue is irrelevant because debt issue does not enable taxpayers to postpone paying for the public service it finances.

This line of argument is most commonly illustrated in a context of war finance. To fight the war, the state must provide various types of military capital, which requires control over productive resources. The state could acquire command over the necessary resources by taxing its citizens at sufficiently high rates. But suppose, instead, that the state acquires command over the resources by selling bonds to some of its citizenry. Regardless of whether the military capital is financed by taxation or by borrowing, the resources required to produce the military capital are extracted from the community at the time of production. This shift from taxation to borrowing as a means of financing the war would seem to be merely a matter of bookkeeping; cost must necessarily be borne at the time of expenditure, so tax finance and debt finance are identical. And if taxing and borrowing are identical, it follows that debt retirement involves nothing more than a redistribution of income from taxpayers to bondholders.

If the cost of the military capital is borne at the time of production, it must be possible to identify just who experiences a reduction in their real income. The cost of the military production is the nonmilitary production that is sacrificed in exchange. There must be identifiable citizens who suffer this loss of real income in order to supply the military capital. With tax finance the issue is clear; the real income of taxpayers is reduced by an amount equal to the transfer of resources to government. The burden of expenditures financed by taxation clearly rests on taxpayers at the time of the expenditure.

But who undergoes a reduction in real income when the military equipment is financed by debt issue? Bondholders transfer command over the necessary real resources to government, but in so doing, their net wealth is not reduced because they receive a promise of greater transfer of resources in the future. Thus, bondholders suffer no reduction in their net wealth; rather, they rearrange their multiperiod pattern of consumption.

But if the bondholders do not pay for debt issue, who does? Someone must. It cannot be the taxpayers because at the time the military capital is supplied, they transfer no resources to government. Bondholders transfer the resources. It must be that the taxpayers pay for the military capital by a reduction in their real income at the time when the debt is amortized. If debt finance places the cost of public services on taxpayers in the future, the retirement of public debt must involve more than merely a redistribution of income from taxpayers to bondholders. Taxpayers are indeed made worse off by debt retirement because of their tax payments. For bondholders, however, because debt retirement involves an exchange of one asset for another, we cannot say that they receive a transfer of income from taxpayers. Taxpayers lose, but bondholders do not gain. Someone must have made a gain at the time of debt creation. These are taxpayers at the time of debt creation, who otherwise would have had to make tax payments.

Debt finance simultaneously involves two distinct transactions. With one transaction, bondholders give up present purchasing power to the state in exchange for a greater amount of purchasing power in the future. With the other transaction, taxpayers avoid paying tax in the present by incurring an obligation to pay tax in the future. Debt finance thus allows taxpayers to defer paying for public services until payments are made on interest and principal. In this respect, the functioning of internal debt is identical to that of external debt. Moreover, the principles of public debt are identical to the principles of private debt.[5]

Bondholders will also be taxpayers, but obviously, not all taxpayers will be bondholders. If, in fact, all taxpayers should buy bonds in proportion to their payments had they been taxed, debt finance would be indistinguishable from tax finance. This situation, however, is inconsistent with the existence of a market in debt instruments, for such a market can exist only if individuals have different relative preferences for present and future consumption. Those individuals with relatively strong desires for present consumption will be borrowers, while those individuals with relatively weak desires for present consumption will be lenders. Because bondholders will also be taxpayers, and because we are interested in individual decisions concerning debt finance or tax finance, we shall distinguish bondholders and nonbondholders rather than bondholders and taxpayers in the following discussion.

When public expenditures are financed by borrowing, alterations will have taken place in intertemporal patterns of personal consumption. The replacement of tax finance by debt finance can be looked on as an agree-

[5] See James M. Buchanan, *Public Principles of Public Debt* (Homewood, Ill.: Irwin, 1958).

ment between bondholders and nonbondholders in which bondholders agree to contribute additional resources toward the supply of public services in exchange for the agreement of nonbondholders to make compensating payments in the future. Debt finance thus allows nonbondholders to defer paying their share of the cost of supplying public services by borrowing from bondholders in the present and repaying them in the future.[6]

Debt finance clearly entails a different intertemporal location of the cost of public services than tax finance. The essence of debt finance is that it accommodates individual differences in time preference by allowing citizens who do not want to reduce their present level of consumption to become nonbondholders rather than taxpayers. Yet when the bonds are amortized in the future, the nonbondholders will be burdened by debt retirement. There is no escape from paying for public services, only deferment.[7]

Because debt finance is a means by which present taxpayers can defer paying for public expenditures, it is an especially suitable means of financing expenditures when the benefits extend into the future. When a public service provides benefits that will extend into the future, tax finance will produce an inequitable distribution of cost on the one hand and an inefficient allocation of resources on the other. Tax finance would be inequitable in that future beneficiaries would escape payment, but receive the benefit. Tax finance would be inefficient in that budgetary outlays chosen by the median voter would be inefficiently low. In effect, debt finance extends credit to the median voter, who will consequently choose a higher rate of public output under debt finance than he would under tax finance.[8]

PUBLIC FINANCING THROUGH MONEY CREATION

Public services also may be financed by creating money, and money creation will differ from both debt finance and tax finance. The impact of money creation as a means of public financing will be substantially different, depending on whether the economy is fully employed or whether substantial unemployment exists. Moreover, an additional dimension arises when we consider the need to allow for growth in the money supply over time.

[6] James M. Ferguson, ed., *Public Debt and Future Generations* (Chapel Hill: University of North Carolina Press, 1964), reprints many articles concerning the controversy surrounding the inter-temporal location of cost under debt finance.
[7] Individual taxpayers may escape payment by migrating or by dying. A taxpayer who dies before payments are made on interest and principal escapes paying for the public services that he would have had to pay for under tax finance. A person may similarly escape payment by migrating.
[8] On these issues of equity and efficiency, see Richard A. Musgrave, *The Theory of Public Finance* (New York: McGraw-Hill, 1959), pp. 556–80.

When unemployment is substantial, the creation of money is a costless means of financing public services. The new money will bring into employment previously unemployed resources. Because those resources previously were producing nothing, the opportunity cost of employing them is zero. Hence, when unemployment is substantial, the creation of money is a costless means of financing public output. We should be careful to note, however, that what is costless is the decision to create money, the decision to employ the previously unemployed resources. Contrary to all too frequent allegations, concepts of opportunity cost remain valid in depressionary conditions. The choice to use resources to supply X still involves the sacrifice of the Y that those resources could have produced.

Unless unemployment is substantial, inflation will result when public services are financed through the creation of money. Inflation, which results when the supply of money expands more rapidly than does the economy's productive capacity, is a tax on the holding of money. Inflation produces revenue both from its tax yield and from its ability to increase the real yield of other taxes. When tax rates are progressive, inflation will increase real rates of tax. If, for instance, nominal income doubles as a result of inflation, tax collections will more than double under progressive taxation.[9] Inflation also directly produces revenue for the government, and the incidence of this tax is borne in proportion to holdings of nominal money balances.[10] This direct yield of revenue takes two forms. On the one hand, there is the tax on existing money balances that results from the rise in prices. On the other hand, there will be the yield from the provision of additional real balances over time. The revenue yield from money creation is the sum of these two yields.[11]

It is often asserted that inflation differs from other forms of taxation in that inflation is a hidden tax. The National Association of Manufacturers, for instance, published a pamphlet on inflation, subtitled "The Silent Tax."[12] Many taxes are hidden, however, so inflation is not unique on this account. Yet it seems hard to claim that inflation is a hidden form of taxation, especially with the periodic announcements on the state of the Consumer Price Index. The important feature about inflation seems to be not so much that the tax is hidden as that it is misperceived. Inflation

[9] For documentation, see Charles J. Goetz and Warren E. Weber, "Intertemporal Changes in Real Federal Income Tax Rates, 1954–70," *National Tax Journal,* 24 (March 1971), 51–63.

[10] Moreover, inflation, like any excise tax, involves a welfare loss. See Martin J. Bailey, "The Welfare Cost of Inflationary Finance," *Journal of Political Economy,* 64 (April 1956), 93–110; and Alvin L. Marty, "Growth and the Welfare Cost of Inflationary Finance," *Journal of Political Economy,* 75 (February 1967), 71–76.

[11] See Milton Friedman, "Government Revenue From Inflation," *Journal of Political Economy,* 79 (No. 4, 1971), 846–56.

[12] *Inflation: The Silent Tax* (New York: National Association of Manufacturers, 1967).

misrepresents itself, and as a result, blame is falsely placed. With an income tax or a property tax, individual citizens directly associate a diminution in their net wealth with a transfer of wealth to government. When taxation takes place through inflation, however, individual citizens associate a diminution in their net wealth with a rise in the prices of products they purchase on the market.[13] This misrepresentation of responsibility for reduction in real personal income is a form of fiscal illusion, which perhaps explains much of the support for price controls. The illusion allows those who benefit from and support inflationary finance to place the blame on others.[14]

In the content of a growing economy, money creation will not necessarily be inflationary. In the absence of shifts in the demand for money, the creation of money at a rate equal to the real rate of growth of the economy is consistent with price level stability. Even if we allow for monetary growth over time, however, there are different means of providing for growth in the money supply. Because this is so, a choice must be made among these means of providing for monetary expansion.

Money may be created through either debt monetization or budget deficits, although budget deficits need not involve the creation of money. Debt monetization takes place when the Federal Reserve system acquires national debt formerly owned by private investors. Although this shift in ownership does not change the nominal amount of national debt, such a shift in ownership transforms public debt into money under American monetary institutions. Budget deficits may also be used to increase the supply of money. If a budget deficit is financed by Federal Reserve purchases of new Treasury debt, the money supply will expand. If the new Treasury debt is sold to the general public, monetary expansion will not take place. Instead, genuine debt will have been created, as distinguished from money creation that is falsely labeled debt. Moreover, the creation of money by budget deficits can result either from an increase in expenditure relative to taxation, or from a reduction in taxation relative to expenditure.

These means of providing for growth in the money supply differ in several respects. The initial impact of debt monetization as a means of providing for growth in the money supply favors the private sector of the economy, although this initial impact becomes diffused through fractional

[13] Under a system of fractional reserve banking, of course, part of the tax proceeds from inflation accrue to the banking system. The initial injection of money will accrue to government, but this creation of money will increase the equilibrium level of bank deposits by some multiple, depending on the reserve requirement.

[14] In this respect, note Arthur Burns' observation that "Now [1968], as in other times of inflation, the administration in power has been blaming greedy businessmen, irresponsible trade union leaders, and unruly congressmen. But the new inflation is mainly the result of the excessively rapid creation of new money." Arthur F. Burns, "The Perils of Inflation," *Tax Review*, 29 (May 1968), 21.

reserve banking. Because debt finance is a means by which taxpayers can postpone paying for public expenditures, debt retirement through debt monetization reduces the burden of taxpayers (more correctly, nonbondholders) in the future. If the money supply is increased through budget deficits, the initial impact favors the growth of the public sector, although, again, this impact is diffused under fractional reserve banking. Budget deficits are financed by reducing taxes in comparison with what would occur under a balanced budget. As a result, a policy of creating money through budget deficits benefits taxpayers in the present.

To summarize, we have essentially two ways of providing for growth in the money supply: (1) Federal Reserve purchases of new Treasury debt and (2) Federal Reserve purchases of privately owned debt. The incidence of these two means of providing for growth in the money supply differs in at least three respects, as we have noted above. One difference rests in the impact on the private-public mix in the economy. The initial injection of new money under debt monetization is used to finance the supply of private goods, whereas the new money is used to finance the supply of public goods under budget deficits. Yet this initial impact tends to become diffused under our system of fractional revenue banking. A second difference between the two means rests in their impact on present and future taxpayers. Injection of new money through budget deficits confers benefits on current taxpayers, whereas debt monetization confers benefits on taxpayers in the future through a reduction in future levels of taxation. A third difference lies in the impact on rates of capital formation. By reducing the supply of bonds, thereby raising the price of bonds, debt monetization lowers the rate of interest, thereby stimulating investment. Budget deficits, by contrast, are more neutral toward capital formation.[15]

DEBT POLICY, MONETARY POLICY, AND FISCAL POLICY

The principles of debt creation and monetary creation that we examined in the preceding two sections are essentially means of financing the supply of public services. As contrasted with tax finance, debt finance places the cost of public services on taxpayers in future time periods when the debt is amortized. Debt finance thus becomes an appropriate means of financing when a desire exists to distribute the burden of public spending over future

[15] In addition, debt monetization and budget deficits will produce different impacts among the various sectors of the economy. For instance, Leonall C. Andersen, "The Incidence of Monetary and Fiscal Measures on the Structure of Output," *Review of Economics and Statistics,* 46 (May 1964), 260–68, found that debt monetization favors the construction and durable goods sectors of the economy while budget deficits favor the consumer goods sectors.

periods of time. Money creation at a rate approximately equal to the real rate of growth in the economy is required to maintain price level stability. One means of injecting this new money into the economy is to run a budget deficit and finance it by Federal Reserve purchases of newly issued Treasury debt. If, for instance, an annual increase in the money supply of $8 billion is desired, a budget deficit of about $1 billion annually would be necessary under present reserve requirements.

In addition to their use as means of financing the supply of public services, however, debt creation and money creation may also affect the short-run stability of the economy. If the economy is experiencing unemployment, an expansionary monetary or fiscal policy can be invoked. Or if the economy is experiencing inflation, a contractionary monetary or fiscal policy can be invoked.

Monetary policy operates through Federal Reserve transactions in government securities. If the Federal Reserve purchases national debt from the general public, the supply of money increases, which operates to alleviate the unemployment. The opposite result occurs if the Federal Reserve sells national debt to the general public, for then the supply of money falls, which operates to dampen inflationary tendencies.

Fiscal policy, in contrast to monetary policy, operates through the public budget. A budget deficit, which may result from either a decrease in taxes or an increase in expenditures, may be expansionary in the same manner as the Federal Reserve purchase of national debt. Similarly, a budget surplus, which may result from either an increase in taxes or a reduction in expenditures, may be contractionary in the same manner as is the Federal Reserve sale of national debt.

However, the impact of fiscal policy depends critically upon the way in which the deficit or surplus is handled. If, in the case of a budget deficit, the Treasury debt is sold to the general public, no expansion should be expected. The present value of the tax reduction or expenditure increase is exactly equal to the present value of the future tax increase. Moreover, while taxpayers have more money because of the deficit, those who loan money to the Treasury have less. Any aggregate impact of fiscal policy in this instance will result only from a redistribution of wealth associated primarily with a rise in interest rates and will be clearly a second-order consequence.[16]

If the budget deficit is to be expansionary, the Treasury debt must be purchased by the Federal Reserve system instead of by the general public. There is a categorical difference between these two means of financing a budget deficit. While the former involves the creation of money, the

---

[16] For a demonstration of this point, see Earl A. Thompson, "Debt Instruments in Both Macroeconomic and Capital Theory," *American Economic Review,* 57 (December 1967), 1196–1210.

latter involves the creation of debt. This categorical difference between these two means of financing budget deficits brings into question the typical distinction between monetary policy and fiscal policy. It serves no useful purpose to label as "fiscal policy" both a budget deficit financed by selling Treasury debt to the general public and a budget deficit financed by Federal Reserve purchases of Treasury debt. The latter transaction is similar to Federal Reserve purchases of national debt instruments from the general public, for both involve the creation of money.

The standard dichotomy between monetary policy and fiscal policy may well be counterproductive, for the monetary-fiscal distinction blurs the essential choice that confronts us in choosing techniques for promoting economic stability. This blurring results because the common reference to an expansionary fiscal policy as one that results from a deliberate budget deficit fails to specify that the deficit may be financed in two ways, one of which is expansionary and one of which is not. Moreover, the expansionary method of financing a deficit involves the creation of money, and money can be created without a budget deficit. The alternatives that confront us in choosing among techniques for short-run stabilization—assuming such an objective is presently attainable, which is not a self-evident assumption—are not Federal Reserve purchases of national debt from the general public and deficits in the public budget. Rather, the alternatives are Federal Reserve purchases of national debt from the general public and Federal Reserve purchases of national debt from the Treasury, which are simply two different techniques for increasing the supply of money. This specification of the alternative techniques for implementing short-run stabilization policy returns us to the theme of the preceding section—the choice we face is among techniques for altering the supply of money. With relatively low reserve requirements, however, the incidence of these alternative techniques is probably quite similar. More than anything else, however, we should distinguish more carefully between debt creation and money creation, for a confounding of this fundamental distinction makes sterile much of the controversy over monetary policy and fiscal policy.[17]

---

[17] The classic source of the importance of this distinction is Henry C. Simons, "On Debt Policy," *Journal of Political Economy,* 52 (December 1944), 356–61; reprinted in his *Economic Policy for a Free Society* (Chicago: University of Chicago Press, 1948), pp. 220–30. Simons proposed to institutionalize the distinction between debt and money by converting all national debt into either consols or money.

Debt management usually is advanced as a third technique for stabilization policy. Yet any possible stabilizing impact of debt management policy is pale by comparison with the impact of monetary change. See, for instance, Phillip Cagan, "A Partial Reconciliation Between Two Views of Debt Management, *Journal of Political Economy,* 74 (December 1966), 624–28, an article that, by the way, essentially supports Simons' proposal for institutionalizing the distinction between debt and money.

III

Denouement

14. Toward a Fiscal Constitution for a Democratic Society

Now that we have concluded our examination of both the institutions of fiscal choice and the instruments of public financing, it is time to conclude our discussion. We shall do this by relating our analysis to the problem of choosing a fiscal constitution for a democratic society. Our aim is not to adopt the posture of an "impartial spectator" and specify the characteristics of an optimal fiscal constitution. Our aim is more modest: to illustrate a few of the issues that face us in choosing the constitutional rules of the game, with consensus over such rules probably being essential for the survival of a basically democratic and liberal society.[1]

We saw earlier that fiscal and political rules may substitute for one another in constraining the budgetary policies likely to be chosen by a legislative assembly. For purposes of our discussion in this chapter, we shall assume that the political constitution permits all nonconstitutional choices to be made by majority consent. Given that majority voting prevails, then, we want to examine the properties of alternative rules concerning the ability of governments to finance public services on the one hand and the processes of making decisions concerning public spending on the other.

The rationale of a fiscal constitution, or of a political constitution for that matter, rests on the possibility that majority voting without constitutional constraints may yield a sequence of outcomes that will be harmful to all members of the collectivity, even though each individual outcome

[1] For perceptive observations on some problems of constitutional choice in relation to the governance of urban areas, see Worth Bateman and Harold M. Hochman, "Social Problems and the Urban Crisis: Can Public Policy Make A Difference?" *American Economic Review,* Proceedings, 61 (May 1971), 346–53.

FIGURE 14-1
Individual Rationality, Constitutional Rules, and Special Tax Privilege

Person *B*

	Privilege	No Privilege
Privilege	3 3	1 4
No Privilege	4 1	2 2

Person *A*

is beneficial to a majority of the collectivity. The phenomenon that the product of a sequence of choices in which the outcome of each choice is beneficial to a majority may be harmful to all participants is labeled the prisoners' dilemma in the theory of two-person, nonconstant sum games. To illustrate how the adoption of a fiscal constitution may be beneficial to all, the remainder of this section will be devoted to a description of two possible instances of large-number analogues to the prisoners' dilemma.

First, consider the fiscal constitution as it relates to the choice of exemptions and deductions from the tax base. In Figure 14-1 each of two persons (or groups), *A* and *B*, is faced with a choice of two options: to seek a special tax privilege by supporting a deduction or exemption from the tax base, or to refuse to seek such a special privilege. The numbers in each cell refer to the ordinal rankings of each of the four possible outcomes, with *A*'s ranking appearing in the northwest quadrant of each cell and *B*'s ranking appearing in the southeast quadrant. Person *A*'s most favorable outcome occurs when he secures a tax privilege while person *B* does not. The outcome when neither *A* nor *B* secures a privilege ranks second, while the outcome when both secure a privilege ranks third. Finally, *A*'s least favorable outcome occurs when he fails to secure a privilege while *B* succeeds. For Person *B*, the first and fourth rankings are a reversal of *A*'s, while the second and third rankings are identical.

If a fiscal constitution does not operate to preclude any of the four possible outcomes, what is the probable outcome? Consider the choice of Person *A* in deciding whether to seek a special tax privilege. If *A* assumes that *B* (the rest of the collectivity) will seek a special privilege, *A*'s dominant strategy is also to seek a special privilege. However, Figure 14-1 shows that if *A* assumes that *B* will not seek a privilege, *A*'s dominant strategy will be to seek a special tax privilege. Person *B* is confronted by the identical situation, with the result that both will seek special privileges. Because all members of the community thus have a demand for special tax privileges, a political supply of such privileges probably will be forthcoming.

In the resulting fiscal equilibrium, both participants secure special privileges and both attain an outcome that they rank third among the four alternatives. It is individually rational for each person to seek a special tax privilege. But when all persons receive similar tax privileges, all participants may be worse off than if no one had received special tax privileges. If both participants described by Figure 14-1 should impose a constitutional constraint on their fiscal choices by prohibiting special deductions and exemptions, both would attain an outcome that each ranked second among the alternatives—and the best attainable alternative that is also a fiscal equilibrium.

Tax revenues, of course, are the product of a tax base and a tax rate. As a matter of arithmetic, the same amount of revenue can be collected from a low rate applied to a broad base or from a high rate applied to a narrow base; we can collect $100 either from a 10 percent tax applied to a $1,000 base or a 20 percent tax applied to a $500 base. The narrower base would indicate the erosion of the tax base through the grant of special tax privileges. While the same amount of revenue is raised under either tax base, the low rate, high base alternative is preferable because there is an excess burden associated with extending tax privileges. Tax privileges require resources for tax administration, and much of the cost of legal and accounting services can be attributed directly to the existence of tax privileges. Moreover, as average rates of tax rise in response to narrowing of the tax base, the stronger will be the incentive to devote resources to avoiding and evading tax, and the excess burden that results is a social waste produced by the low base, high rate alternative. As we have seen in the hypothetical case illustrated by Figure 14-1, it is in the interest of each participant to seek special privileges, but the end result of all the participants securing special privileges is to make all of them worse off than they would have been if no one had acquired privileges. If a fiscal constitution required a comprehensive tax base, the ability of majority coalitions to set in motion such negative sum grants of privilege would be greatly diminished.

FIGURE 14-2
Political Choice and Tax Base Fragmentation

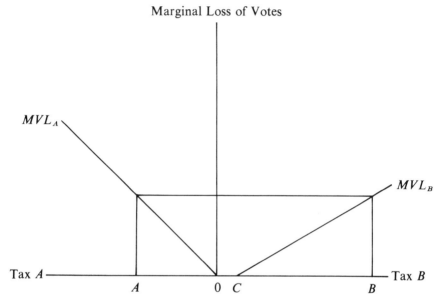

A second illustration of the way in which political competition may produce inefficient outcomes if it is not subjected to the constraining influence of a fiscal constitution revolves around the presence of a multiplicity of tax bases. Tax bases differ in the degree to which taxpayers are aware of the price they are paying for public services. Moreover, for any particular tax base, the degree of awareness seems likely to rise with an increase in the tax rate applied to that base. In Figure 14-2 two taxes, *A* and *B*, differ in the degree of taxpayer awareness concerning the price paid for public services. Tax *A* might represent a personal income tax, which produces a high degree of taxpayer awareness of the price of public services. By contrast, tax *B* might represent a value-added tax of the consumption variety, which would produce a considerably lower degree of taxpayer awareness. Because taxpayer opposition to public expenditure will vary directly with the degree of taxpayer awareness of the price of public services, we can define the degree of awareness in terms of the marginal loss in votes from an expansion in the level of taxation.[2] If we assume in Figure 14-2 that the size of the budget is *AB*, both tax forms will be used to

[2] Increases in public spending provide a marginal gain in votes, and the equilibrium budget results when the marginal gain in votes from spending equals the marginal loss in votes from taxing. See Anthony Downs, *An Economic Theory of Democracy* (New York: Harper & Row, 1957), pp. 51–74.

FIGURE 14-3
Welfare Loss from Tax Base Fragmentation

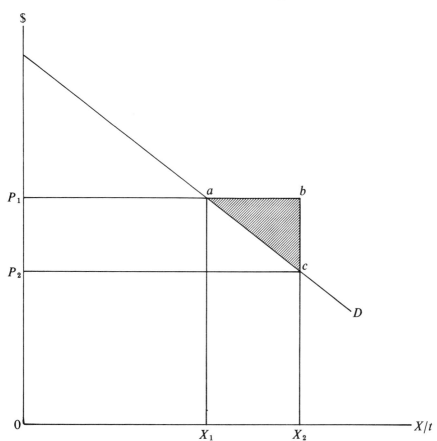

raise revenue, with *OA* raised by the income tax and *OB* raised by the value-added tax.[3]

Let us assume that taxpayer awareness of the price of public services is perfect when a personal income tax is the instrument of public financing. Figure 14-3 depicts the median voter's demand for a collective good, *X*. If *X* is financed by income taxation, the price of *X* appears as P_1. Hence, the resulting budgetary choice is X_1. Suppose, however, that *X* is financed by a value-added tax. Because taxpayers are less aware of the price of *X* when it is financed by a value-added tax, the price of *X* appears to

[3] If the size of the budget should be only *OC*, of course, only Tax *B* would be used to finance public spending.

be P_2. Budgetary choice under the value-added tax would thus yield the output rate X_2. The fiscal illusion that is introduced through the use of indirect taxation generates a dead-weight loss that may be measured by the shaded triangle, *abc*. We have seen that political competition will tend to produce a proliferation of tax bases. Yet the consequence of this proliferation is a welfare loss for all, as illustrated by Figure 14-3. Thus, our analysis suggests that some limitation on the tax forms available for financing public services might be a desirable element of a fiscal constitution, thereby increasing the efficiency with which political coalitions exercise budgetary choices.

Author Index

Subject Index

Date Due

MAR 1 '84			